REEL
THERAPY

REEL THERAPY

HOW MOVIES INSPIRE YOU TO OVERCOME LIFE'S PROBLEMS

Dr. Gary Solomon

M.S.W., Ph.D.

LF LEBHAR-FRIEDMAN BOOKS

NEW YORK · CHICAGO · LOS ANGELES · LONDON · PARIS · TOKYO

To Dr. Robin E. Huhn:

You make every moment of every day the best
dream I could ever imagine. Your love and support
make me forever thankful that we are together.

With all my love, Gary

© 2001 by Dr. Gary Solomon

Lebhar-Friedman Books
425 Park Avenue
New York, NY 10022

All rights reserved. No part of this work covered by the
copyright hereon may be reproduced or used in any form
or by any means—graphic, electronic, or mechanical,
including photocopying, recording, taping, or information storage and retrieval systems—without the written
permission of the publisher.

Published by Lebhar-Friedman Books
Lebhar-Friedman Books is a company of
Lebhar-Friedman, Inc.

Printed in the United States of America

Library of Congress Cataloging-in-Publication Data
on file at the Library of Congress

ISBN 0-86730-834-6

Book design by Erin L. Matherne and Tina Thompson

Visit our Web site at lfbooks.com

Please note: CinemaTherapy® is a registered trademark of
Gary Solomon. The Movie Doctor® is a registered trademark of Gary Solomon.

Volume Discounts
Call (212) 756-5248 for information on volume discounts.

CONTENTS

ACKNOWLEDGMENTS

To Ivy Fischer Stone, my agent, who believes in my work and supports my mission.

To all those from all over the world who have sent me letters thanking me for bringing cinematherapy into their lives.

To the entertainment industry for their continued efforts in bringing movies with healing messages to the public.

And to professor Carlo Defazio, whose energy and belief in my work remind me that I am not alone in my mission.

PREFACE

With the support of my publisher and editor, your interest in reading healing stories, and my research into more healing movies, I have written, *Reel Therapy*. In this book you will find nearly 200 movies to see you through everyday problems ranging from foster parenting, AIDS, relationships, issues on death and dying, and drug abuse to overeating, gambling, stalking, physical and emotional abuse, issues on abortion, and much, much more. *Bastard Out of Carolina* asks you to look at the painful issue of molestation, whereas *Doing Time on Maple Street* may appeal to those of you who are searching for answers about your sexuality. *East of Eden* examines difficult relationships between fathers and sons and learning about a lost parent, whereas *The First Time* takes you back to those beginning moments of sexual awareness and the mother/daughter struggles that often come with growing up. *Crazy from the Heart* helps you get in touch with being a woman and looks at the relationships between men, women, and power. *Keeping Secrets* reminds us of some of the difficulties that come with teenage pregnancy and taking on the responsibility of being a young parent. *Safe Passage* lets all of us look at our family through the eyes of nine people who are struggling to get a handle on being a family unit. And *Waiting to Exhale* touches our soul as four women and men teach us what relationships should, and should *not*, be about.

In this book you will find more ways to help yourself and your friends with some of life's difficult problems. I have worked just as hard as I did on my first book to supply you with analysis of a balanced assortment of movies covering key issues that may confront you on your journey through life. And again, I provide you with index references to help you easily locate discussions of movies that pertain to particular issues. I promise you will enjoy *Reel Therapy* just as much as you did *The Motion Picture Prescription*. So go ahead and start your healing journey today. You're in for a "reel" treat!

—Gary Solomon, M.S.W., Ph.D.
Las Vegas, Nevada

PART ONE

THE STORY BEHIND CINEMATHERAPY

CINEMATHERAPY: HEALING THROUGH THE MOVIES

*More than entertainment, movies are the stories of our lives;
they are the healing messages that guide us through life's journey.*

Many of you have already read my first book, *The Motion Picture Prescription*. It may have been that book and its emotional healing stories that led you to *Reel Therapy*, the second in a series of recovery and self-help books about healing and the movies. If that is the case, I'm thrilled you have come back for more. To you I would like to say, "Welcome back." Now that you've got the hang of it—how to watch the movies I have recommended—you will be able to get the most from *Reel Therapy* right from the start. You're going to enjoy these new healing stories as much as you did those examined in *The Motion Picture Prescription*. Here you have at your fingertips discussions of 200 more movies dealing with a wide range of life's challenges—relationships, emotional and mental illness, sex, drugs, food, gambling, adoption, foster parenting, families, and alcohol, to name a few.

For those of you who are taking your first journey through my look at healing stories, welcome. I know you are going to be thrilled and delighted with the doors that will be opened to help you deal with your most personal issues and questions. You will find, as others have, that the answers to many of life's problems can be found in the movies.

When I began working on the introduction to *Reel Therapy*, I struggled with the fact that most people like to cut right to the chase—to skip the introductions of recovery and healing books and go right to the heart of the matter. And while I understand this desire, I think there are some important concepts to explore before you take on the challenge of your first healing story.

I was in the middle of a promotion tour for *The Motion Picture Prescription* when the solution to getting you involved in the introduction of my next book came to me. I had just finished my third radio interview of the day, the fourteenth interview that week, when I realized that the questions the various interviewers were asking me were some of the same questions you, the reader, would ask if you were talking to me about the book. My answers to those questions, I saw, are what I want you to know before you begin reading about the healing stories covered in this book.

I decided to pull together the television, radio, newspaper, and lecture interviews I've done over a period of months and share them with you in the form of a single interview. I think you will find that reading the interview questions and answers about me and my work is a little more fun than your typical book introduction. So let's get started. Most of the interviews began like this:

INTERVIEWER: "It's a pleasure to introduce our guest for today, Dr. Gary Solomon, also known as The Movie Doctor. Dr. Solomon, welcome to our show."

THE MOVIE DOCTOR: "Thanks. It's wonderful to have an opportunity to be on your show."

I: "Your book is a great concept. I've not seen anything like it before. How did it all come about? I mean . . . where did it begin?"

MD: "I believe it all started in my own childhood. When I was five or six, I actually began using movies to escape from my family life. I used movies to learn about emotions and feelings—although I didn't know it at the time. For the most part, I raised myself. I was a latchkey child; my mother and father worked all day and argued all night. I was left to raise myself. So I was either sitting in a classroom marking time or I was in my room playing my musical instruments to drown out the noise from their yelling and screaming—I learned very young that the way to escape the family arguments was to blend into the woodwork.

"Since I did not learn to read, write, or spell until I was in the tenth grade, I had nothing to do except become absorbed in the radio and television shows I would listen to. I think most people, especially kids, are entertained by the movies. But I got something else from movies: I learned to feel things that my family never taught me to feel. Oh, I had fear down really well. I was scared all the time. My father spent his time scaring my mother, sister, and me half to death. But the rest of the emotional range of feelings, such as love, trust, and empathy, were learned through the movies."

I: "What are some of the movies you remember from your childhood that got you through the tough times?"

MD: "Oh, I can remember some great movies that gave me a sense of life and hope. They taught me that there was more going on in the world than yelling and screaming. *Yankee Doodle Dandy* gave me joy and happiness, while it inspired me to go on with my music. I played clarinet and was further inspired by the *Benny Goodman Story*, which taught me about how loneliness is not only a state of being but has feelings of sadness and emptiness tied to it. I learned that falling in love with someone was a very special thing filled with both joy and pain. *I Was a Fugitive from a Chain Gang* taught me that I never wanted to end up in jail. I had already lived through enough isolation for one lifetime. The last thing I wanted to do was to go through what this guy was experiencing. I also learned that the system can be corrupt. *Hot Spell* confronted me with my own family life. It was not a very pretty picture. *The Wizard of Oz* got me in touch with hope and begged me to ask questions about my life and the journey I was taking. And as strange as it may sound, even back then I always thought I had a greater purpose in this life other than listening to my family feud. I knew it had to do with the movies, I just didn't know what it was. I think I've found my purpose."

I: "You said you were illiterate. How in the world did you ever make it through school? Most kids with your background end up dropping out of school and many drop out of life."

MD: "The truth is I did quit high school in my senior year to travel with a rock-and-roll band. The band broke up shortly after I quit school and I was left with nothing: no education, no band, and no job. However, my high school, Inglewood High School in Inglewood, California, let me back in school and somehow, by some miracle, I graduated. Although I never caught up with the basics—reading, writing, and spelling—I was able to crawl through undergraduate and graduate school at the University of California at Los Angeles. I had to go through two junior colleges and a state college to get to UCLA. I don't mind telling you it was a struggle. It seemed to take me four times as long as everyone else to read a book or write a paper—it still does. But somehow I got through a bachelor's, two master's, and a Ph.D."

I: "You spent a long time in school. Why so much schooling?"

MD: "Oh, that's an easy one: low self-esteem. I was trying to prove to myself and to the world around me that I wasn't stupid. Now that I've got five degrees . . . well, I guess I'm okay with myself. However, for those of you who are listening at home, don't try this without a therapist. It may be harmful to your well-being."

I: "So the process of using movies to deal with your personal problems stayed with you your whole life?"

MD: "I wish it had. Unfortunately, as I grew older, other than being entertained by movies, I forgot those early-childhood lessons. I guess my life turned into what most people's lives are like—keep going and going and going, and don't look back. So I kept on going until my family dysfunction caught up to me. And, oh, did it catch up to me. I did everything a person could possibly do to themselves to reenact a destructive family life. And for a reason that I still do not understand, I lived through my self-destructive behavior and survived to write my recovery and healing books. Here's a story just to let you know how sick I was:

"Some years ago, I was sitting on the edge of a doctor's examining table waiting for some test results. I had just come off years of self-abuse—alcohol, drugs, sex, compulsive spending, you name it. I lost most of a small fortune in the process. I mean, I was sick. Now, for some reason I have always looked significantly younger than my age. When I was thirty, I looked twenty-one, and so on. The doctor came in after going over the results of the blood workups and various other tests. He looked straight into my bloodshot eyes and said, 'I don't know why you're still alive. By all rights, you should be dead. How old are you?' I remember I had answered that challenging question when I got to the office. 'Thirty-eight,' I sputtered. 'No, you're not,' he fired back with doubt and debate in his voice, accusing me of lying or not remembering. Knowing I was not all together, I asked with complete sincerity, 'Oh, how old am I?' as if he were going to cut me in half and count the rings. That's how low I had gone and how far I had removed myself from using movies to keep me centered and alive."

I: "Do you still struggle with those problems or issues that brought you so low in your own life?"

MD: "I certainly have my own life battles to fight. Most of the addictive behavior is behind me, but I still have a major struggle with my relationship with food. Much to my dismay there are not very many movies that deal with food issues. *For the Love of Nancy, Kate's Secret, Eating, The Karen Carpenter Story,* and a few more movies are all that exist on the subject. Unfortunately, most of these movies look at food problems from the female perspective. If all goes well, I will soon have the opportunity to write and produce my own screenplay that deals with the various issues I talk about through the use of cinematherapy."

I: "Does it matter from what perspective the movies come? I'm talking about the sex of the individual using the movie for reasons of personal growth."

MD: "It used to matter a lot. After working with movies for so many years, I have come to realize it's about the problem of food, alcohol, sex, drugs, physical illness, relationships, et cetera, not the gender of the person who has the problem or is portraying the problem in the movies. However, I do find that some of my clients and patients have trouble getting on the other side of that concept. Others are able to jump that hurdle rather quickly."

I: "So when did you rediscover the healing power of movies?"

MD: "It was during the time that I was doing my internship as a psychotherapist that movies as healing stories slipped back into my life. I'll never forget the first time it all came back to me. It was an epiphany.

"I had been working with a young woman for some weeks. I was her social worker. She was very nervous about being in therapy; she received little support from her psychologically abusive fiancé and was afraid to come to her sessions. One day she started to tell me a story about something that happened to her the previous week. As I listened, I remembered an old black-and-white movie that I loved, *The Lost Weekend*. It was clear to me that she was retelling this old movie and living it in her own life. When she was done, I suggested she watch *The Lost Weekend*. 'Let me know what you think. See if you see yourself in one of the characters or if the story is similar to your story.' The next week this rather sullen, previously sedate woman came bounding into my office. 'How did you know? That's exactly what I'm going through. He's always drunk, and I'm always trying to fix him. Is that what you mean when you say codependent?'

"That really started me thinking. One of the most difficult things to do as a therapist is to help people understand concepts like denial, codependency, and addiction. I thought if I could help people understand more about themselves by watching movies, I could reach them more quickly.

"I began asking people to watch certain movies that related to their particular problem. If someone was dealing with alcohol or drug problems, I recommend a movie such as *The Days of Wine and Roses, Clean and Sober, Basketball Diaries, Leaving Las Vegas, Trees Lounge,* and *A Voice in the Mirror*. If the issue was gambling, I asked them to watch *The Lady Gambles*. And if the problem was abuse or abandonment or other childhood issues, I suggested *What Ever Happened to Baby Jane?, The Woman's Room,* or *The Bell Jar*. Sometimes the issues were more specific, such as AIDS or physical illness. Under those circumstances I recommended *An Early Frost, Philadelphia,* or *David*."

I: "And what was their response to this video therapy?"

MD: "It was very positive. They gained so much from seeing themselves in the characters in the movies and the story that was being portrayed right before their eyes. My clients would open up and start talking about the problems that they had not seen or dealt with before. And they were grateful that I was not asking them to read a book."

I: "Come on, Doc, didn't they think you were just a little crazy?"

MD: "A few clients were resistant at first. They could not understand what a movie had to do with their problems or how it was going to help them. But it didn't take more than one or two movies for them to see the benefits. You see, for many of them, their feelings were being validated for the first time. I can't emphasize enough how important cinematherapy can be for people who are trying to take the journey of recovery. Validating your feelings is so important in the recovery process. My patients and clients no longer had to be embarrassed by what they were feeling. They realized they were not alone. And knowing you're not alone is another important awareness in the healing process."

I: "So how did you come to write the book?"

MD: "It was really my wife's idea. Some time after I started using movies as a therapeutic tool, I went to a bookstore to buy a book on the subject. Surely someone had written a book on the movies and their therapeutic value, right? Wrong! Much to my surprise, there was no such book. Using my background in academic research, I investigated at the Arizona State University and found nothing. Again, I found no book or significant research on the subject. When I told Robin, my wife, how frustrating it was not having a reference book to turn to for a list of movies, she said, 'I have an idea.' Well, if you read my first book, you know that her idea became my new career. And I'll always give her credit for being the originator of the idea to write books on the subject." (A side note: It is interesting to me the number of people, interviewers, and the general public who have complimented me on giving the credit to Robin. A couple of interviewers said, "Most people don't like to share the credit. You must feel good about your relationship with Robin to acknowledge her this way." "No question about it," I quickly reply. "I wouldn't have it any other way.")

I: "So do you use these movies in your practice while your patients are in your office, or do you just give them a list of movies and tell them to do it on their own?"

MD: "The movies are used more like homework. On rare occasions I will watch a portion of a movie in my office. But for the most part I ask my clients to rent, buy, or find out when a particular movie is airing on television. Many libraries throughout the country have movies that you can check out for free. Next, I have them watch the movie before the next session so we can discuss what they got from the movie. I look for their response and reaction to the movie."

I: "Now I've got the idea your clients are supposed to get something from the movies. Are they supposed to do something special when they're watching the movies? Do they have to watch them in a certain way?"

MD: "Good question. There must be a little piece of a therapist in you. I take pre-scribing movies very seriously. So yes, there is a particular way I like my clients and patients to watch the movies. In general, I prefer they watch the movies in the safety and privacy of their own home. That's not to say I don't want people going to movie theaters. Movie theaters are fine when the goal is to be entertained. But when it comes to taking the healing/therapeutic journey, I want people to experience a silent and a safe, familiar setting. Next, I ask them to focus on a character—or characters—and a story theme or a story idea. I tell them to look for similarities between what they're seeing in the movie and the events in their own life. I also suggest they journal their feelings, their own emotions, as they watch the movies. The journal becomes a useful tool to use in working through problems and issues in the future. Also, I ask them to make sure that they watch the movie without any chance of being disturbed: phone off the hook; children tucked away in bed; sign on the front door that reads, 'Do Not Disturb'; and no food, drugs, cigarettes, or alcohol before, during, or after the movie."

I: "Do you tell them in advance what to look for in the movie?"

MD: "No. I prefer they watch the movie and get what they can see and feel, or want to see and feel. If they return to my office with, 'Dr. Solomon, I didn't get a thing from this movie,' I help them move on to something different to watch. Therapy is, and should always be, a journey of choice. If I tell them what to get from the movie, they lose sight of their own choices. I often find that when they return they see something in the movie that I did not see or I had not expected them to focus on. I invite them to talk about their experience from their perspective."

I: "I'm going to be completely honest with you. This all seems a little strange to me. How are your peers taking to this whole thing? Do they think you've lost it?"

MD: "Well, I know this may surprise you, but therapists and hospitals have been using this approach for years. I'm simply the first person to write a book on the subject. As I said earlier, when I couldn't find a book on movies and therapy, I wrote the book. It's quite exciting to be the first person to write on the subject of movies and therapy. I'm enjoying the acknowledgment of being the first."

I: "Dr. Solomon, you talk about a couple of concepts in your book that I'm not familiar with. One of them is suspension of disbelief and the other is paradoxical healing."

MD: "Let's first talk about a basic therapeutic dilemma. In my opinion, the most challenging job of the therapist is to help the client or patient out of denial. Helping them out of their denial can be a very difficult, time-intensive experience. Denial is the inability to see a situation, a life problem, as it really is, as it is affecting their lives, their future. One way I have found to help them out of denial is to use what the movie industry calls *suspension of disbelief.* Suspending one's disbelief comes about when a movie or book is so strong, so real in its presentation, that the viewer forgets that he or she is watching a story. Here's an example:

"You might recall the movie *The Bridges of Madison County.* This is a wonderful love story with some basic moral problems—for example, the female character is having an affair. The characters and story are so strong that people suspend their disbelief and believe *The Bridges of Madison County* is a true story about real people. The male lead plays the role of a photographer for *National Geographic*. Some people called or wrote to *National Geographic* requesting copies of his photographs. That is suspension of disbelief. That's what makes the healing stories so powerful. When people suspended their disbelief they can see themselves as the gambler in *The Lady Gambles* or as the architect in *The Fountainhead*. They find themselves inside of the sick relationships portrayed in *Fool for Love* or *Passages*. They see their own role of being a parent or the children in *Imaginary Crimes*. So, to sum it up, with suspension of disbelief, we believe what we're seeing before our eyes, if only for a moment.

"If I can get people to suspend their disbelief and accept the story or characters as real-life situations, I can help them see themselves, their family, or friends through the movie they're watching. You see, suspension of disbelief is the mirror image of denial. Each of the movies can, for many people, bring out some emotional attachment to the stories and characters long enough to help them deal with their own problems and issues. My experience in using movies for this purpose is that clients and patients move more rapidly through the denial stage of their treatment when they use the movies I have recommended to bring themselves out of denial. It's really quite miraculous to watch. To sum it up, we do the opposite of what we see or expreience."

I: "Is that part of paradoxical healing? Is it the same as healing by proxy?"

MD: "Yes, but not completely. Not all movies have a positive or happy ending. Foreign films often end very dark, with the evil character getting away with something or a couple ending in a bitter breakup. People have questioned some of the movies I have chosen for my book because of the negative or dark endings. But we learn what we should do in life by watching the opposite; we can learn what to do by seeing the wrong way of doing things.

"For instance, you may have received a traffic ticket at some time in your life and ended up going to traffic school. And you may recall they showed you a movie of a very bad accident. They showed you that movie not because they wanted you to get in a bad accident. Rather, they wanted you to do just the opposite; they wanted you to learn by proxy—through someone else's bad mistake. Given that understanding, paradoxical healing comes about by learning through another person, or that person's life events, no matter the outcome. Take *Leaving Las Vegas*, for example. Here is a man who has given up on life and decides to drink himself to death. He meets a woman who tries, in her own way, to stop him. You might think of this couple as a bad accident waiting to happen. By watching their behavior, I believe we can learn through their mistakes so we can do just the opposite. That is paradoxical healing and healing by proxy."

I: "There have been a number of politicians—Bill Clinton and Bob Dole to name two—who have come out against violence and sex in the movies. Basically, they say that violence and sex in the movies is bad. What do you think?"

MD: "During the time I was writing *The Motion Picture Prescription* and after its release, there was a lot of talk about violence and sex in the movies. Coincidentally, I was writing this section of the opening of *Reel Therapy* the day before and after President Clinton gave his State of the Union address.

"In Clinton's speech, he suggests that the movie and television industry need to police themselves with respect to sex and violence in the movies. A number of politicians, including the ones I've mentioned, have stated quite emphatically that sex and violence in the movies have a negative effect on people, especially our youth. They have gone on the airways and newspapers reporting their beliefs, stated as if they were fact, which have rippled their way into the ears of movie, television, and radio talk-show viewers and listeners. At the time of the writing of this book, the idea had gained so much momentum that a bill was entered into congress forcing electronics manufacturers to install what they called the V chip—a computer chip that would allow parents to monitor what their children watched on television by blocking selected programs. It's all a wonderful notion with one very big problem: We don't know that violence and sex in the movies or on television have a negative or a positive effect on our children or adults. Simply stated: There is no scientific proof or solid evidence in this area.

"You see, it is very important that we know something has an effect on something else before we decide that we need or want to do anything about it. How do we know that our societal problems relating to sex and violence are not caused by changes in food processing, chemicals in the air, pressures imposed through the increase in technology, or social pressures that come from fashion or the economy unless we do some scientific testing to learn more about this phenomenon?

"And what about the problems that come from not watching the violence? Could it be that there is something to be gained by watching Sylvester Stallone or Arnold Schwarzenegger duke it out with the bad guys? My generation grew up on westerns and the Three Stooges. Visually they were violent experiences. Is there any data to show these events had a positive or negative long-term effect? Not to my knowledge. Maybe the violence is an outlet. Possibly, simply watching the violence stops people from acting out their fantasies. Could it be that sex scenes acted out on screen decrease sexual assaults? Possibly, these movies represent a way to indulge in some of our inner fantasies so that we do not need to act them out in real life.

"Have you ever heard the word *ignoratioelenchi?* This is a wonderful word that describes so accurately what is happening here. First, let me give you the heady definition: A belief or conclusion based on a supposition founded in presupposition(s) based in emotion. Now let me give you a layperson's explanation:

"I'm going to tell you a story, and you tell me the conclusion you come to from the story. Yesterday, I saw Mary, at twelve midnight, petting a black cat while sitting in front of a fire under a full moon. Today, Billy was walking by Mary and tripped and broke his leg. What's your conclusion?

"'Mary must be a witch' is the natural conclusion that people came to in the late seventeenth century. Of course, today most of us know that is nonsense. Yet simply because Johnny and Sally saw a violent movie, we come to believe that they are violent because of the movie. That, my friend, is *ignoratioelenchi.*"

I: "Can you give me an example of what you mean when you suggest that monitoring this kind of viewing many have a negative effect?"

MD: "Imagine that your children have five very close friends. They do everything together, from attending school to going to the mall. And like most kids and adults they share their personal experiences, some of which are things related to what they are watching on television or in the movies. You know: 'I saw this movie last night. You should have seen these two guys. One of them hits the other dude with this brick and . . .' You get the idea.

"Now, in the process of trying to decide what your children will watch, you elect to stop them from watching the *Mighty Morphin Power Rangers* or the latest Bruce Willis movie. But at the same time, the parents of the other five children let their children continue to view these shows or movies. What effect will be introduced into your children's life? Do you think your children will feel rejected or left out? Possibly, they will begin to act out because they were not allowed to watch the movie. Will we then say that they have problems because they were not allowed to watch violence or sex? Is it possible that the sense of isolation and rejection they feel may cause problems later on in life?"

I: "So you're saying it's not having an effect on people?"

MD: "I'm saying that sex and violence *may* have an effect on our society. I am also saying that I don't know—and other scientific investigators don't know—whether sex and violence in the movies is having a positive, negative, or neutral effect on the human race. To properly make good, sound judgments in this area we must do the research necessary to learn what effects, if any, movies are having on various parts of our culture."

I: "I had not considered some of what you're suggesting prior to this interview."

MD: "I think the whole subject is quite thought-provoking. Here's another problem: Who will decide what we should watch with respect to sex and violence? How do we know what is harmful and what is helpful? Let me give you an example: In *The Motion Picture Prescription,* I suggested watching the healing movie *The Women of Brewster Place.* In the first twenty minutes of the movie, Matty, played by Oprah Winfrey, has sex in the middle of a field with a man she barely knows. She becomes pregnant. When her father finds out she's pregnant, he beats her viciously. This scene is a very important part of the movie. And it's an important part of the total healing process; the scene teaches us some things in life about what to do and not to do. Would you want this scene removed? Do you want someone else to decide what you can and cannot watch? I don't think so. In *Darkness Before Dawn,* Meredith Baxter plays the role of a young nurse who is addicted to drugs and addicted to another addict. She has a flashback to her childhood. In the flashback she is beaten by her father for leaving a light on in the house. Should the scene be removed? I think you get the idea."

I: "So what's the bottom line to all this?"

MD: "We must be very careful when we decide to give power and control to someone or an agency with respect to removing violence and sex from movies. We must not jump to conclusions without the proper information and research, or we will relive the Salem witch trials. Instead of just watching these movies and internalizing the stories, spend time with your family to discuss each other's feelings about a particular movie or a scene in a movie. I truly believe there is a far greater benefit to interacting with your family about the contents of a movie than spending the time monitoring what they are watching."

I: "I have heard a lot of people compare movies to dreams. I'm not sure what that idea means."

MD: "I was in the bookstore the other day and saw a rack of books on dreams. I spent some time going through a few of the books. Much to my surprise, there were a few of my healing stories being used as examples to explain the meaning of dreams. To tell you the truth, it actually bothered me. It bothered me because some people still suggest that our dreams can be interpreted by someone else. I have said this before and I will say it again: There is no science that can prove what dreams mean. You can interpret your dreams, and I can interpret mine. That's as far as we can go. No one can tell you what your dreams mean. Yes, it is true that some movies are dreamlike in the way they are presented. Movies such as *Hook, The Wizard of Oz, Dreamscape,* and *Alice in Wonderland* are but a few examples. But only the writers can tell you what they meant when they wrote those stories."

I: "So why do we dream, and how might that relate to watching your healing movies?"

MD: "Dreams are probably the human body's way of dealing with conflict and unwanted or unneeded material. Dreams are to the brain what the process of elimination is to the colon. When we dream, we are experiencing our individual way of trying to deal with conflict. There is no way of knowing if the house you dream about is the same as the house I dream about. If I dream about a sexual experience, it may not have anything to do with sex. There is simply no way of knowing. So please don't let someone try to tell you what your dreams mean. What is important is that you may begin to feel better after your dream, as if you were relieved—and that's where the movies come into play.

"Now to the question 'How might dreams relate to watching healing movies?' Again, only the individual can get something out of a dream and relate it to a movie. If it works for you, that's all that matters.

"Remember, one of the goals is to use the movies to unlock the doors in your memories, those doors that have been sealed shut for one reason or another. Well, I believe that the movies can unlock the doors to some of those memories that you might have been trying to process in your dreams. If I can get you to watch a movie that helps you deal with your healing, you may find that a dream is a continuation of that healing process or that previous dreams are similar to what you see and feel by watching the movies. The movies may help you put to rest those conflicting feelings that you have been carrying around for so many years. Possibly, you have been carrying them around in the form of weight, drowning them in alcohol, dealing with them by having indiscriminate sex, or getting lost in your work. Maybe the nightmare is that you can't have a good, healthy relationship or you have a terrible fear of death and dying. You will be quite amazed at the outcome when you let yourself feel free to heal. And part of that healing will be in the dreaming process and movie watching."

I: "Are there movies for men and movies for women? I mean, do you find there are differences among some movies as they relate to men's and women's issues?"

MD: "Yes. In fact, in this book I have added "Men's Stories" and "Women's Stories" to the cross-reference section. Over the years that I have been practicing, men's and women's issues are unquestionably the most common recurring theme. 'He never listens to me. It's like talking to a brick wall.' 'We used to have sex all the time. Since we started living together, I might as well be a celibate.' 'She won't do anything around the house. I'm getting tired of this stuff.' Sound familiar? Well, movies do a wonderful job of confronting all of these issues and more. They can help you see your problems and lead you to some solutions that you might have otherwise not seen."

I: "So do you categorize movies?"

MD: "A section in the book cross-references each movie into twenty separate categories. These categories help you find your issue more quickly. Movies such as *A Woman's Room, Waiting to Exhale,* and *Steaming* open doors for women to see what is happening in their own lives. *Fresh Horses, The Good-bye Girl,* and *Love Story* take a different kind of look at the way men and women interact with each other and how relationships can either grow together or fall apart. *Let's Talk about Men* and *Let's Talk about Women* are wonderful character studies that supply us with lessons for our own lives.

"Families can watch movies together to get in touch with their own feelings.

Trading Moms, The Summer My Father Grew Up, Like Mom Like Me, East of Eden, and *The Restless Years* can set the groundwork for real family discussions on subjects ranging from growing up to problems communicating with parents and children. *Scared Straight* and *Everybody's Baby: The Rescue of Jessica McClure* help bring the whole family together in dealing with a family crisis."

HOW TO USE THIS BOOK

At the beginning of this book is a table of contents that tells you, from A to Z, which movies are discussed. I have set up each separate entry to contain one and only one movie. I know you will find this approach easier to read and understand than other movie guide books. The top of each movie section contains the title of the movie. This is the actual **movie title**. Immediately following the title is the name of the **movie company**, the **year** the movie was released, status of the movie with respect to **color** verses **B & W** (black & white) presentation, **length** of the running time of the movie in minutes, and movie **rating**. The ratings, including many of the movies made for television (which until recently had no industry rating), are identified with the following letters:

G   General audiences. All ages admitted.

PG   Parental guidance suggested. Some material may not be
        suitable for children.

PG-13   Parents strongly cautioned. Some material may be
        inappropriate for children under 13.

R   Restricted. Children under 17 require accompanying parent
        or adult guardian.

NC-17   No children under 17 admitted.

Next comes the **Healing Themes** heading. Here I supply you with four or five key healing themes or ideas on which the movie focuses. For instance, in *Avalon,* the healing themes are: Looking at family issues; Starting fresh; Growing up with brothers and sisters; Coping when family conflict is pulling you apart; and Losing contact with your past and your family history. These healing themes will act as an overall guide to the general themes written in the movie. However, please note that each movie contains many hidden themes. I invite you to discover and experience other themes in each film.

Following the healing themes are the names of the **Director** and the writer of the **Screenplay** if it is a theatrical release or **Teleplay** if it is a television production. By the way, if you see that the movie was written by a screenwriter, it means that it was originally made for the big screen. Conversely, if you see that the movie was written by a teleplay writer, it means the movie was originally made for television release. However, these days, simply because the movie was made for television does not mean you will not be able to find a copy of it at your local video store.

For those who like to know the **Cast**, I've given you a list of each main performer and the name of the character they play in the movie. In looking for movies that contain healing themes, I have noticed that certain actors and actresses seem to return to making films with these healing story lines. In time, you may find a certain actor or actress whom you particularly enjoy seeing. The next thing you will find on the page is the **Synopsis,** which gives you a brief idea of what the movie is about: the story line. In many cases I use the main characters' names so you will have a sense of the names of the individuals you will be following throughout the picture.

Finally, what you have been waiting for, **Cinematherapy**. It is in this section that I provide you with an idea of what you might experience during your healing journey of movie watching. While on your path to understanding the various messages the movie might be sending you, I will ask you questions such as: "Is that what it was like growing up in your family?" "Are you part of an abusive relationship like the one you are watching?" "Do you know someone like her who has to drink to get happy?" The queries are offered to create thoughts and feelings about what you have experienced in your life or what you are currently undergoing.

The cinematherapy section also supplies you with an analysis or statements about what you are seeing in the movie. Keep in mind that each movie contains a great deal of information, far more than I could possibly write about and analyze within the confines of this book. The ultimate goal is to help you or someone whom you care for make positive changes for the future. I support you in going the distance and seeking the inner meaning beyond those comments that I have made about the picture under discussion. Note: In some of the cinematherapy sections, I have mentioned other movies that you may want to view. These movies are in bold type and italicized.

Most people tend to ignore the closing pages of a book. However, you are going to find these sections quite useful on your trip through my healing movies.

In the Useful Resources section, you will find a **Healing Movies Prescription List.** This is a handy list for therapists to give to their patients and clients when they want them to watch a particular movie. It's also an easy reference list to use when you are at your local video store. It will help you keep track of what you have watched and what you want to view. Following the list are two **Healing Movies Prescription Pads.** I have included these prescription pads primarily for therapists. Simply fill out the pad and give them to your clients and patients for their weekly movie assignment. By the way, you have my permission to copy these two sections from the book to use at your convenience.

Following the prescription pads is the **Subject Index**, which contains twenty-one key issues offered in the movies. Here you will find headings of: Abandonment, Abuse, Adoption, Alcohol, Codependency, Death/Dying, Denial, Divorce, Drugs, Family, Food, Friends, Gambling, Men's Stories, Mental/Emotional Illness, Physical Illness, Relationships, Sex/Sexuality, Women's Stories, Okay for Under Fifteen, and Special Issues. The references will help you turn right to issues that interest you.

Let's say your issue is divorce and you want to find movies that focus on the topic. Simply turn to the cross reference index, look up the heading, Divorce, and go to those movies in the book that are listed in the index. You will also find the same movie in some of the other categories. For instance, a movie may be listed under Divorce but also categorized under Alcohol, Abuse, and Abandonment because those healing themes are also a part of that movie. So, as you can see, you will find this cross reference index a very helpful tool.

Also included in this book is a list of **Support, Recovery, and Outreach Organizations** with their toll-free phone numbers. This is a handy resource for locating your local chapter of Overeaters Anonymous, Cocaine Anonymous, etc. Additionally, you will find contact numbers of groups dealing with cancer, Alzheimer, AIDS, etc. Be sure to use your local phone book as an additional resource. Please keep in mind that the name of the organizations and their phone numbers may vary from state to state. Use these contact names as a guide to finding the support group or individual in your part of the world.

And for those of you who may want to give the World Wide Web a try, read **For Those Who Enjoy the Internet** . . . and **Just For Fun.** Currently there is not a Web site targeted to healing movies exclusively. However, you may find a news/user group on the Internet willing to give the topic a try. For that matter, why not start your own Internet site.

Now comes the **Suggestion Box.** Here I am inviting you to send me your thoughts about the book and a list of movies you would like to see included in subsequent editions. Then there is a page that shows you a way to contact the movie doctor.

Now it's time to take the journey. You should now have a solid foundation for understanding what this book is all about. Take time to thumb through the pages of the book and understand how it is organized. Then HAVE FUN and enjoy the wonderful journey to self-improvement, awareness, and enlightenment through the use of cinematherapy.

PART
TWO

MOVIES
FROM *A* TO *Z*

ALWAYS

(United Artists, 1989), color, 121 minutes, PG-rated

HEALING THEMES:

Pushing life to the limit
Learning that someone you love has died
Grieving the death of a loved one
Letting go of the past
Starting all over again

DIRECTOR: Steven Spielberg; SCREENPLAY: Jerry Belson; CAST: Richard Dreyfuss (Pete); Holly Hunter (Dorinda); John Goodman (Al); Brad Johnson (Ted); Audrey Hepburn (Hap); Roberts Blossom (Dave); Keith David (Powerhouse); Marg Helgenberger (Rachel)

SYNOPSIS: Pete is a pilot who takes one too many risks and dies in a plane crash. Dorinda, his girlfriend, is devastated by the loss and has trouble getting her life back on track. Pete is sent back to earth to be a guiding light for Ted, a young pilot who happens to fall in love with Dorinda. Pete and Dorinda learn to let go and say goodbye to the past.

CINEMATHERAPY: I couldn't have been ten years old when I saw *A Guy Named Joe* (1943), the movie on which *Always* is based. At the time, I didn't know much about love and I certainly had not seen anything that looked like love in my family. However, I was taken by how strongly these two characters felt about each other. When *Always* came out, I was so deeply touched by the film that I watched it several times. I could not imagine what it would be like to lose someone I felt dearly about. Have you lost someone who you felt was your soul mate? Maybe they didn't die, but they might have moved away or possibly they just didn't feel the same way about you. Well, *Always* is as much about letting go and moving on with your life as it is about love and the belief that there will never be anyone else in your life whom you could possibly love. Get in touch with what Dorinda experiences as she grieves the loss of Pete. Maybe you're someone who has always denied those feelings. You simply put the relationship behind you and decided that it was not going to affect you. But it's there, isn't it? You might find yourself looking at those who remind you of that special person from your past. Possibly you have held on to special memorabilia. Or, like Dorinda, you might have this strange feeling that this special someone is still with you, looking over your shoulder, looking after you. Grieving and letting go is an important phase of life's healing process. It takes a great deal of courage and strength to embrace a brand-new day. And it takes opening your eyes to those around you who want to live in the here and now and who want to share themselves with you—*if* you will simply give them a chance. This is one of those movies you can watch by yourself or with that special someone. Don't hold back the tears. Experience the cleansing power of this film. Don't fight it. And when it's over, commit to moving on with your life.

AMERICAN GRAFFITI
(Universal, 1973), color, 110 minutes, PG-rated

HEALING THEMES:
Remembering when you were young
Knowing when it's time to grow up and move on
Love at first sight
Cruising the night away
Trying to grow up too quickly
Making the most of your youth

DIRECTOR: George Lucas; SCREENPLAY: George Lucas, Gloria Katz, and Willard Huyck; CAST: Richard Dreyfuss (Curt); Ron Howard (Steve); Cindy Williams (Laurie); Mackenzie Phillips (Carol); Paul LeMat (John); Charles Martin Smith (Terry); Suzanne Sommers (blonde in Thunderbird); Candy Clark (Debbie); Harrison Ford (Falfa); Bo Hopkins (Joe); Joe Spano (Vic); Kathleen Quinlan (Peg)

SYNOPSIS: It's the early 1960s and a group of kids—Steve, Curt, and others—are out cruising the streets of a small town. Some of them have just graduated from high school and are looking to have a big night on the town, and others are just out to make trouble. They're all experiencing the thrill of finishing school, the excitement of coming of age, and the fear of what tomorrow may bring.

CINEMATHERAPY: I was absolutely terrified when I graduated from high school. Where would I go? What would I do? Who would I be? I grew up in Inglewood, California. There was a place there called the Witch Stand. We'd line up at the drive-in in our cars for hours just to have a reason to be out for the night and maybe get a burger. Cruising was the name of the game. That was a long time ago, but *American Graffiti* brings it all back and helps us get in touch with our school years. Really try to get into this movie and work to identify yourself with one of the characters. You may have been Steve, the good kid, or John, the tough guy. Maybe you were one of the popular kids, or possibly you were the class nerd. Do you recall being like Carol, trying to grow up way before your time? Were you the illusive, no-name blonde from the other town whom no one knew? Whoever you were, this is an opportunity to open yourself up to memories, both good and bad. I found myself wanting to go back to some of those roots. Why not return to the place where you grew up? Visit your old high school or take a drive through your childhood neighborhood. You will be amazed at the feelings that will come from the process. How about calling old friends with whom you've lost contact? Phone your high school and learn when they're holding your next class reunion. Make plans to attend and reunite with some of these old friends. Doing these positive things can be quite a nurturing experience. But first, watch this nostalgic film and get in touch with your feelings about all your yesterdays. You'll find, when you do, that you will be a little more free to really experience all your todays. (A personal note: When I was young, I worked for radio disc jockey Wolfman Jack, who plays the deejay in this movie. I even performed at a few of his concerts. I forgot all about those times. See, it's working already.)

AMERICAN HEART

(Triton, 1993), color, 113 minutes, R-rated

HEALING THEMES:
Growing up without a parent
Coping when one of your parents drinks
Being abandoned by someone you love
Feeling like you have no place to go
Being told you're not wanted
Taking on the responsibilities of being a parent

DIRECTOR: Martin Bell; SCREENPLAY: Peter Silverman; CAST: Jeff Bridges (Jack); Edward Furlong (Nick); Lucinda Jenney (Charlotte); Tracey Kapisky (Molly); Don Harvey (Rainey); Margaret Welsh (Freddie)

SYNOPSIS: Jack is released from jail and returns into the mainstream of society. He doesn't have to start over, since he didn't have anything to begin with. His son, Nick, would prefer not to be around. Jack does what he can to support him, but he's not much good at it. It doesn't help that Jack spends most of his time drunk and one step ahead of his probation officer and his landlord. His life ends at the moment he becomes a real father.

CINEMATHERAPY: Over the years, I've observed a lot of people work to make the transition from being an alcoholic or a drug addict to living a clean and sober, responsible life—and what a struggle. Often I find that people who don't understand what these individuals go through become very angry at these "slackers." Now, don't get me wrong; I'm not saying it's not their responsibility to get clean. I'm simply saying it's difficult. And from that point of view, *American Heart* has something unique to show us. First, look at our ex-con. He's a broken spirit who's taking his last shot at life. What events in his history might have caused him to turn out the way he did? Maybe he grew up in a home with parents who weren't around enough. Or possibly they drank and never could care for him. Now look at his son. Is anything making sense here? The boy is a reflection of the father. You can see he's a bright kid. He wants to have a relationship with a dad who doesn't have much time for him, drinks, and is constantly manipulating the system. Do you have concerns he will grow up just like his father, who grew up like his father, who . . . That's why I wanted you to watch this movie. Maybe you've been struggling to get a foothold on life but don't know how to do it because you were never taught. Possibly you work at having relationships but they never seem to pan out. You could be caught in your own issues. You are responsible for your actions and you need to spend the time to get in touch with why you are the way you are. Did you grow up in an alcoholic home? Were you raised by a parent who wasn't around or sent you the message that he or she couldn't be bothered with you? Use this movie to begin the process of healing from the effects of your past. I suggest you view this film alone and let yourself feel what you're watching. I believe you will be as deeply touched as I was. And after you're done, embark on the healing journey by letting go of those old memories. Begin the first day of the rest of your life.

AND THE BAND PLAYED ON

(HBO-Cable, 1993), color, 155 minutes, PG-rated

HEALING THEMES:
Understanding AIDS
Dealing with ignorance and prejudice
Losing someone to AIDS
Gaining an appreciation for how we build knowledge
Grieving over the death of a friend

DIRECTOR: Roger Spottiswoode; TELEPLAY: Arnold Schulman; CAST: Matthew Modine (Dr. Don Francis); Alan Alda (Dr. Robert Gallo); Phil Collins (Eddie); Richard Gere (choreographer); Angelica Huston (Dr. Betsy Reiz); Steve Martin (brother); Lily Tomlin (Dr. Selma Dritz); Glenne Headly (Mary); Swoosie Kurtz (Mrs. Johnstone); Richard Masur (William); Saul Rubinek (Dr. Curran); Charles Martin Smith (Dr. Harold Jaffe); B. D. Wong (Kico)

SYNOPSIS: It's the late 1970s. A medical researcher, Don Francis, is called to work on an unusual case involving unexplained deaths. Over the years, a link is made to those fatalities and a plague of viral disease that will soon be called AIDS. Francis and the rest of the research investigators continue to work on a cure for the disease, but with little success, leaving them baffled.

CINEMATHERAPY: I remember as if it were yesterday the rumblings about a new, unexplained virus called AIDS. "It's those damn homosexuals. They're givin' everyone that gay people's disease and there ain't no cure. You can't breathe the air, stand next to them, or even live in the same community. They need to be sent off to some other country to die," and on and on went the ignorant masses. People were blaming everyone they could point a finger at. However, over the decades we have come to understand that everyone is at risk for both transmitting and acquiring AIDS. So, what's this got to do with healing stories? you ask. As we also see in *Choices of the Heart: The Margaret Sanger Story*, we can all heal by comprehending where major problems and issues have their origin. With education and awareness comes understanding. And this brings healing. I lose my sense of prejudice about anything when I let go of my ignorance of a subject. As you watch this movie, you can't help but go back in your own memory to the people we've lost to AIDS: entertainers, sports figures, friends, and friends of friends. This immune deficiency disease has touched each and every one of us in one way or another. We do not need to point a finger at any one group or population and exclaim, "It's your fault! You are the cause of this mess!" The truth is we still don't know the full cause and we don't know the actual cure. However, we do know we must work together as a community, a world, to get on the other side of this horrible, deadly virus. This is a wonderful movie for families and educators to use to help deal with the misunderstanding and prejudice surrounding the scourge called AIDS. Heal and grow as a person by lifting you and your family out of ignorance over this global plight. Avoid being a party to narrow-minded thinking. And most of all, don't put yourself and your family at risk by having unprotected sex.

AND THEN THERE WAS ONE

(Lifetime-TV, 1994), color, 100 minutes, PG-rated

HEALING THEMES:
Dealing with the illness of someone you know
Issues on AIDS
Dealing with death and dying
Learning to let go
Making the best of every moment of your life
Turning to friends in a time of need
Accepting life on life's terms

DIRECTOR: David Jones; **TELEPLAY**: Rama Laurie Stagner; **CAST**: Amy Madigan (Roxie); Dennis Boutsikaris (Vinnie); Jane Daly (Lorrie); Jennifer Hetrick (Janet); Kenneth Welsh (David); Richard Monette (Dr. Lloyd)

SYNOPSIS: Vinney and Roxie Glasser are up-and-coming television writers who want to have a baby. In the process of trying to conceive, Roxie receives a blood transfusion, which gives her, Vinnie, and their unborn child AIDS. They have their child, struggle to live with the virus, and struggle to die with dignity.

CINEMATHERAPY: Of those people I have worked with who are HIV positive, I can assure you that none of them planned to acquire the disease. Oh, some of them knew they were at a higher risk than others, but getting sick was definitely not part of the game plan. However, this story offers us much more than a glimpse of a family's struggle to deal with AIDS. It offers us courage, strength, and hope through a portrayal of a couple who strive to maintain the quality of their lives. As you watch this movie, you will notice the emotional roller coaster that Vinnie and Roxie embark on. None of us is taught how to die, yet each of us knows it is inevitable. Notice the transition from disbelief to anger to denial to depression and finally to acceptance. "What have I done to deserve this? Why me? Bad things happen to good people." Have any of these thoughts ever crossed your mind? It seems I've been in that place a few times myself. What would you have done if you knew you had to go through what they experienced? And what about their baby, Miranda? Did you find yourself blaming Roxie because the AIDS virus came from her, or were you angry at a system that was not efficient enough to guard against this accident happening to her? And what of their social circle? How did you feel about the way Roxie and Vinnie were treated? One day they were all the best of friends, and the next some of their pals wanted nothing to do with them. Were you angry at this? Did you want to lash out at those friends? Maybe you felt they were justified? This will not be an easy movie to watch. Emotional healing occurs when you come to realize how vulnerable we all are in this complex world. Take the time to watch this as a couple or with a group of friends. Have an honest, open discussion about how you would handle your relationship if a catastrophic event happened in your life. Discuss your definition of an acceptable quality of life and how you want to live and die. Get in touch with your vulnerability about these key issues. You will grow in the process.

ANGEL BABY

(Meridian Films/Stamen,1995), color, 105 minutes, not rated

HEALING THEMES:
Living with a mental disorder
Trying to have a normal life

Caring for someone who can't take care of him- or herself
Standing up for what you believe
Suicide

DIRECTOR: Michael Rymer; SCREENPLAY: Michael Rymer; CAST: John Lynch (Harry); Jacqueline MacKenzie (Kate); Colin Friels (Morris); Deborra-Lee Furness (Louise)

SYNOPSIS: Harry and Kate, both of whom have psychological problems requiring drug treatment, fall in love. When Kate gets pregnant, they decide to stop taking their medication. Although she has the baby, the end result is disaster, with both Harry and Katie struggling to stay connected to the real world.

CINEMATHERAPY: If a member of your family is mentally challenged or you know someone who suffers from a mental illness, *Angel Baby* may offer you insight about the many trials in his or her life. It may also give you some validation that coping with a mentally challenged person is a big job. How easy it is for me to be critical of those who don't appear to function as well as I do. More than once in my life I have been impatient with people who can't seem to keep their life on track, who act funny, and have ways that seem strange. But maybe there was something wrong with them, something they could not control. Many people think that the solution to mental illness is medication. Unfortunately, that is not the case. Each of us has an individual reaction to such treatment. So it's not as simple as giving every person with a special problem the same drugs. Let me invite you to see that regardless of the degree of the problem, those who are mentally challenged have dreams and hopes just like you. Harry and Kate wanted to be married and have children. Can you appreciate how difficult it must have been for them to struggle with their schizophrenia in a world that makes no allowances for their problem? Do you know anyone who wants to lead a normal life but can't seem to make it because of being challenged in one way or another? What are your thoughts about those who are mentally challenged choosing to have a baby? Some think such people should be sterilized. Should the government intervene in their lives and force them to become sterile? Kate decided she no longer wanted to live. Should she have the right to take her own life? Do you think she is capable of making that choice? This movie is not going to make you feel good. Perhaps it will educate you and stir up some questions that you might otherwise never have an opportunity to think about. Above all, it may show you that you should learn to be patient with those who require extra love and care. They need your support and understanding.

ANGEL HEART

(TriStar, 1987), color, 113 minutes, R-rated

HEALING THEMES:

Selling your soul too cheaply
Taking care of the wreckage from your past
Memories that haunt you
Dealing with someone who wants to hold you accountable
Being caught between heaven and hell

DIRECTOR: Alan Parker; **SCREENPLAY**: Alan Parker; **CAST**: Mickey Rourke (Harry); Robert De Niro (Louis Cyphre); Lisa Bonet (Epiphany); Charlotte Rampling (Margaret); Stocker Fountelieu (Ethan); Brownie McGhee (Toots); Michael Higgins (Dr. Fowler); Charles Gordone (Spider)

SYNOPSIS: A private detective is hired to find a missing person, someone who has an outstanding debt. While on the hunt, he begins to realize that something is quite strange about the investigation and the mysterious man who hired him. As he delves deeper into the complex case, he wonders if he is looking for himself.

CINEMATHERAPY: Here's the situation: You want something in life—a lot of money, to be the best at something, people to see you as a beautiful-looking person, et cetera. Now you get a chance to make a deal for that to happen. But it does *not* come for free. You're going to have to give up your soul. What do you do? You'd do it in a second, you say. There is no such thing as a soul. Well, maybe not. However, there are those who believe very strongly in heaven and hell and everything that goes with it. This is one of several movies I have found that offer a different version of the concept of heaven, hell, and how we get there. Why do I include this type of film in this book? Because each of us absorbs life's messages in different ways. Some want a direct way to deal with questions and issues. Others prefer a more abstract approach. *Angel Heart* forces us to look at the bargains and deals we make with ourselves and at what cost they are really made. Note how Harry is constantly haunted by the repetition of the trumpet melody throughout the movie. That music still haunts me to this day. Are there things in your past that play like that trumpet in your mind? Do you try to shake them away, only to hear a voice in your head drawing you back to an experience you're trying to forget? Possibly you cheated on someone or lied at the expense of others. In the movie, Louis Cyphre—Lucifer, or the devil—can haunt our minds until we are willing to make amends, until we hit bottom. And sometimes hitting bottom is the epiphany; it certainly was for him. Once enlightened you have the chance to heal, to recover from the repercussions of all those bad deals you made when you tried to take a shortcut in life. Warning: This is the kind of movie that can create nightmares. Prepare yourself. You might want to invite a friend along for the ride.

ANIMAL FARM

(RKO, 1955), color, 75 minutes, PG-rated

HEALING THEMES:
Being dominated by others
Having a chance to be equal in the world
Working toward a common goal
Being taken advantage of
Being dominated by other people

Directors: John Halas, Joy Batchelor; **SCREENPLAY:** John Halas, Joy Batchelor, Lothar Wolff, Borden Mace, Philip Stapp; **CAST:** Maurice Denham (voices of the animals); Gordon Heath (Narrator)

SYNOPSIS: When a farmer dies, the animals must fend for themselves. Having lived under the dictatorship of the farmer and his rules, the animals choose to live in a democracy, with all animals being equal. However, in time, some animals become "more equal than others." Eventually they end up as they began, being ruled by those animals who saw themselves as superior to the others.

CINEMATHERAPY: Some of you may feel that the animated *Animal Farm* has nothing to do with healing. However, I would like to invite you to open your mind to the idea that we heal on many levels. Most of the stories in this book I share with you on a personal, intimate level. A few of the movies show you issues relating to groups and communities. *Animal Farm* asks us to examine our ethical and moral beliefs about ourselves and those around us. Do you remember when you were young and you promised that when you grew up you were going to be more fair with your children than your parents were with you? Or possibly you resented being told what to do at school, always feeling that you were being treated unfairly. Have you kept your promise? Do you treat people with equality and humanity? Are you prejudiced against some because you have a personal agenda or you don't feel they're as good as you? As you watch *Animal Farm,* keep in touch with how this story relates to your own life and the world around you. Notice the way things progressively get worse for some of the animals when other animals take charge and take advantage. Is that how you view life? Have you been a party to dominating those around you? Use the movie and its therapeutic message to make a commitment in your life to teach your children about the pitfalls that come with trying to be superior in a world given to all of us equally. This is a wonderful film to watch as a group. Invite open and honest discussion about how the movie affects everyone. It's a rare and special opportunity to see recovery on a global level.

THE APPRENTICESHIP
OF DUDDY KRAVITZ

(International Cinemedia Centre Paramount, 1974), color, 120 minutes, PG-rated

HEALING THEMES:
Feeling used by someone you care about
Trying to get ahead at other people's expense
Relationships that take and don't give
Taking steps to get out of an unhealthy relationship

DIRECTOR: Ted Kotcheff; SCREENPLAY: Mordecai Richler; CAST: Richard Dreyfuss (Duddy); Randy Quaid (Virgil); Denholm Elliott (Friar); Jack Warden (Max); Micheline Lanctot (Yvette); Joe Silver (Farber); Joseph Wiseman (Uncle Benjy); Zvee Scooler (grandfather)

SYNOPSIS: Duddy Kravitz is a young boy living in Canada. He comes from a middle-class family that has everything but money. Duddy finds a piece of land that he believes will make him rich. He schemes to acquire the property. Along the way, he forgets those who love him.

CINEMATHERAPY: *The Apprenticeship of Duddy Kravitz* left a deep impression on me. I'm a bit embarrassed to say there was once a great deal of Duddy Kravitz in me. You, too? I forgot all the reasons I was working so hard. I turned my back on those who cared about me and gravitated to those who offered me nothing unless I could give them something in exchange. I wish I had gotten the message much sooner. I know Duddy feels the same way. We have all known someone who would do anything to get to the top—to make a buck. Maybe one of the reasons you have sought recovery is that you are beginning to question the motives for why you want to fight your way up the ladder. Have you had a fall and are now wondering what happened to your life? *The Apprenticeship of Duddy Kravitz* vividly portrays this kind of experience. Watch as Duddy loses all sense of purpose and morality. Notice his willingness to say and do anything to get what he wants. Does this ring a bell for you? Have there been times you said something or made a promise you knew you wouldn't keep? Have you lost contact with people who loved you? Some of you may still be in relationships of one kind or another with people like Duddy. Why do you stay with that person? Listen to the way the people around Duddy continue to "buy into" his manipulation. Do they remind you of yourself? What kinds of feelings are brought up as you watch their responses? Are you angry? Sad? Hurt? They all have the choice to stay or go just like you. Here's an opportunity to gather friends together and watch a film that will open up deep feelings about love, trust, and friendship. Afterward, gather the courage to confront that individual who's abusing the relationship in which you've invested so much. Let them know how you feel, and set boundaries. You can heal yourself and that friendship bond that is wearing away. Take a chance. You will grow in the process!

AS GOOD AS IT GETS

(TriStar, 1997), color, 138 minutes, PG-13-rated

HEALING THEME:

Admitting you have a problem
Being obsessive-compulsive
Just getting by
Raising a physically challenged child
Seeing the good through the bad
Taking chances

DIRECTOR: James L. Brooks; SCREENPLAY: Mark Andrus, James L. Brooks; CAST: Jack Nicholson (Melvin); Helen Hunt (Carol); Greg Kinnear (Simon); Cuba Gooding Jr. (Frank); Skeet Ulrich (Vincent); Shirley Knight (Beverly); Yeardley Smith (Jackie)

SYNOPSIS: Melvin is no ordinary guy. He certainly doesn't have ordinary problems. Suffering from obsessive-compulsive disorder, he seems to hate everything and everyone unless, of course, he's not trying to avoid stepping on the cracks in the sidewalk. When Melvin's lifestyle collides with those of Carol and his neighbor Simon, he sees that there is more to living than rewashing his hands.

CINEMATHERAPY: It's probably the therapist in me that would not allow me to enjoy this movie. No, I'm not saying that it was not a good film. (As you know, that's not the purpose of my work here.) Rather, I'm saying that Melvin's problem is so disturbing that I had a difficult time seeing anything else in the story line. Several of my clients saw this picture, and they returned for their next appointment somewhat relieved. "Remember I told you my sister used to wash her hands until they would bleed? Well, until I saw this movie I thought she was the only person in the world who did that kind of thing to herself." "Am I crazy? Sometimes I check three or four times to see if I've closed the garage door!" Make no mistake, obsessive-compulsive disorder is no laughing matter. It can destroy a person's life by taking over their will, making them do things they really do not want to do. I wish I could tell you that the solution to the problem is as simple as finding the right person to love. But unfortunately, that is not the case. The treatment of this disorder can be long and painful, requiring both therapy and medication. In some severe cases, a brain surgery procedure may be performed. However, even in these instances, there are no guarantees of success. So why would I want those of you who have no connection to this problem to become involved with this movie? It is my personal mission to make this a kinder, more gentle world in which to live. How wonderful it would be to give more understanding to those who cannot help themselves instead of mocking and tormenting them. So watch this healing story and learn to be patient with those who endure such unimaginable problems. And if you are someone who suffers from this difficult disorder, please get help. The good years are right before you, in between the cracks.

AVALON
(TriStar, 1990), color, 126 minutes, PG-rated

HEALING THEMES:
Looking at family issues
Starting fresh
Growing up with brothers and sisters
Coping when family conflict is pulling you apart
Losing contact with your past and your family history

DIRECTOR: Barry Levinson; SCREENPLAY: Barry Levinson; CAST: Leo Fuchs (Hymie); Eve Gordon (Dottie); Lou Jacobi (Gabriel); Armin Mueller-Stahl (Sam); Elizabeth Perkins (Ann); Joan Plowright (Eva); Kevin Pollack (Izzy); Aidan Quinn (Jules)

SYNOPSIS: Hymie Krichinsky and the rest of his family finally have a real chance at life. After immigrating to Baltimore, Maryland, from Russia, Hymie and his brothers work hard to get ahead in their new homeland. But the years take their toll on the family as each member responds in a different way to time slipping out of their hands.

CINEMATHERAPY: I don't know about you, but I did not experience much of a family life. There were only four of us, and for the most part we existed in separate houses together. Can you relate? Most of the time, we were strangers. If it were not for the violence that came from yelling and screaming, I would not have known that I had relatives at all. *Avalon* is a rich compilation of domestic issues. Let me warn you not to get caught up in the fact that these people are new to this country or that they come from an ethnic or religious background different from yours. For the most part, we are all the same. Look for yourself in one or more of the characters. Were you the follower or the leader? Did you feel you always lived in the shadow of your brothers' or sisters' successes? Maybe you were the one who ruled how the household functioned. What kind of relationship do you have with your family today? Is it strained due to problems that the family has never been able to resolve? Do you have trouble communicating your feelings to your relatives for fear they will negate them or put them down? And what of the wives of these brothers in the film? Can you see how they each work to resolve the family issues yet get caught up in the concerns at the same time? *Avalon* is a wonderful portrayal of what we have come to call a nuclear family and what such family units go through to survive. You will get a chance to look at your own history as this group reminds you about the importance of strong blood ties. If you're working to hold your family together, give this film a try. Gather the members of your family together and watch *Avalon*. Open up the doors to discussion, and listen to one another's thoughts and feelings. This is a beautiful way to heal yesterday's wounds and rebond as a family unit.

AWAKENINGS
(Columbia, 1990), color, 120 minutes, PG-13-rated

HEALING THEMES:
Dealing with a serious mental illness
Finding the courage to make changes
Reaching out to those who need your help
Never giving up
Learning to love those who can't love themselves

DIRECTOR: Penny Marshall; SCREENPLAY: Steven Zaillian; CAST: Robin Williams (Dr. Malcolm Sayer); Robert De Niro (Leonard); John Heard (Dr. Kaufman); Julie Kavner (Eleanor); Penelope Ann Miller (Paula); Max Von Sydow (Dr. Peter Ingham); Anne Meara (Miriam)

SYNOPSIS: Dr. Malcom Sayer is assigned to a Bronx, New York, hospital ward full of comatose patients. Sayer discovers and uses a drug that dramatically brings them out of their longtime catatonic state. The patients face both joy and sadness about their lives. Sayer is eventually confronted with his own humanness and feelings of inadequacy as one by one the patients regress back to darkness.

CINEMATHERAPY: There is little question that those who suffer from this severe mental illness are not readers of this book. So why did I want you to watch this movie? Because Dr. Sayer offers us courage to go forward in the face of adversity, and we can all gain something by learning to be more empathetic to those who have lost their ability to function in the real world. Have you ever wanted to do something, only to hear people around you tell you it is impossible? "Forget it. It can't be done." Sound familiar? That has happened more than once in my life. And each time I accomplish my goal in the wake of disapproval and lack of support, I realize that it is others' fear of failure that stops people from going forward. Has anyone ever told you that you couldn't make it in school or in that business? Maybe you were informed you weren't "good enough" to learn how to play a musical instrument or paint. Were they fearful or jealous of your potential and future success? Follow in the footsteps of Sayer. Just keep trying. Don't buy into other people's fears. Gather your own inner strength and do it anyway. How did you feel about these patients? Have there been times that you have wanted to burrow inside yourself and never come back? As you will see, these people have lost control over their own existence. Don't let that happen to you. Don't let your life slip away in regret, coming alive only for brief periods of time, filled with remorse about the time you've lost. You can experience healing when you come to realize that you must venture out on your own regardless of the views and ideas of others. And there is self-nurturing when you realize how important it is to live every day in the here and now. Let yourself be touched by this movie and learn from Sayer's self-awakening. Remember that there are no failures in life except the failure to try. You've *got* to try.

THE BAD SEED

(Warner Bros., 1956), color, 129 minutes, not rated

HEALING THEMES:
Abusive children
Refusing to see children for who they really are
Accepting that children can do harm
Getting help for a child before it is too late
What goes around comes around

DIRECTOR: Mervyn LeRoy; SCREENPLAY: John Lee Mahin; CAST: Patty McCormack (Rhonda); Nancy Kelly (Mrs. Christine); Eileen Heckart (Mrs. Daigle); Henry Jones (LeRoy); Evelyn Varden (Monica); William Hooper (Kenneth)

SYNOPSIS: Rhonda lives around the corner in small-town, Middle America. She's blond and cute, but this little girl does horrible and evil things to get what she wants, including murder. She becomes more and more aggressive in her attacks on people who she thinks are standing in her way. Eventually lightning takes our bad seed away, as death becomes her.

CINEMATHERAPY: I don't know what came first, this movie or the expression "bad seed," as in "He's a real bad seed, that one is" or "You can't trust him. He's a bad seed." I can tell you this: When the various versions of *The Bad Seed* came out, they struck fear in the hearts of many people. And from that point forward, any kid who even looked like they were doing something wrong was "a bad seed." Now, I don't know about you, but I did just a few things wrong when I was a kid and a few more things as an adult—the devil made me do it.

I wonder if you grew up believing you were bad no matter what you did. I have seen a lot of people in my office who have a pretty skewed message about themselves. Do you tend to think of yourself as someone who is not as good as the next person? Do you feel like you will never be anybody in life but do not know why? Maybe you keep on replaying the "bad seed" message over and over again. It could be you're in a relationship where your partner keeps reinforcing that old childhood message: "No one else would have you. You're a loser, a bad seed." I'm not suggesting you are like our little blond friend on screen, make no mistake—this little girl is a sick child and she needs lots of help. I simply want you to take time and reflect on your life today and how you feel about yourself. I have no doubt you did a few things in your past that you'd like to forget, but you were probably nothing like this youngster. Tell yourself you're okay. Give yourself some hugs and go through the healing that comes from realizing you're not the bad person your parents may have made you out to be. If they made you feel bad about yourself, they were sick themselves. They were the bad seeds. Give this film a try. Don't be afraid to show it to the whole family. I have no doubt it will prompt some interesting discussions.

THE BASKETBALL DIARIES

(New Line Cinema, 1995), color, 102 minutes, R-rated

HEALING THEMES:
Getting caught up in drugs and alcohol
Giving up the opportunity of a lifetime
Living on the streets
Having no place to turn
Turning your life around

DIRECTOR: Scott Kalvert; SCREENPLAY: Bryan Goluboff; CAST: Leonardo DiCaprio (Jim); Lorraine Bracco (Jim's mother); Bruno Kirby (Swifty); Mark Wahlberg (Mickey); James Madio (Pedro); Ernie Hudson (Reggie); Barton Heyman (confessional priest); Juliette Lewis (Diane)

SYNOPSIS: With the exception of basketball, Jim hated just about everything in his high school years. Eventually he finds relief in street life and heroin. Strung out and near death, he turns to his mother, who can no longer endure watching her son kill himself. Although he briefly quits his drug use, he jumps right back on the dangerous merry-go-round to give it one more try.

CINEMATHERAPY: An addiction doesn't happen overnight. And whether it's drugs, alcohol, food, sex, cigarettes, et cetera, the climb all the way up from the depths of an addiction is a very long journey. It takes time and lots of self-nurturing to get that low in your life. I'll bet you never thought of it that way, but it's true. That's how it's done. If you know anyone who is suffering from an addiction, *The Basketball Diaries* is going to pull him or her out of denial about as fast as any movie I can think of. Remember, the idea of recovery through cinematherapy is based, in part, on helping you to *see* what is happening to yourself or someone you know. This is accomplished through watching your life, or that of someone you know, through the characters and story lines in the movies. Do you know someone who is on a downward spiral from a dependency? Are you struggling from day to day to try to keep away from your own self-destructive behavior? Like Jim, what chances are you destroying in your life so that you can go from one high to the next, to the next? . . . I apologize if I sound preachy, but this one really hits home for me. I took Jim's path. I only wish I had seen this and other movies before I hit bottom. In the end, Jim reminds us that the only person who can decide to no longer take the road to destruction is ourself. So if you, or someone you care about is in emotional trouble, you will want to experience this movie. Force yourself to confront your emotions. Don't turn away from the movie to seek the security of denial. Take the time to face up to yourself and get on the recovery track. No matter where you live, there are support groups and meetings to see you through to recovery.

BASTARD OUT OF CAROLINA

(Showtime-Cable, 1996), color, 101 minutes, R-rated

HEALING THEMES:
Being abused
Living with a stepparent
Losing those you love
Denial, denial, denial
Keeping secrets
Protecting a parent from the truth

DIRECTOR: Angelica Huston; TELEPLAY: Anne Meredith; CAST: Jennifer Jason Leigh (Anney); Jena Malone (Bone); Ron Eldard (Glen); Glenne Headly (Ruth); Lyle Lovett (Wade); Dermot Mulroney (Lyle); Christina Ricci (Dee Dee); Michael Rooker (Earle); Diana Scarwid (Raylene); Susan Traylor (Alma); Grace Zabriskie (Granny); Richard Todd Sullivan (Travis); Pat Hiengle (Mr. Waddell); Laura Dern (Narrator)

SYNOPSIS: Life was never what anyone would call easy for Bone. Being poor was not that difficult. Living with Glen, her stepfather, is what made every day a living nightmare. After years of mental, physical, and sexual abuse, Bone finally leaves her mother and sister for a safer life with relatives.

CINEMATHERAPY: You may be asking, "Doc, why would you want us to watch a movie like *Bastard Out of Carolina*? Who needs to watch all that horrible abuse?" The answer is simple: We must never, ever forget the devastation brought about by an emotionally sick parent—no, not just Glen, the stepfather. Anney, Bone's mother, is just as ill as Glen. She knows what he is doing to her daughter, yet she remains with him. Now, some of you may not like what you are about to read because it hits too close to home. But then, I'm not in the business of beating around the bush. Bone's mother sold her daughter down the river. She needed to stay with her sick husband for unhealthy, selfish reasons and she was willing to overlook little things like Glen beating and molesting her daughter. You may not have grown up dirt poor like Bone. However, if you were abused or molested as a child, this film will make you feel every corner of your body. And that is exactly what I want to happen. Were you raised in a home with no boundaries? Did one parent overlook the behavior of the other just so they could get what they needed out of their relationship? Are you someone who is ignoring things that are taking place in the house to avoid dealing with the pain and loneliness of not having a relationship? If ever I have used a movie to help people come out of denial, it is *Bastard Out of Carolina*. If you have been keeping your childhood memories to yourself, get help. Reach out to those who can hear your pain. There are support groups, counselors, therapists, teachers, and religious leaders to see you through to a brighter tomorrow. To those who can't seem to get the message, try this: Leave our children to grow in peace. They're all tomorrow has to offer.

BEAUTIFUL GIRLS

(Miramax, 1996), color, 107 minutes, R-rated

HEALING THEMES:

Growing up
Having an affair
Alcohol becoming the center of your life
Feeling like you're going nowhere
Falling for someone who is too young for you
Making life choices

DIRECTOR: Ted Demme; SCREENPLAY: Scott Rosenberg; CAST: Timothy Hutton (Willie); Matt Dillon (Tommy [Birdman]); Noah Emmerich (Michael [Mo]); Annabeth Gish (Tracy); Lauren Holly (Darian); Rosie O'Donnell (Gina); Max Perlich (Kev); Martha Plimpton (Jan); Natalie Portman (Marty); Michael Rapaport (Paul); Mira Sorvino (Sharon); Uma Thurman (Andrea); Pruitt Taylor Vince (Stanley [Stinky]); Anne Bobby (Sarah); Richard Bright (Dick); Sam Robards (Steve); David Arquette (Bobby)

SYNOPSIS: The gang's complete when Willie, a struggling musican, comes back to his hometown to visit his high school friends. Still drinking, having affairs, and talking about women passing through his life, Willie is confronted with his inability to make a decision to commit to his girlfriend, who stayed behind in Manhattan. Before his visit is over, Willie, along with the others, takes a long-delayed giant leap toward maturity.

CINEMATHERAPY: Here's another film that did not do well at the box office. However, it is so rich with messages that I can't possibly offer all of them to you here. Maybe you are someone who is unable to make a commitment, so you latch on to more than one intimate relationship at a time. Possibly you have waited too long to make a permanent attachment to someone who has now decided to move on with his or her life. Perhaps you're angry at other people because they thought you did not fit the model of how an attractive person should look. Or maybe you just can't let go of the old gang so you keep on doing the same things you used to do. Can you relate? Are you feeling emotionally stuck, like you can't move forward and yet you can't move back? Listen as each of these young men expresses his fears through his own immature behavior. Notice the way the characters qualify women in terms of physical looks, with little or no concern about substance and values. And now the most difficult problem of all: What about the fantasy relationship between Marty and Willie? Have you ever felt the way they did, caught up in your emotions, torn between what society expects you to do or feel or think and what *you* want to do or feel or think? Many people have been in Willie's place. And most of us have had to deal with the pain of doing the right thing. Make no mistake: In spite of its title, this is a great movie for both men and women to use as a means to open up a discussion of true feelings and thoughts about relationships. Invite your friends over for a cinematherapy session. After the film, let down your guard and experience some real self-growth.

BED OF ROSES

(New Line Cinema, 1996), color, 87 minutes, PG-rated

HEALING THEMES:
Losing someone you love
Building emotional walls
Falling in love too fast
Taking time to smell the roses
Learning to love again

DIRECTOR: Michael Goldenberg; SCREENPLAY: Laura Jones; CAST: Christian Slater (Lewis); Mary Stuart Masterson (Lisa); Pamela Segall (Kim); Josh Grolin (Danny); Ally Walker (Wendy); Debra Monk (Lewis's mom)

SYNOPSIS: Lewis and Lisa are two young adults with something crucial missing from their lives—each other. The problem is that they must heal the pain of previous relationships before they can reach an emotional understanding with each other. When Lisa lets down her guard, true intimacy prevails.

CINEMATHERAPY: "I like him, but he's moving too fast." "She's pushing me to meet her parents." "We've known each other for a month and he's already talking about marriage." Any of this sound familiar? Do you feel you may have found the right person but are being overwhelmed with the pace of the relationship? And what about healing wounds from past relationships gone bad? Or feeling like you will never be involved again after losing the one you love to a tragic accident? *Bed of Roses* asks these questions, tugging at your innermost feelings to make you confront your fears of intimacy. It seems that we all start life off guard, with a wide-open heart, willing to let life happen. However, with each emotional injury, another brick is cemented in a wall that grows higher and thicker. So *not* letting someone in emotionally may become less painful than being alone. As you're watching this movie, notice how Lisa handles the feelings of intimacy encroaching on her life, how she sets herself up to avoid having a true involvement even with someone for whom she cares a lot. Be careful men, you may try to write off this film as another "chick flick." But let's not forget that Lewis is a man struggling with his own emotions. And it doesn't matter whether he owns a flower shop or a steel mill. Why deny your own feelings just to seem strong, to look like you are emotionally unbreakable? Did you notice the way his family spent their time with one another? Even I could be jealous of his family. So, if those are the problems, what are the solutions? Be open and honest with your partner. Tell him or her how fast or slow you can handle moving forward in the relationship. Let the person know that just because you need space does not mean you're running away. Communicate. Communicate. Communicate. Now go plant your own bed of roses.

BEFORE WOMEN HAD WINGS

(ABC-TV, 1997), color, 100 minutes, G-rated

HEALING THEMES:
Growing up with parents who abuse each other
Feeling like you're nobody
Someone you love committing suicide
Being abused and neglected
Finding someone who will teach you how to fly

DIRECTOR: Lloyd Kramer; TELEPLAY: Connie May Fowler; CAST: Ellen Barkin (Gloria [Mamma]); Oprah Winfrey (Zora); Tina Majorino (Bird); Julia Stiles (Phoebe); Burt Young (Mr. Ippolito); John Savage (Billy); William Lee Scott (Hank)

SYNOPSIS: After Bird's abusive, drunken father commits suicide, her homeless family resorts to living in a trailer. When Gloria, Bird's mother, becomes just as abusive toward Bird as her dad had been, she finds a friend in Zora, a kind and loving woman living in the same trailer park. Gloria's abuse eventually drives Zora, Bird, and Phoebe away from the park.

CINEMATHERAPY: It doesn't matter who you are or where you came from—you will be touched by this story. For those of you who grew up in abusive or neglectful homes, I recommend you hold on to your seats—it's going to be a bumpy ride. It is not difficult to see what alcohol and immaturity are doing to these very sick parents. But what is hidden, at least for a while, is the effect that the poor and almost nonexistent parenting is doing to Bird and Phoebe. Did you grow up in a home with chaotic parents? Were alcohol and violence the main themes? Did the local police know where to go whenever they heard your family's name? How do you feel when Mamma constantly puts her children down and blames Bird for their father's suicide? If you got a bad sensation in the pit of your stomach, I would suggest you examine your own childhood issues. A childhood laced with such memories can be devastating. And when physical and psychological abuse is figured into your life equation, the world can forever appear to be an unsafe, hostile place in which to live. Possibly, like Bird, you got lucky and met someone like Zora, a person who would just listen to you. Watch how Zora weaves her magic of love around a child who has never heard or seen love like Zora's. Notice the way Zora takes the time to nurture Bird's childhood with the realization that Bird is living in an abusive home. I don't know about you, but I was never lucky enough to find anyone like Zora—someone to take me under their wing and help me feel good about myself, to let me just be a kid when I was one. And it can be difficult when you don't have relatives or friends to step in and protect you from the very person, like your mom or dad, who should be loving you more than anyone. If this movie touches you the way it did me, consider joining a support group such as Adult Children of Alcoholics or Codependency Anonymous. Seek the assistance of a therapist who can help you through the pain and the memories that still linger. Work for the recovery and, in turn, the healthy life you so richly deserve. When you do this, you will soon learn to grow wings and fly.

BELL, BOOK AND CANDLE

(Columbia, 1959), color, 106 minutes, not rated

HEALING THEMES:

Trying to get someone to notice you
Letting go of control

Breaking old habits
Belief in the supernatural
Letting love come in

DIRECTOR: Richard Quine; **SCREENPLAY**: Daniel Taradash; **CAST**: James Stewart (Sheperd); Kim Novak (Gillian); Jack Lemmon (Nicky); Elsa Lanchester (Queenie); Ernie Kovacs (Sidney); Hermione Gingold (Mrs. De Pass); Janice Rule (Meile)

SYNOPSIS: Sheperd moves into his new apartment. The residents of the building are not quite your average tenants. One of them, a witch, decides she is no longer going to use her special powers to get what she wishes. Now she wants to live life like most people. She ends up breaking the promise to herself and creates a spell using her powers to attract the eligible tenant. Eventually, she abandons her ploys and true love conquers all.

CINEMATHERAPY: Did you ever wish you had special powers you could use to get whatever you wanted whenever you wished it? I know I've had those thoughts. There were times I would fantasize about knowing the outcome of a horse race, betting a lot of money, and really making a fortune. Maybe you wish you had the power to get someone like this kindly witch to love you. Well, the truth is you don't have to be a witch or use secret powers to have someone love you. You see, you already have the power; all you have to do is learn to use it. That's what comes as a result of the healing process. You learn to be who you really are, and when you do that, people are naturally attracted to you. Did you ever wonder how that kid in school, the not-so-attractive one, had so many friends? He knew his power because he knew who he was inside. We receive that message as we watch this film. I acknowledge that some of you will watch this movie and think, "nonsense." You might feel the same way about *The Butcher's Wife*, since it has a similar theme. However, give both movies a try. Can you see that this is really about destiny and the way things are supposed to happen? All Gillian has to do is let go and let the love come her way. Have you ever worked hard at trying to get someone to really care for you, only to have them ignore you? Perhaps when you stopped working at the goal, they suddenly knew you were gone and began to pay attention to you. And why spend your time on someone who doesn't care for you anyway? Focus your energy, your love, on those who appreciate you and who have the ability to see all you have to offer. Just enjoy this wonderful, uplifting film. Remember, when you can shed a real tear, you're at home with the person you really are.

THE BELL JAR

(Avco Embassy, 1979), color, 117 minutes, R-rated

HEALING THEMES:

Feeling like you can't take it anymore
Never letting people see the real you
Living with a mental illness
Coping when those who say they love you won't listen
Making the long climb to wellness

DIRECTOR: Larry Peerce; SCREENPLAY: Marjorie Kellogg; CAST: Marilyn Hassett (Esther); Julie Harris (Mrs. Greenwood); Anne Jackson (Dr. Nolan); Barbara Barrie (Jay); Robert Klein (Lenny); Donna Mitchell (Jean); Jameson Parker (Buddy); Thaao Penghlis (Marco)

SYNOPSIS: Esther has been pushed to the edge. When she can't take life any longer, she falls into a deep, dark, black depression, believing it will swallow her for life. Her climb back to mental health is difficult. It comes at great expense—losses on which she never counted.

CINEMATHERAPY: "No one knows who I really am. Not even you, Doc. Oh, you think you do, but you don't. I go to work every day, keep a smile on my face, and outperform everyone else. They all think I'm great. But I'm not, you know. I'm losing it. I don't know how much longer I can hold on." Does any part of that little speech apply to you? Have you ever felt you were going crazy, like you were hiding a big secret of insanity? We've all been there from time to time. Esther gives us bits and pieces of ourselves by letting us into her life through the "bell jar" in which she exists. What did Esther go through in her life that you can identify with? Have you been in a relationship that demanded everything from you but gave you nothing in return? Notice the movie's climax, in which Esther's boyfriend visits her in the mental hospital and acts as if nothing happened. He is still demanding what he wants, never concerned for her requirements. And what about Esther's relationship with her mother? Listen to the conversation about her father. Do you feel her mother was keeping secrets? Secrets will eventually destroy any relationship. Can you relate? I sure could! I could see and hear the words of my own family. It really hit home. You're going to get in touch with a lot of memories with this movie. And some of you may not like what you find in yourself. You may see your role in making demands and being unfair with people. I suggest you watch this one alone. Sit with your emotions. Let yourself be absorbed into Esther's thinking, and look for yourself in her. You will be amazed at the fear you feel and the healing that comes in confronting yourself with your own feelings. Watch and feel Esther's courage, and reach for that courage within your own heart. Her self-enlightenment can be yours. Just watch, listen, and learn to take the world one day at a time. If you feel you need extra help with your healing, seek the support of a close friend, a loved one, a therapist, or a religious group to see you through the difficult times.

THE BEST YEARS OF OUR LIVES

(Samuel Goldwyn Pictures/RKO, 1946), B & W, 172 minutes, not rated

HEALING THEMES:
Being away from home for a long time
Your lover leaving you
Accepting your physical handicap
Learning the true meaning of love
Trying to get on track with a career
Finding the true meaning of friends and family

DIRECTOR: William Wyler; **SCREENPLAY**: Robert Sherwood; **CAST**: Fredric March (Al); Myrna Loy (Milly); Teresa Wright (Peggy); Dana Andrews (Fred); Virginia Mayo (Marie); Harold Russell (Homer); Hoagy Carmichael (Butch); Gladys George (Hortense); Roman Bohnen (Pat); Steve Cochran (Cliff)

SYNOPSIS: Homer, Al, and Fred return home from the war. Although they reside in the same town, they each come from different walks of life. Each of them works to adjust to their new world. In the process, they learn some of life's most important lessons.

CINEMATHERAPY: I've said it before, and it bears repeating: Often older movies provide the strongest gifts of healing. I don't know if it's because they are in black and white, the actor's interpretations, or the way the screenplays were written, but these movies from decades ago reach into our souls and strike a very special chord. *The Best Years of Our Lives* is one of those movies that has it all: relationship issues, physical and emotional loss, family confrontation, alcohol abuse, abandonment, becoming an adult, and so on. If you're anything like me, you probably take your physical health for granted. When I see what people like the double amputee Homer go through, gratitude comes rushing into my life; I realize how truly lucky I am. How did you feel as you watched him struggle through the process of accepting life without arms and hands? Maybe you or someone you know is physically or mentally challenged. What did you learn from Homer's courage and the love of his family and fiancée? (By the way, Harold Russell was playing what was for him a true-to-life role: He really lost his arms and hands in the war.) What about our comfortable banker? Notice how he struggles at becoming part of his family again. Did you grow up in a home where one of your parents would come and go for weeks or months at a time? What memories returned as you watched Al try to be part of the household again? Listen to his daughter talk about her affair with a married man. Bring back any memories? Can you hear her denial and lack of understanding about what it means to have an affair? Maybe there was a time when someone you loved and cared for was not faithful to you. Possibly you grew up in a home that was torn apart because of an affair. This movie is three hours of healing, growing, and understanding. Watch *The Best Years of Our Lives* with those you care for. You're going to grow emotionally from this one. Sit back and enjoy this enlightening journey.

BOB & CAROL & TED & ALICE

(Columbia, 1969), color, 104 minutes, R-rated

HEALING THEMES:
Doing the "swing thing"
Being reminded what intimacy is all about
Experimenting with drugs
Being bored with life
Taking things too far
Putting your relationship at risk

DIRECTOR: Paul Mazursky; SCREENPLAY: Paul Mazursky, Larry Tucker; CAST: Natalie Wood (Carol); Robert Culp (Bob); Elliott Gould (Ted); Dyan Cannon (Alice); Horst Ebersberg (Horst); Lee Bergere (Emelio)

SYNOPSIS: Bob, Carol, Ted, and Alice are the best of friends. They do just about everything together. The group decides they want to take their friendship a step further and try swinging—swapping partners. When all is said and done, they realize the importance and meaning of their marriages and friendship.

CINEMATHERAPY: Swinging—swapping partners—or having sex with friends is one of the more common fantasies people have. "We've been together for more than three years. It's not that I don't love him, it's just that I'm getting bored of doing the same, you know, thing all the time. We need some new and exciting sex in our lives." "In the last few years, I've found myself attracted to the wife of my best friend. I think she's attracted to me, too. I'm thinking about approaching them to see if they want to swap. What do you think?" I have told my readers that my goal is to open the door to discussion and self-examination, *not* to pass judgment about individual choices and lifestyle. However, practicing this kind of lifestyles comes with risks. You must be solid in your primary relationship before you can venture into swinging with friends. You have the additional danger of contracting a potentially fatal sexually transmitted disease, which puts not only you in jeopardy but also your significant other and the rest of your family. If you're having contact with more than one couple, the risk increases exponentially. And it is possible that by watching what Bob, Carol, Ted, and Alice experience in the movie, you might feel differently about trying this. How did you feel when they proposed this sophisticated idea to one another? Maybe you questioned if their relationships were really grounded in love and caring. Which one of the group were you? The aggressive, take-charge person who initiates the first step? Maybe you were the individual who went along for the ride. What part did you feel drugs played in their lives? Were the drugs responsible for lowering their inhibitions? And what about the effect their behavior had on their children? Possibly the children were put in second place, ignored, while the parents were taking the drugs and considering this most personal and intimate step. Try using this movie to help you think through this difficult life decision. Make sure that all concerned are in complete agreement before you take this step.

THE BOSTON STRANGLER

(Twentieth Century-Fox, 1968), color, 116 minutes, not rated

HEALING THEMES:
Living life with reasonable caution
Spending the time to know your neighbor
Knowing what to do if someone around you is not mentally stable
Learning to protect yourself
Realizing that people can go over the edge

DIRECTOR: Richard Fleischer; **SCREENPLAY:** Edward Anhalt; **CAST:** Tony Curtis (Albert); Henry Fonda (John); George Kennedy (Phil); Murray Hamilton (Frank); Mike Kellin (Julian); George Voskovec (Peter); William Hickey (Eugene); James Brolin (Sergeant Lisi); Hurd Hatfield (Terence); William Marshall (Edward); Jeff Corey (John); Sally Kellerman (Dianne); Leora Dana (Mary)

SYNOPSIS: Tony Curtis is the Boston Strangler, not your average American guy. This serial killer gets up every day and goes to work to support his family. However, he has a bad habit of strangling women to death. He terrorizes the city of Boston before being caught. He eventually succumbs to his own mental instability.

CINEMATHERAPY: This is the only movie in the book that deals with violence of this sort. Quite honestly, this film is not for everyone. However, you have an excellent opportunity to learn from this movie to help you see things you may be avoiding. The mere fact that someone seems nice and fits into the neighborhood does not mean he or she is incapable of commiting a heinous crime. We have seen the "nice guy" profile fit many murderers, molesters, and rapists. I make this point not to cause you to be suspicious of every neighbor or friend, but rather to make you aware of this reality: Some people go over the edge, and we simply cannot predict who they are or when it will happen. At times, each of us feels as if we are being pushed to the edge. And although we may experience being shoved too far, we have the capability to hold on; we can stay within the normal bounds of human behavior. Notice the different crafty ways the Boston Strangler gains access to his victims' homes. As I look back on my own life, I can recall how I put myself in jeopardy from time to time. I just wasn't thinking. I opened doors to people I didn't know, went to parts of town that were dangerous, and spent time with people whose backgrounds were completely unknown to me. Take the time to learn how to protect yourself. Avoid risky, life-threatening situations. If you have children, teach them early how to recognize dangerous people and environments. Instructing them today may save their lives tomorrow. If this movie strikes a chord with you, I suggest that you also watch *Falling Down* (1993). Both of these movies give us an opportunity to observe what can happen when we don't resolve our problems before it's too late. People can stretch themselves too far and snap if they don't resolve their own issues. There's healing from just knowing you don't have to let things get that far. Don't wait. Let people know what's going on with you, and seek the support you need to enjoy a happy, healthy life.

THE BOY WHO COULD FLY
(Twentieth Century-Fox, 1986), color, 114 minutes, PG-rated

HEALING THEMES:
Living in a fantasy
Trying to escape painful memories
Learning that you've lost your mother and/or father
Living in another world
Accepting there are those who are different
Falling in love

DIRECTOR: Nick Castle; SCREENPLAY: Nick Castle; CAST: Lucy Deakins (Milly); Jay Underwood (Eric); Bonnie Bedelia (Charlene); Colleen Dewhurst (Mrs. Sherman); Fred Savage (Louis); Fred Gwynne (Uncle Hugo); Louise Fletcher (psychiatrist); Jason Priestley (Gary); Mindy Cohn (Geneva)

SYNOPSIS: Eric loses his parents in a plane crash. Soon afterward, he is befriended by a young girl, Milly, who lives in the house across from him. Milly is given the job of getting Eric to come out of his shell. She knows he needs to escape from his own mind, but she doesn't know how to assist him. Eventually his dreams come true and he flies into the sunset.

CINEMATHERAPY: Did you ever feel as if you just wanted to fly away or change your name and move somewhere to have a fresh start on life? That's a pretty common fantasy. Have there been times you wanted to shut yourself off from everyone, to live as if you were floating through the world and no one could see you or hurt you? Many of us hit a point in our lives where we just don't think we can or want to take it any more. And sometimes we just don't have control over when that moment strikes. Focus on the idea that Eric is trying to escape for all of us; he is the fantasy and the metaphor for escaping the pain and turmoil that come with living life. Think back to a time you had something traumatic happen. Maybe you lost your job, had a difficult or destructive breakup of a relationship, lost a great deal of money, or lost a loved one. How did you handle that bad time in your life? Did you turn to food, drugs, alcohol, or gambling? Maybe you became depressed and didn't go to work or couldn't even get out of bed. Weren't you escaping from reality just as Eric does? Times such as these can be painful and overwhelming. They prompt us to want to fly away and turn the present into our past so we can have a future. In many ways, people like Eric are reflections of ourselves. Try watching this movie alone. Stay with what it is trying to show you in your own life. If you're going through difficult times, try to stop yourself from escaping into other thoughts. Reach out to a therapist, minister, school counselor, or support group and let them help you with your healing. They will guide you to ask the questions What is it you would like to fly away from in your life? and What healing must you undertake so you can stay and enjoy the here and now and all that life has to offer?

THE BOYS NEXT DOOR

(CBS-TV, 1996), color, 100 minutes, G-rated

HEALING THEMES:
Dealing with a member of the family who is mentally challenged
Understanding more about those who have special needs
Learning to reach out and help
Supporting those who are mentally challenged
Trying to handle your own life
Knowing when it's time to move on

DIRECTOR: John Erman; TELEPLAY: William Blinn; CAST: Nathan Lane (Norman); Robert Sean Leonard (Barry); Tony Goldwyn (Jack); Michael Jeter (Arnold); Courtney B. Vance (Lucien); Mare Winningham (Sheila); Elizabeth Wilson (Mary); Jenny Robertson (Rena); Lynne Thigpen (Mrs. Tracy)

SYNOPSIS: Arnold, Norman, Barry, and Lucien live in a group home for the mentally challenged. Each has a special need. When they learn that their social worker, Jack, is leaving, the members struggle with the idea that they no longer have a leader. In the end they realize that, in time, everyone must move on.

CINEMATHERAPY: I'll admit something to you. There are times that I have actually envied those who are mentally challenged. Why not? They're being taken care of and appear to live in their own private world with no responsibilities. Life seems to be blissful. On the other hand, I've learned to better appreciate and enjoy the luxuries in life that I have around me—my friends, my ability to come and go as I please, and the privilege of having a handicap-free life. Notice the way each of the characters in this film tries earnestly to deal with life. Maybe you know someone who is mentally challenged or you grew up with a family member who was handicapped. This film is going to bring back memories. Some of them may be painful, whereas others might remind you of the special moments that can only come from caring for someone who truly needs you. How do you feel about the idea of two mentally challenged individuals having a relationship? Should they be allowed to become intimate? Many people believe we should forestall intimate involvement between the mentally challenged. Were you angry because the people at the store were taking advantage of Lucien? I've seen it before, and it amazes me that people would consider doing such a thing. How did you feel about Jack, the caseworker? He is a rare individual who is willing to reach out to help others. Maybe there are things that you could do to help people with special needs. Volunteer some of your time to help out those who are mentally or physically challenged. The Boys Next Door are just that—the people down the block or in the next building who are struggling to have a normal life. This movie gives us a way of learning more about what this special group endures to survive. Be gentle and kind to such needy people. Also, learn to appreciate your own journey in the process.

BOYS ON THE SIDE

(Warner Bros., 1995), color, 117 minutes, R-rated

HEALING THEMES:
Starting over
Being in an abusive relationship
Dealing with issues of being a lesbian
Knowing someone who has AIDS
Paying the consequences of your past

DIRECTOR: Herbert Ross; SCREENPLAY: Don Roos; CAST: Whoopi Goldberg (Jane); Drew Barrymore (Holly); Mary-Louise Parker (Robin); James Remar (Alex); Anita Gillette (Elaine); Matthew McConaughey (Abe); Belly Wirth (Nick); Bennis Boutsikaris (Massarelle), Estella Parsons (Louise); Anay Agruno (Anna)

SYNOPSIS: Jane's out of work, Robin needs a fresh start, and Holly's on the run. They take a shot at starting new lives together. They each are confronted by their personal problems and are forced to deal with the consequences of their past. In the end everything turns out exactly as it was intended, but not without the tears that accompany self-growth and death.

CINEMATHERAPY: I can remember a few times in my life when I wanted to pull up stakes and move some place where no one knew me—a place where I could have a fresh start. Have you ever felt that way? Maybe you're in an abusive relationship and you feel the only way out is to run. Possibly you're ill and think you can escape the reality of your sickness. *Boys on the Side* gives us some insight into those issues, and more, through the lives of three women. Do you see yourself in one of them? Let yourself identify with these characters or their desire to start a new life. How would you handle falling in love with someone who is ill? Could you deal with a person of the same sex falling in love with you? Maybe something like that has already happened to you. How did you handle the experience? Notice the way Robin works at trying to resolve her past. Her running away is just a metaphor for the emotional running she has done all of her life. Is that what it's been like for you, always trying to avoid the reality of your past? Pay close attention to the bond these three women have with one another. I was envious of their close relationship. How about you? Are there people from your past with whom you've lost contact? Try to locate them and talk over old memories. You will be amazed at how healing it can be and how free you will feel. And what of the dying process? Notice the way they all strive to put Robin's death to rest within themselves. Have you ever lost someone close to you? Could you relate to the emotions you were seeing these two experience? This is a special movie, particularly for women. Sometimes we can heal ourselves through the adventures, excitement, and crises that others experience in their lives. Work to get in touch with their feelings and relate those feelings to yourself. These three musketeers have a lot to share with you. Allow them in, and your emotions will do the rest.

BREAKFAST AT TIFFANY'S

(Paramount, 1961), color, 115 minutes, not rated

HEALING THEMES:
Escaping your past
Living in a fantasy world
Falling in love when you least expect it
Getting caught up in drugs and alcohol
Learning to live in the moment

DIRECTOR: Blake Edwards; SCREENPLAY: George Axelrod; CAST: Audrey Hepburn (Holly Golightly); George Peppard (Paul); Patricia Neal (2-E); Buddy Ebsen (Doc); Mickey Rooney (Mr. Yunioshi); Martin Balsam (O. Berman); John McGwen (Tiffany's clerk)

SYNOPSIS: For Holly Golighty, New York is a magical city—the kind of place where fanciful young woman like Holly can get lost. She lives in a fantasy world surrounded by those who know nothing of her except her kindness to others. Reality sets in when Paul enters her life and she falls in love with him. Holly Golightly can no longer avoid living in the real world.

CINEMATHERAPY: As a therapist, I have witnessed people getting stuck in life's day-to-day routine. They come to my office because they want to escape the reality. Many people have a fantasy about slipping away into another life, doing something completely different and frivolous with their life. They dream of existing from moment to moment in a style that is anything but conventional. *Breakfast at Tiffany's* reminds us that people can live their fantasy if they choose. Holly Golightly is a good example of someone who is living a fantasy. She's the kind of woman who lives for every moment of every day. Have you ever known anybody like Holly? Someone who could just get up in the morning and take life for what it's worth? Maybe you, like Holly, have tried to escape your past so that you could be someone different and new. Possibly, like our young writer in the film, you're trying to make it on your own but still rely on others (for example, people, parents, friends, or lovers) to get you through life. What is it about these two people that captivates you? Which of them would you like to be? What fantasies do you have about escaping your current life to live a carefree existence? Here's an idea: Why not try getting up on a Saturday or a Sunday morning and just letting the day be a beautiful experience? Take a walk down a wonderful street where there are shops and pastry stores and embrace the moment for what it is. Try to live a little bit like Holly—in spirit. Enjoy life's journey and the wonderful experiences that each day has to offer. What an incredible thing to learn to live in the moment. I'm not suggesting that, like Holly, you give up everything for a fantasy world. However, every once in a while, it's okay to just enjoy the fun that living can offer. Give this movie a try. I think you'll find yourself falling in love with someone named Holly Golightly. In fact, maybe there's a Holly Golightly in real life waiting for you. At the very least, this film helps you to learn to enjoy your own moon river anytime you wish.

BREAKING AWAY

(20th Century-Fox, 1979), color, 100 minutes, PG-rated

HEALING THEMES:
Feeling good about your accomplishments
Getting support from your family
Being the best of friends
Growing up and moving on

Fighting against all odds
Digging deep for the courage to keep on going
Having people look down on you for who you are

DIRECTOR: Peter Yates; SCREENPLAY: Steve Tesich; CAST: Dennis Christopher (Dave); Dennis Quaid (Mike); Daniel Stern (Cyril); Jackie Earle Haley (Moocher); Barbara Barrie (Mrs. Stohler); Paul Dooley (Mr. Stohler); Amy Wright (Nancy); Robyn Douglas (Katherine); Hart Bochner (Rod); John Ashton (Mike's brother)

SYNOPSIS: Four friends from the other side of the tracks take a challenge to compete in a yearly bike race. The local college, whose team always wins the race, doesn't want to have anything to do with this low-life group. As they go through their personal and joint struggles, and as they learn to deal with the town's prejudices, the four pals grow closer. When the race is over, the young men emerge triumphant.

CINEMATHERAPY: *Breaking Away* is a very special movie. When I started to research movies for this book, I wanted to be sure there would be movies that focused on concerns relevent to both men and women. There was no problem choosing films that dealt with men and violence. Movies with stories presenting real feelings are pretty rare, but *Breaking Away* fits that description just perfectly. To top it off, this group of men are really boys, and for young males to get in touch with their feelings and what's going on in their lives is quite difficult. You can hear the issues of rejection because one group is not as good as the next. And you have an opportunity to observe how one of the on-camera families communicates and the difficult time one father has demonstrating his feelings for his son. What kinds of feelings do you have when you watch this group of friends together? You can easily observe that these guys have a very special bond with one another. Is this something you're still missing in your life? Have you ever felt you didn't belong in that "special group"? Or did you have a tendency to turn your back on those who didn't come from wealthy families? What was it like dealing with those feelings as a young child or adolescent? Let the feelings come to the surface. Tell yourself you are a worthy person and those who would reject you because of where you come from are not worthy of being with you. What about the relationship between the father and son? Were you able to see yourself in their awkward atttempts at communication, trying to reach out to each other? Have there been times you've just given up on something because someone else said you couldn't do it or you were not good at it? You can experience a sense of triumph and healing by capturing the power and energy when you break out of the mold cast by those who would try to hold you back. Be all you can be and you will have a life rich in personal success and fulfillment.

BRIAN'S SONG

(ABC-TV, 1970), color, 73 minutes, G-rated

HEALING THEMES:
Making a friend for life
Learning that someone you love is going to die
Dealing with feelings of not being able to help someone you love
Grieving the loss of a friend
Saying goodbye
Learning to let go and go on with your life

DIRECTOR: Buzz Kulik; TELEPLAY: William Blinn; CAST: James Caan (Brian); Billy Dee Williams (Gale); Jack Warden (Coach George Halas); Shelley Fabares (Joy); Judy Pace (Linda); Bernie Casey (J. C. Caroline); Daivd Huddleston (Ed); Abe Gibson, Jack Concannon, Ed O'Bradovich (themselves)

SYNOPSIS: When professional football player Brian Piccolo and Gale Sayers meet, their relationship is rocky and competitive. In time, they become close friends. Gale becomes worried when Brian is unable to function and Brian loses his place on the team. He eventually learns that Brian has terminal cancer. They both struggle with the inevitability of death.

CINEMATHERAPY: For those of you who have lost someone you care about, this movie offers a sensitive look at dealing with the issues of dying and death. You may have known someone, possibly from childhood, whom you considered your best friend. You did everything together. You experienced the good times and the bad together. Maybe you parted for some time because you had a falling-out or you moved and lost touch. That is a kind of death, isn't it? As you view this movie, you may be able to get in touch with some of your feelings about losing a friend or family member. When you do this exercise, your self-healing begins. Whereas Gale lost his friend Brian to cancer, you may have lost your friend for other reasons. How did you handle your feelings? What kinds of emotions did you bury that you know are there but you are still afraid to let surface? When that person comes to mind, do you just shake the memories away? It's important to keep our emotions current and not let them build up. If we carry them around as baggage, they will begin to affect us negatively. Possibly the pressure of keeping those feelings hidden has caused you to have your own psychological or physical problems. Are you someone who can't sleep or be at peace with yourself at night? Do you use food, alcohol, drugs, or gambling to keep your emotions in check? What's really bothering you? When you watch this film, let your feelings run free and focus on how it relates to your own life. Let yourself feel Gale's loss and your own losses. Experience the stages of grieving Gale undergoes and the healing you experience in the process. That's what my healing stories are all about—learning to let go by watching the process before you. Stay with this one and go on the self-recovery journey. You will free yourself from the pain and loss that you have been carrying within you.

THE BRIDGES OF MADISON COUNTY

(Warner Bros., 1995), color, 135 minutes, PG-13-rated

HEALING THEMES:

Meeting someone special
Having an affair
Trying to fill a void in your life
Living in a lie
Going on when all you have are memories

DIRECTOR: Clint Eastwood; SCREENPLAY: Richard LaGravenese; CAST: Clint Eastwood (Robert); Meryl Streep (Francesca); Annie Corley (Carolyn); Victor Slezak (Michael); Jim Haynie (Richard)

SYNOPSIS: Robert is a photographer working for *National Geographic* magazine. His new assignment is to photograph the bridges of Madison County in Iowa. He meets Francesca, a married woman, whose husband is away on business. They have a love affair that lasts for the rest of their lives.

CINEMATHERAPY: Of the many reasons people come to my office, love is the most often discussed issue. "Dr. Solomon, I feel empty, like I'm dead inside. We've been married for nine years and there's nothing left. It's like I'm obligated, but not in love." "I'm forty years old and I feel like my life is over. What love is there for someone my age? It seems like love is for people under thirty." Now, hold on just one minute. I'm over thirty and I experience love *every* day. Don't be so quick to put yourself in a locked room. Are you someone who feels you're missing something in your life—the excitement that comes from having someone special to hold you and tell you that they care? Do you wonder if that special person can ever come into your life? *The Bridges of Madison County* lets us know that love is as near as the next person you meet, that you simply must keep your eyes open and listen for the sounds of love when they are near. As you watch this movie, stay in touch with your feelings. What did you think of Francesca's having an affair? Do you think that having an affair is ever acceptable? Can you see that she was lying to her family and her children? Have you had an affair, or are you in the middle of one right now? What's missing in your relationship that you need to turn to someone outside of your relationship to feel whole? Have you ever experienced the emotional intensity that Robert and Francesca feel for each other? Maybe you have a memorabilia box that holds pieces of your past and memories of a love lost. If you are in a relationship with someone now, watch this movie with them. Open up to discussing your feelings. If there are problems, work at solving them through more movies, counselors, and groups. You had a love with this person once, and that emotion can come rushing back if you work at it. If you feel that it's over, say goodbye. Having an affair is never an acceptable way to enjoy love. And if you're looking for someone special in your life, just hold on. The right person is just on the other side of the bridge.

THE BUTCHER'S WIFE
(Paramount, 1991), color, 105 minutes, PG-13-rated

HEALING THEMES:
Belief in destiny
Clairvoyance
Learning to listen to your instinct, not your intellect
Living life philosophically
Following the dream where ever it takes you
Letting your guard down while allowing other people into your life

DIRECTOR: Terry Hughes; **SCREENPLAY:** Ezra Litwak and Marjorie Schwartz; **CAST:** Demi Moore (Marina); Jeff Daniels (Dr. Alex Tremor); Mary Steenburgen (Stella); George Dzundza (Leo); Frances McDormand (Grace); Margaret Colin (Robyn); Maz Peelich (Eugene); Mirian Margolyes (Gina); Christopher Durang (Mr. Liddle); Helen Hanft (Moely)

SYNOPSIS: A young woman, Marina, believes in her destiny. She is able to tell what has been and what will be. She marries a man who turns out to be destined for someone else. At the same time, she realizes her own destiny and falls in love with a psychiatrist, her true "split-a-part." In spite of all his efforts to be logical about his feelings for Marina, he gives in to his emotions and follows her to the ends of the earth.

CINEMATHERAPY: I remember when I was a child, I had a friend whose parents were wonderfully affectionate toward each other. They always held hands, they said kind words to each other frequently, and they often embraced each other. They seemed to glow. Their relationship was foreign to me. In my home, my parents had little contact. I decided way back then there was someone out there who was special for me—someone with whom I would be connected to on all levels. *The Butcher's Wife* helps us see how important it is to permit that special someone into our lives. Now, you may think that Marina is a bit strange. Many people don't believe in destiny or clairvoyance. However, if you do, you're going to love this movie. Are you looking for your split-a-part, your other half, your soul mate? Do you have difficulty listening to your inner self and letting that someone special into your life? I know I fought those feelings for years. However, when I finally let my instincts lead me rather than my intellect, I experienced the healing that comes from enjoying a deep, rich love. What did you think of Marina? I saw her as a philosopher, always able to cut to the chase. "What's meant to be can't be changed." "If it's wrong, listen to yourself, don't fight it." These are some of the perfect thoughts to live by. Did you notice how the psychiatrist in the film couldn't accept any of her ideas? He needed to be logical about everything. Most important is knowing, believing there is someone out there who's meant for you. You won't know when and you won't know where, but if you listen to your intuition, you'll find the special person. Have some fun with this picture. Let yourself be part of Marina's world and feel her joy and experiences. Try *On a Clear Day You Can See Forever* (1970) for similar ideas. Try watching both these films back-to-back. You'll laugh and get close at the same time. *Note:* I've said it before and I'll say it again: It's never acceptable, as in *On a Clear Day You Can See Forever,* for a therapist to become involved with a client/patient—never!

BYE BYE, LOVE

(Twentieth Century-Fox, 1995), color, 106 minutes, PG-13-rated

HEALING THEMES:
Dealing with divorce
Living the playboy life
Trying to get on with life
Leaving the past behind you
Failing to understand what caused a breakup
Growing up in a broken home

DIRECTOR: Sam Weisman; SCREENPLAY: Gary David Goldberg, Brad Hall; CAST: Matthew Modine (Dave); Randy Quaid (Vic); Paul Reiser (Donny); Janeane Garofalo (Lucille); Rob Reiner (Dr. Townsend); Amy Brenneman (Susan); Eliza Dushku (Emma); Ed Flanders (Walter); Maria Pitillo (Kim); Lindsay Crouse (Grace); Johnny Whitworth (Max); Ross Malinger (Ben); Pamela Dillman (Sheila)

SYNOPSIS: Three divorced dads have been buddies since before their days of marital bliss. Left out in the cold, each tries to succeed as a single father. While on the hunt to find happiness in other relationships, work, sports, and so on, they come to realize that the single life is not what they hoped it would be.

CINEMATHERAPY: You know I don't mind telling you that there have been a few times in my life when I thought I'd found the perfect relationship, only to realize months later that it was not going to work. I was devastated. Lonely and depressed, I was out on my own one more time. I know that men don't like to admit it, be we hurt just as much as women when relationships fall apart. Sometimes I wondered if I was ever going to find my true mate. When I saw *Bye Bye, Love,* it reminded me of those rough times as a single. Are you someone who has or is dealing with a divorce? Did you have a family and a home you thought represented your life's dream, only to have it fall apart? How are you coping now? Are there times when you're depressed, feeling like trying to be happy is a waste of time? The wonderful thing about *Bye Bye, Love* is that it looks at the humorous side of divorce and single parenthood, yet deals with the reality of a wide variety of situations that revolve around marital splits. How did you feel about these three guys? Which one of them were you? The one who was always out, running around, and having the next affair? Maybe you were the one who wanted the relationship back. Or were you the individual who was always in an argument with the ex-spouse but couldn't let go? And what did you think of the relationships each of them tried to get involved in? Did that bring back any old memories for you? I recall meeting some crazy people. I got involved because I was desperate to go out and do something. Anything! I couldn't handle being alone. And what about the children? Did you grow up in a broken home? Did you resent your parents for leaving? Possibly it felt as if they never did anything for you, or maybe when you look back it was that they never could do enough for you. I'm sure a lot of feelings are going to get kicked up as you watch this movie. Experience your feelings. If you're having problems coping with your divorce, get involved in singles or parent support groups. Seek direction from a therapist or trusted spiritual leader. And remember, there is a wonderful relationship waiting for you just around the corner.

CAN'T BUY ME LOVE

(Touchstone, 1987) color, 94 minutes, PG-13-rated

HEALING THEMES:
Getting in touch with your high school years
Accepting yourself for who you are
Being left behind by a best friend
Putting up a front to get what you want
Trying to buy friends and influence people
Remembering a time when you were young

DIRECTOR: Steve Rash; **SCREENPLAY:** Michael Swerdlick; **CAST:** Patrick Dempsey (Ronald); Amanda Peterson (Cindy); Courtney Gains (Kenneth); Tina Caspary (Barbara); Seth Green (Chuckie); Sharon Farrell (Mrs. Mancini)

SYNOPSIS: A high school nerd is in love with the class queen who also happens to be his neighbor. He loans her $1,000, provided she agrees to pretend to be his girlfriend for a month. Things go well for a while, but eventually everything blows up in his face. In time, true love takes the place of the business deal.

CINEMATHERAPY: Once in a while I find that a movie really helps me get in touch with my school days. We all had different experiences in school. Some people were loners, while others were part of the in crowd. Some did exactly what they were told, and others were troublemakers. There were those who were at the top of the class academically and those who barely squeaked by. If you're anything like me, some high school memories are a little difficult to deal with. I know when I flash back to those times, I have some sadness. How about you? Did you feel left out of what was going on? Did you struggle to fit in with your peers? Maybe you kept up a front just so you could be accepted. Try to get involved with the characters in this movie. Which one are you? How did you handle those tough kids who always wanted to start a fight or teased you whenever they had a chance? Perhaps you were the one who did the teasing. How do you feel when you see yourself through this film? Was there someone at school whom you wanted to be with but never had the courage to talk to? Maybe you tried to be with that person but were rejected because they thought you weren't good enough. I was angry when the Ronald character forgot about his best friend. What about you? Did you turn your back on someone just so you could be popular? Being who you are and feeling good about yourself is the foundation for a healthy, happy existence in life. And that's *really* being self-aware. Here's a suggestion: Call your old high school and find out when they're having the next class reunion. Try watching *Can't Buy Me Love* or one of the other movies I've recommended that help you deal with similar issues. Then attend your reunion with the goal of asking people how they felt about their high school experience. You will find it to be enlightening. You will have the opportunity to put your past behind you and move on to a better, richer life.

CASABLANCA

(Warner Bros., 1942), B & W, 102 minutes, PG-rated

HEALING THEMES:
Memories of a lost love
Letting go of the past
Being confronted by your feelings for someone
Realizing you have to get on with your life
Learning to live in the here and now

DIRECTOR: Michael Curtiz; SCREENPLAY: Julian Epstein, Philip Epstein, Howard Koch; CAST: Humphrey Bogart (Rick); Ingrid Bergman (Ilsa); Paul Henreid (Victor); Claude Rains (Capt. Louis Renault); Conrad Veidt

(Maj. Heinrich Strasser); Peter Lorre (Ugarte); Sydney Greenstreet (Señor Ferrari); Dooley Wilson (Sam); Marcel Dalio (Emil); S. Z. Sakoll (Carl); Leonard Kinskey (Sascha); Margaret Le Beau (Yvonne); Joy Page (Annina)

SYNOPSIS: Having escaped the immediate peril of war-torn Europe, Rick is confronted by his emotions when Ilsa, the love of his life, walks into his Moroccan nightclub. Rick is put to the test as he puts his own needs aside and works to save her and her husband, Victor, from imminent danger.

CINEMATHERAPY: Just before I released *The Motion Picture Prescription*, I decided that it would contain a form that invited people to let me know what movies they would like me to include in my next book. I was amazed at how many people requested *Casablanca*. I even got requests for *Casablanca* while I was doing radio and television interviews. The truth is I passed on *Casablanca*. The movie was devoid of any healing themes. Well, the Movie Doctor missed the boat. And so my apologies to all those who saw the vision and had the feelings. Do you remember a time in your life when you loved someone with all your heart and soul? Just the mere mention of their name sent your mind swirling with images from the past. Maybe it was the girl across the classroom or the guy who worked in the next office, or the husband or wife of your best friend. Oh, the both of you knew the secret of your passion. Surely no one in the history of humankind ever felt the way you two did about each other. However, for some reason it just couldn't happen—circumstances tore you apart, your family moved away, college or careers sent you both in different directions, one or the other of you decided to be with someone else for some unthinkable, irrational reason. So where's the healing? you ask. It's in the fantasy, the memories. And provided you don't live in, or for, those fantasies and memories, you're doing just fine. But some people can't let go. Their life slips by them as they lose day after week after month, longing for the past to be rewritten. Take a message from Rick and the others at the café: Learn to let go and get on with your life. Put that love memory on the last plane out of town. Start living in the moment and release the past. And when you do, you will find there is someone ready to come into your life who can love you for today. So go ahead, watch this movie, enjoy the high from all the emotional intrigue, and then let go. And remember: "This one's for you, kid."

CAT'S EYE
(MGM/UA, 1985), color, 93 minutes, PG-13-rated

HEALING THEMES:
Kicking the smoking habit
Fighting an addiction

Being out of control
Putting someone you love at risk because of your behavior
Going to extremes to stop someone from practicing their addiction

DIRECTOR: Lewis Teague; SCREENPLAY: Stephen King; CAST: Drew Barrymore (Our Girl); James Woods (Dick Morrison); Alan King (Dr. Donatti); Kenneth McMillan (Creszner); Robert Hays (Norris); Candy Clark (Sally); James Naughton (Hugh); Patricia Kalember (Marcia); Charles Duttone (Dom)

SYNOPSIS: Dick Morrison goes to a rather special clinic to stop smoking. He gets in over his head when he realizes that the people at the facility go to extremes to make sure he stops his smoking. Every time he slips and has a cigarette, his family is punished.

CINEMATHERAPY: *Cat's Eye* is the only movie I found that focuses on the issue of smoking. You may be surprised to learn that it was written by horror specialist Stephen King. But many people describe smoking as their own personal nightmare, so maybe it is appropriate that he wrote this story. Have you tried to stop smoking and been unable to quit? What have you done to break the habit? Avoided any and every place where people were smoking? Put patches on your body? Took drugs? Promised a higher power that if you could stop smoking you would start attending church? Well, this movie is going to hit home for you. I realize this is a rather bizarre way to get you to see the problem, but the reality is that the movie hits the nail right on the head: You must make a serious commitment to quit your addiction or it won't happen. Are you like the alcoholic, hiding your cigarettes so no one will find them? Do you look for excuses to get away from people so you can satisfy your nicotine craving? Maybe you're with someone who smokes. Have you watched them play the "I'll quit tomorrow" game? Samuel Clemens said, and I paraphrase: "It's not a problem to stop smoking. I've done it hundreds of times." Notice how the character in this film puts his wife and children in jeopardy. Are you doing the same thing by smoking around your loved ones, taking the chance of your children picking up the habit, spending money on cigarettes instead of on the family, putting your health at risk? Can you see it's the same thing that Dick is doing but with a twist? Make a real commitment to stop smoking. Seek help from a clinic or professional. Go to support group meetings. Work at being honest with your family and friends, and reach out for their support. Do it for yourself first and you will be healing yourself and everyone who cares about you. What a beautiful gift that would be. *Note: Cat's Eye* is actually a series of three stories. Look for different messages about obsession and desire in the other two sections of the film. You'll enjoy this picture.

THE CELLULOID CLOSET

(Brillstein-Grey Entertainment, 1995), color, 102 minutes, R-rated

HEALING THEMES:
Feeling free to be who you are
Understanding the gay and lesbian lifestyle
Prejudice
Knowing that love is always spelled L-O-V-E no matter who you are
Viewing life through someone else's eyes

Directors: Rob Epstein, Jeffrey Friedman; SCREENPLAY: Rob Epstein, Jeffrey Friedman, Armistead Maupin; CAST: Narrated by Lily Tomlin

SYNOPSIS: Lily Tomlin, aided by numerous interviews of screenwriters, directors, and actors, takes you on a journey though the history of homosexuality as depicted in the cinema. The public perception of the homosexual community is also discussed, showing how attitudes have changed over the decades.

CINEMATHERAPY: Only on rare occasions do I come across a documentary that is so intense that I decide to include the work in my cinematherapy. This beacon of sunshine was recommended to me just as I reached my movie quota. There is a remarkable message in *The Celluloid Closet* that I would like you all to hear. Listen closely as each individual interviewed reminds us that if you look for a message in a movie, eventually you will find it, even if the signals being sent are unintended. Have you ever talked to someone about a film, only to learn that he or she received from the picture a message very different from the one you received? One movie clip after another is shown with the claim that there is a message about homosexuality in the footage. I consider myself pretty insightful, but I must admit that I had a difficult time seeing the point. About halfway though the screening I realized that I did not see it because I was not looking from their perspective—possibly, I didn't want to see or hear the message. This movie taught me to open more than my ears and eyes. I learned that I must alter my way of perceiving the world. If you are not a homosexual, let yourself feel the discomfort when two people of the same sex show more than just affection to each other. Try to get in touch with the way a homosexual might feel when they watch heterosexuals experience love and emotion on the screen. More than anything, I would like you to understand the concept that no matter if you are straight, lesbian, gay, or bisexual, the emotion of love is the *same* for each of us. Why not learn to accept one another for who we are instead of who we want one another to be?

CHASING AMY

(Miramax, 1997), color, 111 minutes, R-rated

HEALING THEMES:
Falling in love
Accepting one's past
Feeling abandoned
Being honest
Gays and lesbians
Learning that we're all the same
Waiting until it's too late

DIRECTOR: Kevin Smith; SCREENPLAY: Kevin Smith; CAST: Ben Affleck (Holden); Joey Lauren Adams (Alyssa); Jason Lee (Banky); Dwight Ewell (Hooper); Jason Mewes (Jay); Kevin Smith (Silent Bob); Matt Damon (executive); Casey Affleck (little kid)

SYNOPSIS: It can take a long time for some people to find the right love match. When Holden meets Alyssa he believes he has found his soul mate. One problem: She's gay. Her sexual preference and her indiscreet past create barriers for Holden. When he is finally ready to let her into his life, it's too late.

CINEMATHERAPY: Here are the big questions: Can someone who is heterosexual become homosexual? Can someone who is homosexual become heterosexual? Can someone who is homosexual or heterosexual become bisexual? The answer to all these questions is yes. However, *Chasing Amy* moves beyond those basic questions and asks: Can you forget my past so that we can have a future? And as you can perhaps tell, this is a question for anyone, no matter their sexual preference. If you're like me, you have a few skeletons in the closet that you would just as soon never see the light of day. But if and when they do emerge, will other people be able to accept you for who you are, or will they reject you for who you were? While Holden struggles with Alyssa's sexual choice, he simply cannot accept some of her past sexual behavior. Can you relate? Have you lost a relationship because someone you loved could not cope with knowing your past? Have you turned your back on an individual because of stories you have heard or people with whom they have had sexual contact? Are you having trouble letting go of your past, embarrassed by your actions and behavior? Some years ago I heard a song from the musical *A Chorus Line* that stays with me to this day, a song about doing what "I had to do for love." And when I remind myself that I was just trying to get through to the next day, week, month, and so on, I can forgive myself for all those occasions when I did what I had to do for love. My significant other has her own past, and I have mine. But together, today, we have each other. Try using this movie to let go of the past. If you're in a relationship that keeps bringing your history to the surface, watch this movie as a couple. Learn to accept each other for who you are now. Oh, and one more thing: Gay, straight, lesbian, bisexual, we're all looking for love. Let's just accept one another's sexual identity instead of rejecting one another for our differences.

CHILD OF RAGE

(CBS-TV, 1992), color, 120 minutes, PG-rated

HEALING THEMES:
Being foster parents
Adopting a child
Nightmares of sexual abuse
Trying to cope with a violent child
Learning to deal with your anger and rage
Being a molestation victim

DIRECTOR: Larry Peerce; TELEPLAY: Phil Penningroth, Suzette Couture; CAST: Mel Harris (Jill); Dwight Schultz (Rob); Mariette Hartley (Rosemary); Ashley Peldon (Catherine); Rosana Desoto (Doris); Sam Gifaldi (Eric); Nan Martin (Barbara); George D. Wallace (Henry)

SYNOPSIS: A reverend and his wife become foster parents. Catherine (Kat) and Eric are the children they have always wanted. But something is terribly wrong with Kat. She has temper tantrums and likes hurting people. Her parents take Kat to a therapist, who helps her deal with her anger.

CINEMATHERAPY: *Child of Rage* not only gives us insight into problems related to adoption and foster parenting, but also helps us get in touch with issues connected to molestation. Are you considering adopting a child? Maybe you have adopted a child and are experiencing unexpected problems, such as those portrayed in this TV movie. As you will see, Kat has rage stemming from what her father did to her. It is difficult for most of us to imagine that anyone would want to hurt a child in any way, let alone take advantage of them sexually. This man is sick, and he is passing his sickness along not only to Kat, but to everyone with whom she has contact. They are molested by proxy—she passes the effects of her assualt to those around her, even if, unlike her father, they love her in an appropriate manner. Do you have any childhood experiences that you have a difficult time explaining? Were you always angry? Did you set fires, get into fights, hide in the closet, or refuse to eat? I am not suggesting that everyone who had these problems was once molested. I am saying that if you had some of these problems, you may find yourself beginning to question what really happened to you as you watch this movie. Did you escape to the recesses of your mind to protect yourself from the unpleasantness? Possibly that's what you did as a child. Being a foster parent and adopting a child who comes from a background you know nothing about can be an overwhelming responsibility. Are you seeing Kat's behavior in the children you are trying to raise? There are counselors, therapists, support groups, and religious organizations to help you through these difficult times. With a lot of love and understanding, you can see and appreciate the nurturing and healing. *Note:* Holding Therapy—embracing the child until he or she becomes calm—as detailed in this movie, is one of a number of techniques used in dealing with this problem. You must find the form of treatment with which you are most comfortable.

CHOICES OF THE HEART: THE MARGARET SANGER STORY

(Lifetime-TV, 1995), color, 100 minutes, PG-rated

HEALING THEMES:

Standing up for what you believe
Learning about where your right to practice contraception came from
Responding when someone wants to stand in the way of your life's work
Having to choose your life mission over those you love
Dealing with someone who fights you every inch of the way
Having the courage to keep going

DIRECTOR: Paul Shapiro; TELEPLAY: Matt Dorff; CAST: Dana Delany (Margaret); Rod Steiger (Comstock); Henry Czerny (Bill); Julie Khaner (Anita); Tom McCamus (Arnold); Wayne Robson (Arthur); Yank Azman (Arnold); Jeff Pustil (Robinson); Kenneth Welsh (Margaret's husband)

SYNOPSIS: Margaret Sanger is a woman with a mission in life. Having witnessed one too many women die after attempting to self-abort, Margaret campaigns to teach women how to practice safe contraception. In spite of attempts to persecute and prosecute her, Margaret emerges triumphant in her quest to give women and men the option of planned parenthood.

CINEMATHERAPY: "Every life is a journey along an unfamiliar road." "Who has the right to play God?" Those lines from the movie really stuck with me. When I was growing up, I took a great many things for granted. I assumed the world always operated just the way I saw it. I thought things like radios, televisions, cars, and freedom always existed. As I grew older, I came to realize that many people fought and struggled so I could live in a world that was more equal and fair. Margaret Sanger reminds us that the fight can come at a great personal expense. We didn't always have the right to hear or even read about family planning. She reminds us that the choices of the heart are often the most difficult to make. Can you imagine a time when people were so closed-minded that you would not even be allowed to learn about contraception?

How do you feel about the choice today? What would it have been like if your freedom to practice contraception was taken away from you? Have you ever met anyone like Anthony Comstock? I know I have. People like Comstock live their lives making decisions for other people regardless of what these people want. Could you have done what Margaret did when she chose her cause over her children? What did you feel when her youngster died? It was as if her ability to grieve was burned out of her. Were you angry at her for staying true to her cause, or did you admire her for what she was doing? Maybe you're someone who's against birth control. Possibly you were angry at Margaret for taking a stand on this still-controversial issue. *Choices of the Heart* gives you an opportunity to work through very personal life decisions. It may inspire you to move forward on an issue you've been struggling with in your life. Taking action and making a stand are both healing and nurturing. Feel her courage and get in touch with your own courage. Make your choice of the heart.

CITIZEN KANE

(RKO, 1941), B & W, 119 minutes, not rated

HEALING THEMES:
Obsession with money
Being hung up on your power
When having an affair turns to unhappiness
Learning there is more to life than material objects
Longing to go back to a childhood of innocence

DIRECTOR: Orson Welles; SCREENPLAY: Orson Welles, Herman J. Mankiewicz; CAST: Orson Welles (Charles Foster Kane); Joseph Cotten (Jedediah); Everett Sloane (Mr. Bernstein); Dorothy Comingore (Susan); Ruth Warrick (Emily); George Coulouris (Walter); Ray Collins (Big Jim); William Alland (Jerry); Paul Stewart (Raymond); Erskine Sandford (Herbert); Agnes Moorehead (Mary); Philip Van Zandt (Mr. Rawlson); Harry Shannon (Jim); Sonny Bupp (Kane III)

SYNOPSIS: A young boy, Charles Foster Kane, suddenly inherits a great deal of money. Part of his inheritance is a broken-down newspaper publishing company that he decides to operate himself. He builds the newspaper into one of the largest fortunes the world has ever known. In the process, he has financial successes and personal failures. As Charles's life ends, he regrets the loss of his childhood.

CINEMATHERAPY: I grew up in a part of Inglewood, California, where the line between the rich and the not-so-rich was very clear. No, there weren't any railroad tracks, but there might as well have been. I would get on my bike and ride through the wealthy neighborhoods wishing I could have the money those people had. "If only I were rich, I could be happy. How could someone be anything but happy with all that money?" Much later in life, I learned what movies like *Citizen Kane* can teach me: Money can't heal the emptiness that comes from not loving yourself or the life you were given. And for that single reason I have included *Citizen Kane* in this book. This message is driven home at the end of the movie when Charles utters his dying words: "Rosebud," the name of the sled he owned as a child. At life's end he is saying that he would gladly exchange all of his fortune for the pleasures and simple life of his youth. Many people feel this way, although they don't talk about it. Some are unhappy in their jobs, their relationships, or the place they live. However, they don't do anything constructive about it. What can you do to get into action and alter your life *today* instead of tomorrow? Are you tired of living under all those financial pressures that link you to your job? Could you trim down your standard of living and start a new career? Maybe you're a lawyer who always wanted to be a gardener. Possibly you're a real estate entrepreneur who would like to teach children. You don't have to remain in your unhappiness. Learn to make healing changes that will give you the things in life that will make you happy. Don't worry about what people think or the other pressures in your life. You've got one shot at this life—make it the best and happiest time it can be. When you're centered in the world, you experience a joy unmatched by money or material objects. Remember, it is true that money can't buy happiness.

CITIZEN RUTH

(Miramax , 1996), 109 minutes, color, R-rated

HEALING THEMES:
Right to life vs. right to choose
Confronting irresponsibility
Homelessness
Being addicted
Taking advantage of others
Codependency
Trying to take control of someone's life

DIRECTOR: Alexander Payne; **SCREENPLAY:** Alexander Payne, Jim Taylor III; **CAST:** Laura Dern (Ruth); Swoosie Kurtz (Diane); Mary Kay Place (Gail); Kurtwood Smith (Norm); Kelly Preston (Rachel); M. C. Gainey (Harlan); Kenneth Mars (Dr. Charlie Rollins); Burt Reynolds (Blaine); Tippi Hedren (Jessica); Kathleen Noone (Pat)

SYNOPSIS: Ruth is a pregnant, homeless addict who has never been able to get her life together. Good fortune comes her way when she finds herself in the midst of a battle between right-to-life and right-to-choose groups. Contibutions come flowing in to support her rights. While these two factions battle it out, Ruth slips out the back door, pregnant and addicted, with more money than she's ever seen in her life.

CINEMATHERAPY: If I've told you once, I've told you a thousand . . . Well, you get my point. *Citizen Ruth* is just one more way to look at all the issues that revolve around taking responsibility for your actions. On more than one occasion I have been in the middle of the battle between the right-to-life and the right-to-choose groups involving someone who simply did not know what she wanted to do or how to take responsibility for her actions. Without taking a side in this ongoing problem, my major concern was, and still is: If we enter into the decision-making process for someone else, do they ever have to take responsibility for their actions? Think about how this might apply to your life. Maybe you are someone who looks to others to make decisions for you, only to be angry at them for their direction. Possibly you have made a life choice and blamed someone else because it was their idea. It seems to me that as long as Ruth and those who live life by her "me, me, me" philosophy aren't held accountable for their actions, we enable them to do the same thing repeatedly while they remain unaccountable. "But Doc," you say, "we're not just talking about some simple-minded decision here. We're talking about abortion." It's all the same. If we take away Ruth's responsibilities, don't we perpetuate her behavior? When others rush in to rescue her, don't they take on accountability for her? And if she does not have to make her own decisions, her own choices, will the same thing happen repeatedly? Try watching this film through the eyes of all the characters *except* Ruth. Now what do you think should be done?

CITY SLICKERS
(Columbia, 1991), color, 112 minutes, PG-13-rated

HEALING THEMES:
Trying to find yourself
Being stuck in a relationship
Saying goodbye to a marriage that doesn't work
Going on life's journeys
Taking risks
Emerging to be the new you

DIRECTOR: Ron Underwood; SCREENPLAY: Lowell Ganz, Babaloo Mandel; CAST: Billy Crystal (Mitch); Daniel Stern (Phil); Bruno Kirby (Ed); Patricia Wettig (Barbara); Helen Slater (Bonnie); Jack Palance (Curly); Noble Willingham (Clay); Tracey Walter (Cookie); Josh Mostel (Barry); David Paymer (Ira); Bill Henderson (Ben); Jeffrey Tambor (Lou); Phill Lewis (Steve); Kyle Secor (Jeff)

SYNOPSIS: Mitch and his two friends, Phil and Ed, all approaching middle age, decide to take a great adventure: a cattle drive. While on their journey they meet other people who are seeking the answers to some of life's questions. By the time they reach the end of the trail, they all learn a most important lesson: Home is where the heart is.

CINEMATHERAPY: Like *Bye Bye, Love, City Slickers* is a great tale about men who are on a journey to find themselves. And isn't that what our existence is all about, a journey of self-discovery? A search for the answer to life's unanswerable questions? Are you someone who feels stuck in an emotional rut? Are you in a relationship that you feel isn't going anywhere? Maybe, like Ed, you can't find the right relationship so you keep hopping from one affair to the next. Or, like Mitch, you might be someone who is very much in love with your significant other but feel you've lost your purpose in life. Sometimes we just have to let go and put ourselves in a different place by finding a change of scenery. What would it be like to take that river rafting trip that you've always dreamed about? How about renting a motorcycle and taking a cross-country road trip, just to see what's on the other side of the mountains? Or what would it be like to put it all behind you, pack your bags, and hit the road for a few months or years? You know there are a lot of conventions in life that teach us that we're supposed to get up and work nine to five, month after month, year after year. However, that isn't necessarily what life is all about. In fact, it may be one of life's major problems. I've seen a lot of people who feel stuck in their everyday existence. It is a hole they dug themselves. But these three guys on-screen remind us that at the end of the trail, many of life's questions can be answered. I invite you to watch *City Slickers*. Yes, I know that it's a comedy, but there is nothing wrong with laughing and learning at the same time. When Curly says there is only one thing to find out in this life, I believe he reminds us that we must learn to find love for ourselves before we can love someone else.

A CLOCKWORK ORANGE

(Warner Bros., 1971), color, 137 minutes, R-rated

HEALING THEMES:
Taking a look into the future
Does crime really pay?
Dealing with your fear of violence
Taking the wrong road in life
What alcohol and drugs can lead to

DIRECTOR: Stanley Kubrick; SCREENPLAY: Stanley Kubrick; CAST: Malcolm McDowell (Alex); Patrick Magee (Mr. Alexander); Michael Bales (Chief Guard); Adrienne Corri (Mrs. Alexander); David Prowse (Julian); Warren Clarke (Dim)

SYNOPSIS: Alex is a sadistic psychopath who heads up a gang of rapists and robbers. The thugs spend their days in bed and their nights under the influence of drugs. Alex is caught and sent into rehabilitation, where behavior modification is used to cure him of his sociopathic behavior. It all backfires, and Alex is soon on his way back to his old tricks.

CINEMATHERAPY: *A Clockwork Orange* is almost thirty years old, yet it's more a reality today than a futuristic fantasy. In so many ways the movie is a model of the current epidemic of gangs in the United States and Europe. But why include the movie in this book? What has *A Clockwork Orange* got to offer us on the subject of healing? We heal on many levels. Healing comes when we look to our doctor to mend a wound or cure a physical ailment. We turn to a teacher to help us solve a problem in math or English. If you go to a therapist, a counselor, or those who guide us through our spiritual beliefs, you experience an inner healing that comes from emerging out of your own darkness and into a bright light of inner peace and awareness. But what of the world and its healing? How do we come to understand the healing we need to go through as a community? *A Clockwork Orange* forces us to look at our community, our world. It asks the questions: What have we come to? Where are we going? What's it all for? And when we can ask the questions, we take our first step toward the solutions. Eldridge Cleaver once said, "If you're not part of the solution, you must be part of the problem." *A Clockwork Orange* throws the problem in our face. It makes us look not only at ourselves and the role we play in our individual healing, but also at the part we can have in the healing of our community. The meaning of violence, drugs, sex, and self-indulgence is made clear to us. It's pure chaos, and Alex is a metaphor for all who create that chaos. He is merely a reflection of our own individual chaos, our own dysfunction. If we are not chaotic individually, we certainly will not be chaotic as a whole. Get in touch with the healing we must do as a community. Look inside yourself to find the role you can play to achieve that goal. Can you get involved in the community? Could you start working with youth groups? Can you make sure your children are taking the right paths in life? You get the idea. When we heal individually, we heal as a whole. *Warning:* This movie is extremely violent and may not be for everyone. If you get to a point where you cannot go on watching, it's okay to turn it off. You've made that first step and you're going to get the message very quickly.

THE COCAINE FIENDS
(Kent Productions, 1936), B & W, 68 minutes, not rated

HEALING THEMES:
Drug use
Knowing when your addiction is ruling your life

Trying to understand the strange behavior of someone you love
Being confronted with your denial
Obsessions

DIRECTOR: William A. O'Connor; SCREENPLAY: Willis Kent; CAST: Noel Madison (Nick); Dean Benton (Eddie); Lois January; Sheila Manners; Lois Lindsay; Eddie Phillips

SYNOPSIS: A rather rough group make their living selling cocaine, the drug of the day. They meet a young girl while running from the law. In the process of getting to know her, they turn her on to cocaine and she gets hooked. After her brother enters the picture, he becomes as consumed with the drug as the rest of them.

CINEMATHERAPY: First, take note of the year *The Cocaine Fiends* was made: 1936. Some people think cocaine addiction is a new problem. That's what I used to think before I became involved in recovery work. The fact is that cocaine has been around for centuries. The reason I include *Reefer Madness* and *The Cocaine Fiends* in this book is that it can be a bit of a shock for people to see an old movie that deals with addictions. These vintage films send the viewer a strong message about drug addiction and the power drugs can have over the mind and body. And if it takes watching an old black-and-white film to bring a viewer around, then so be it. People can really fall into denial about their drug use. "Hey, I'm just havin' a little fun. Okay, so I missed a little work and my car was repossessed. That's got nothing to do with using cocaine." "Life's stressful. What do you do to get rid of the stress, Doc, watch a movie?" Well, now that you mention it, that's exactly what I do. And that's what I'm suggesting you do also. Are you or someone you care about caught up in your addiction? If it's someone you care about, do you see their life slipping away before your eyes? Maybe you've tried to reach out and you can't seem to get through—their denial is great and their addiction is even greater. Perhaps by watching what other people are doing in movies, they can see themselves. And that's when their recovery begins, with the first vision in the mirror. Sit down and give the older movies a try. When you're done, get started on some of the new releases—*The Boost, Rush, Bright Lights, Big City,* and *Clean and Sober,* to name a few. When you start watching these movies, I think you'll be quite surprised about the effect it will have on you. After viewing the picture, take action in your life and begin the recovery process. Join a support group that will help see you through the beginning stages of breaking your addictive pattern. Make this one a gift for life. (*Note:* This movie also goes by the title *The Pace That Kills.*)

COME BACK, LITTLE SHEBA

(Paramount, 1952), B & W, 99 minutes, not rated

HEALING THEMES:

Trying to be clean and sober
Living in the past
Becoming obsessed with someone else
Being pushed into something you don't want to do
Slipping back into dependency on alcohol
Starting again

DIRECTOR: Daniel Mann; SCREENPLAY: Ketti Frings; CAST: Burt Lancaster (Doc); Shirley Booth (Lola); Terry Moore (Marie); Richard Jaeckel (Turk); Philip Ober (Ed); Lya Golm (Mrs. Goffman)

SYNOPSIS: Doc is a man struggling to stay sober, and Lola, his wife, sees him through his sobriety. Doc is pushed to the limit when he becomes obsessed with Marie, a young woman who is renting a room from them. In the end, Doc finds his sobriety and a renewed love for Lola.

CINEMATHERAPY: If you or someone you know is dealing with alcohol issues, this movie is for you. Some of the best films dealing with alcohol and recovery are the older ones. Maybe because they're in black-and-white, the stark images and messages are much more clear. *Come Back, Little Sheba* has some tremendous healing messages. Listen to the way the characters talk about Alcoholics Anonymous: One day at a time; easy does it; you've got to do the steps; the first step is admitting you're an alcoholic; the twelfth step is helping others. The movie is a nonstop meeting. It's wonderful! Now, here's where some of the film's more complicated messages come into play: Can you see how Doc has transferred his obsession and need for alcohol to Marie? And if he can't—or shouldn't—have her, he decides, then he must have his alcohol. Did you notice the scene where Doc tried to replace the bottle he took with another bottle? How about when his personality changed? Whom do you know who's like Doc? That's what happens to some people. It's called a cross-addiction. Some turn to gambling, others to smoking, and so on. Now, what about Lola, the classic codependent? She's falling apart, living in a fantasy world, and still checking on "Daddy," her pet name for Doc. Can you see that hoping Sheba, her dog, will come back is the same as her hopes and dreams for her youth to come back? Like *Hot Spell, Voice in the Mirror, My Name Is Bill W.,* and *Clean and Sober, Come Back, Little Sheba* reminds us to live not in our addiction or the past but rather in the here and now. And without living life in the moment, there can be no healing for a person. Try this movie alone or in a group. Use it as the focus for a discussion meeting and spend whatever time is needed to explore the issues at hand. You're going to grow in the process and emerge triumphant over your addiction.

CORRINA, CORRINA

(New Line Cinema, 1994), color, 114 minutes, PG-rated

HEALING THEMES:

Dealing with the loss of a spouse
Grieving over the death of a parent
Learning to live life all over again
Making room for someone new in your life
Falling in love when you least expect it
Dealing with the prejudice of others

DIRECTOR: Jessie Nelson; SCREENPLAY: Jessie Nelson; CAST: Whoopi Goldberg (Corrina); Ray Liotta (Manny); Don Ameche (Grandpa); Tina Majorino (Molly); Wendy Crewson (Jenny); Jenifer Lewis (Jevina); Larry Miller (Sid); Erica Yohn (Grandma); Joan Cussack (Jonesy)

SYNOPSIS: Corrina is a woman who needs a job. She finds a job as a housekeeper for little girl whose mother has just died. In time, the youngster opens up to her, and in the process Corrina falls in love with the girl's father. Although conflict arises, they put their differences behind them and start a life as a new family.

CINEMATHERAPY: *Corrina, Corrina* is a very rare and special movie. It deals with several issues that most of us will have to confront at some point in our lives. My heart goes out to those who come to my office trying to comprehend and cope with the loss of a loved one. When a child is grieving, it can even be more heart-rending. Are you someone who lost a parent or grandparent when you were young? How did you handle the experience? Some children ignore the loss and go on as if it never happened; some have family and friends to see them through the pain; and others, like this little girl, withdraw into themselves. Can you identify with her? What memories do you have? Maybe you're a parent who is trying to help your youngster deal with the pain. And what of the relationship between Corrina and the newly widowed father? Does it seem wrong to you that he is becoming romantically involved so soon? Are you bothered because it is an interracial relationship? Many people feel this is wrong. But why does it matter? Isn't it really about two people falling in love and trying to be more at peace in this world? Finally, how do you feel about the way the characters handle their relationship? Are you someone who feels strongly that you could not accept this kind of situation? Maybe you're in a relationship with someone from a different race or someone of the same sex. Do you find that people treat you differently? Use *Corrina, Corrina* as a way to open up the doors to experience the healing you need in your life. Eventually, we will all lose a loved one in our lives. And some of us need to recover from that loss, mend our wounds, and let someone new into our lives. I suggest you make this a family movie. After you have watched it, ask others how the film made them feel. What would they want if something like this happened to a member of the family? I know you will grow and feel that much closer in the process.

COURAGE

(CBS-TV, 1986), color, 150 minutes, not rated

HEALING THEMES:
Being concerned about what is happening to your children
Feeling like you have no place to turn for help
Refusing to turn your back on your children
Getting into action
Coming out of denial about your family

DIRECTOR: Jeremy Paul Kagan; TELEPLAY: E. Jack Neuman; CAST: Sophia Loren (Marianna); Billy Dee Williams (Bobby); Hector Elizondo (Nick); Val Avery (Pete); Ron Rifkin (Eppy); Jose Perez (Jose); Mary McDonnell (Gabriella); Dan Hedaya (John); Cosey Parker (Tony)

SYNOPSIS: A parent finds out that her son is addicted to drugs. She does not know what to do or whom to turn to for help. It is beyond her imagination that her boy would be someone who would abuse drugs. She decides the solution is to jail her son's suppliers. She goes undercover to help a federal drug-enforcement agency apprehend the dealers. Eventually, she gets her son back.

CINEMATHERAPY: Are you in denial about who your children really are and what they're doing with their lives? Do you ever ask yourself if you're just too busy to keep track of what they're doing? "I've raised my kid so he wouldn't turn to drugs and alcohol." "Those problems happen to other people's children, not mine." "My daughter knows better. Anyway, if I saw her doing something like that, I'd kill her." Well, here's another question for you: Do you really think any parent raises their children to be an alcoholic, drug addict, or thief? Coming out of denial is the first step in the healing process. Do you feel as if your children are distancing themselves from you? Do you see them isolating themselves, having fits of anger, refusing to be involved with the family, or getting lower grades? These are all signs of a child who is in trouble or on his way to trouble. Ask yourself how far you are willing to go to rescue your child from impending disaster? More to the point, what are you willing to do to ensure that what has happened to the family in this movie does *not* happen to yours? Here are a few ideas: First, ask your family to watch *Courage* and a few of the other movies I've suggested. Spend time talking about each other's perception of the film. Let your children express their thoughts openly without feeling as if they will be chastised or lectured to. If you discover problems in the process, turn to professional help through your religious community or a therapeutic group. There's nothing wrong with seeking support to help you through rocky times. With this kind of open and honest approach to life, you can recover as a family and you will have a much brighter future.

CRAZY FROM THE HEART

(TNT-Cable, 1994), color, 94 minutes, not rated

HEALING THEMES:

Keeping up a front
Letting love in
Knowing that relationships come when you least expect them
Dealing with prejudice
Letting yourself be the person you really are
Learning to live in the moment
Ignoring people's opinions

DIRECTOR: Thomas Schlamne; TELEPLAY: Linda Voorhess; CAST: Christine Lahti (Charlotte); Ruben Blades (Ernesto); William Russ (Dewey); Louise Latham (Mae); Tommy Muniz (Tomas); Fran Bennett (Judge Sandra Farrell); Kamala Lopez (Alcina); Bibi Besch (Cynthia); Robyn Lively (Franny)

SYNOPSIS: A janitor, Ernesto, is attracted to the school principal, Charlotte. She turns her back on him to maintain a good social front. The fact that he's Spanish makes matters even more difficult for Charlotte. He is persistent, and eventually they get together. In the end, she learns the true meaning of love.

CINEMATHERAPY: I love stories like *Crazy From the Heart*. They remind me that romance is all around us but sometimes we just can't see it. I remember watching a news show about executive women who fell in love with men who were postal workers, janitors, mechanics, et cetera. The program pointed out how much in love the women were with these average working guys. As a therapist, I am concerned by the number of clients who are lonely and want a relationship yet will not settle for anyone who does not meet their social standards. We have so much pressure in our lives to perform up to other people's expectations that we forget what life is all about. Are you someone who has turned your back on others simply because of who they are, what they look like, or where they come from? Do you have a difficult time following your heart and ignoring the thoughts and visions of others? What good do we accomplish having prejudice and bias around us? What do we gain by not letting people into our lives simply because of their background? I would suggest we gain nothing but our own lack of personal growth. How did you feel about the way the principal rejected Ernesto? Would you have stuck around as long as he did? And what about the coach? This guy was a real jerk. How did he make you feel? Do you know anybody like him? *Crazy From the Heart* is a wonderful love story that reminds us that true love has no social, ethnic, or economic boundaries. We all have something to learn from the characters' relationship. I invite you to sit down, relax, give this movie a try, and let the message in. There are lots of life's lessons to be learned. Open yourself to the belief that it's okay to follow your heart and let your mind take a rest.

CURSE OF THE STARVING CLASS

(Trimark, 1995), color, 102 minutes, R-rated

HEALING THEMES:
Growing up in an alcoholic home
Coping when your family is nothing but chaos
Trying to survive your childhood
Breaking the codependent chain
Taking the easy way out
Becoming your worst nightmare

DIRECTOR: J. Michael McClary; SCREENPLAY: Bruce Beresford; CAST: James Woods (Weston); Kathy Bates (Ella); Randy Quaid (Taylor); Lou Gossett Jr. (Ellis); Henry Thomas (Wesley); Kristin Fiorella (Emma); James Fitzpatrick (Emerson)

SYNOPSIS: Weston Tate is an alcoholic who's at the breaking point. His wife, Ella, does what she can to keep the family together, but the cards are stacked against her. Weston runs from his debts, and their daughter, Emma, abandons the family. Ella and her son, Wesley, are all that's left of the family.

CINEMATHERAPY: I remember seeing *Curse of the Starving Class* when it was a stage play. I was stunned. Here is a drama that portrays every dysfunction a family can have. I grew up with most of them. Sam Shepard, the playwright, had it down pat. I was thrilled to find that the play had been made into a movie. Those of you who came from alcoholic homes are going to experience the same emotional roller coaster. The title of the movie is perfect, but it has little to do with food. Rather, it deals with a lack of healthy nurturing, which everyone needs to grow. The first thing you will notice is the chaos. Everything this family does is based on chaos. Whom does Weston remind you of in your family? Is your father one who was always going from job to job, or the next big deal to the next big deal? Maybe he reminds you of yourself. And what of Ella? Can you see her codependency as she copes with his erratic behavior? It doesn't matter that they're living on a farm in the middle of nowhere. They could just as easily be struggling in the big city. Listen to Emma as she comes to realize how the family is emotionally diseased. She sees that the gene pool has been passed down through her and on to her children. Do you think that is the way it happens? One of the things I identified with was Wesley playing the cello to occasionally escape to "normalcy." I escaped into my clarinet. What did you do? Play sports? Hide under the bed? Drink? Smoke? Eat? I really appreciated Wesley's description of the changing of the guards. He puts on Weston's old clothes and says, "I feel like I'm leaving and he's comin' in." This is a wonderful example of paradoxical healing. Maybe if you can see what's happening to the Tates you can make the necessary changes to put a stop to dysfunctional family patterns in your life. It is said that family dysfunction is the gift that keeps on giving. Here's your chance to stop giving the gift. Go ahead and take the chance.

DANCING IN THE DARK

(Lifetime, 1995), color, 100 minutes, PG-rated

HEALING THEMES:
Knowing what to do when a friend or relative makes advances
Being afraid to stand up to your parents
Feeling abandoned by your significant other
Being abused by the system
Learning you have the power and how to use it

DIRECTOR: Bill Corcoran; TELEPLAY: Jacqueline Feather, David Leidler; CAST: Victoria Principal (Anna); Nicholas Campbell (Mark); Kenneth Welsh (Dr. Bell); Robert Vaughn (Dennis); Marcia Bennett (Nurse Susan); Anna Louise Richardson (Elaine); Robert Wagner (Dennis)

SYNOPSIS: Anna is molested by Dennis, her father-in-law. When she tries to tell Mark, her husband, what happened, he rejects what she tells him as delusional and has her institutionalized. It all backfires on Mark when she is physically and emotionally mistreated by hospital attendants and staff. Anna learns to stand up for her rights as she and Mark confront Dennis.

CINEMATHERAPY: As you go through my library of healing stories, you will find several movies that deal with molestation and stalking. The emotional trauma that arises as a result of these acts can be devastating. *Dancing in the Dark* gives you an additional perspective, one that is important for all of us to see, the power and effect a parent can have over a child. Do you recall when you were growing up that when your parents said something to you, it was law? It was difficult to see that they would do anything wrong; they were all-knowing. Well, for most people, this view of mothers and fathers never changes. Yet clients come to my office wanting to break the hold their parents have over them. "I don't know what's wrong. I have a family of my own. I know what I'm doing, but when my mother walks into the room, I quiver and I hop to it as if I were five years old again." Can you relate? Do you find yourself feeling like a child around your parents, unable to stand up for what you believe? Do you have trouble letting go of their authority over you? This film will confront you with those issues and more. Watch how Mark initially accepts anything his father says. He emotionally can't handle confronting Dennis, and in the process abandons Anna. Have you been sexually approached by a friend or relative? Are you afraid to tell the person you're with now what has happened? Listen to the line "The more he drinks, the worse he gets." Isn't it interesting how people use their addiction to give themselves permission to do other unacceptable acts? Is it possible that you use your addiction as an excuse to cover up your real desires? "Oh, that was the alcohol, not me." Use this film as a stepping-stone to gather courage and the strength to heal. Seek the love and support of those who can help you express the person you are inside. Make a commitment to take charge and get into action. You have the power. Use it.

THE DEVIL AND DANIEL WEBSTER

(RKO, 1941), B & W, 85 minutes, not rated

HEALING THEMES:
Persevering when nothing in your life seems to work
Selling yourself short
Turning your back on your own morals
Being tempted
Giving up who you really are
Losing your dignity
Reaching out for help

DIRECTOR: William Dieterle; SCREENPLAY: Dan Totheroh; CAST: Edward Arnold (Daniel Webster); Walter Huston (Mr. Scratch); James Craig (Jabez); Anne Shirely (Mary); Simone Simon (Belle); Gene Lockhart (Squire Slossum); John Qualen (Miser Stevens); H. B. Warner (Justice Hawthorne); Jeff Corey (Tom)

SYNOPSIS: Life is difficult for Jabez. Nothing in his life seems to work out for him. He wants the best for his family, but in spite of his efforts he always seems to fail. He sells his soul to the devil. When it's time to pay up, he turns to Daniel Webster to defend him. Good is triumphant over evil.

CINEMATHERAPY: There has been more than one time in my life when I felt I'd sell my soul to get the results I wanted. How about you? "I'd do anything to get that job. Why, I'd be willing to sell my soul to the devil." "If I had all the money in the world, I wouldn't need a soul." Have you ever lied or cheated to get what you wanted? That's like selling your soul, isn't it? The foundation of the soul are your moral and philosophical beliefs about life. However, sometimes beliefs are put to a big test. *The Devil and Daniel Webster* begs us to look at those issues and more. We have all had a Mr. Scratch, the devil, tempt us at one time or another. He may not look like the Mr. Scratch portrayed in the movie, but he's been around. Maybe you've been contemplating an affair. Mr. Scratch was there. Possibly you could close that big deal if you didn't disclose some pertinent information. Mr. Scratch was there. Perhaps you cheated on a test because you needed a certain grade. That's good old Mr. Scratch pulling at you. But what if you don't have a Daniel Webster to get you off the hook? We must seek the truth and look inside ourselves for the moral and honest thing to do before we get in too deep in any given situation. If we end up selling our souls for the money, sex, alcohol, drugs, fame, et cetera, we eventually have to pay the price. So what's going on in your life that puts your soul in such jeopardy? To whom would you make amends to get that piece of your soul back? What friends and family have you lost or put at risk of losing because you've sold your principles? The point is, we have a life to live on this earth. We can get lost in the process if we make deals and bargains for things we think we need, but for all the wrong reasons. So make yourself a promise: Let the devil have his or her due, and live your own life in peace. Remember, your healing life comes from your self-healing actions. And that is true inner peace. (*Note:* This film is also known as *All That Money Can Buy, Here Is a Man,* and *A Certain Mr. Scratch.*)

DISCLOSURE

(Warner Bros., 1994), color, 126 minutes, R-rated

HEALING THEMES:

Being sexually harassed
Turning your back on temptation
Being falsely accused
Standing up for your rights
Coping when your friends turn their backs on you

DIRECTOR: Barry Levinson; SCREENPLAY: Paul Attanasio; CAST: Michael Douglas (Tom); Demi Moore (Meredith); Donald Sutherland (Bob); Caroline Goodall (Susan); Dylan Baker (Philip); Roma Maffia (Catherine); Dennis Miller (Marc); Allan Rich (Ben); Nicholas Sadler (Don)

SYNOPSIS: Tom Sanders is an executive whose loyalty to the company is beyond reproach. Meredith, his new boss, accuses him of sexual harassment when he won't have sex with her. He refuses to accept her lies and files a sexual harassment suit. In spite of a lack of support, Tom emerges triumphant.

CINEMATHERAPY: I was a little skeptical about putting *Disclosure* on my list of healing stories. The sexual harassment issues seemed unreal to me. And then I realized I had fallen prey to a misconception about this troublesome topic. What makes the problem of sexual harassment stand out in this film is that the tables are turned, because most of us expect the male to make an inappropriate approach in the workplace. Unless you have been molested in this manner, it is difficult to comprehend the emotional pain that comes from such abuse. So what I would like you to do is to focus on those scenes involving the legal mediations. Whom do you find yourself believing? Isn't it interesting that even though you know it was his boss that made the advance, you still found it difficult to acknowledge that a woman would do such a thing? Make no mistake, Tom was a party to the sexual contact. However, it was his commitment to himself and his relationship to his wife that caused him to terminate the relationship. The truth is, men can have the same sense of loyalty to themselves and their mates as women can. Listen to Meredith speak about sex. Did she sound like a man or a woman? You see, she makes the point that her interests and rights are no different from those of a male. It is simply society that puts those male/female roles in such polarized positions. Have you ever been sexually harassed? Maybe this is happening in your life today. Possibly you are the one doing the harassing. Can you see the boundaries you are crossing? These lines are crossed when you physically or verbally approach someone without their permission. No matter what your role in such activity, it is important that you put a stop to your inappropriate actions. Stand up for your rights and file a report with your employer. If you're the perpetrator, seek the support of a counselor or group who can see you through these difficult times. Healing is acknowledging mutual respect and living with that respect in your life.

DIVIDED MEMORIES

(PBS, Frontline, 1995), color, 180 minutes, not rated

HEALING THEMES:
Being a victim of sexual molestation
Being led down a false track
Understanding your hidden thoughts
Learning more about repressed memories
Seeing two sides to the memory
Finding out about how therapists think and work

CAST: Documentary; interviews with various therapists, patients, family members, and researchers.

SYNOPSIS: Memories of childhood molestation come to the surface as a therapist works to unearth family secrets. But with each accusation comes the denial and pain on the part of the accused family members. We are left with more questions to be answered.

CINEMATHERAPY: Occasionally I come across material that is not in the form of a fictional movie and it is simply too good to pass up. You may recall that in my first book, I included the documentary *Dialogues with Madwomen*, a wonderful piece of screen work dealing with five women who have experienced serious mental and emotional disturbances. *Divided Memories*, a three-hour documentary, asks all of us to look at a relatively new process occurring with patients, clients, and therapists: to question whether repressed memories, memories we keep stuffed inside, are real. Some people have claimed that through the process of various kinds of therapy, they can now recall being abused and molested in years gone by. In general, I have tried to let my readers come up with their own opinion of the meaning behind the movies. I would like you to watch *Divided Memories* from the same perspective. Use this documentary film to gain a better understanding about repressed memory. Understand the difference between fact and fiction. Learn more about the way therapists work with their clients and patients and then make your own decision. Each of you is going to feel differently. Those who do not believe in repressed memories will find themselves siding with the researchers. Others, who have recalled or are beginning to recall early-childhood experiences, will align themselves with the therapists, patients, and clients. Whoever you are, let me leave you with a few thoughts: The ultimate goal is to go on the healing journey to recover from the wounds that restrict you. Along the way you will encounter roadblocks that may sway you from your journey, sometimes for years, even decades. But when you're done, the rebirth is in the form of a whole new person who emerges triumphant from a battle with the self, able to have a rich and full existence in the world. Give this film a try and watch it with those who can accept your beliefs without debate. Good luck!

DOLORES CLAIBORNE
(Columbia, 1995), color, 131 minutes, R-rated

HEALING THEMES:
Memories of the past
Growing up in a violent home
Living with a lie
Confronting a parent
Standing up for your rights
Putting your past behind you

DIRECTOR: Taylor Hackford; SCREENPLAY: Tony Gilroy; CAST: Kathy Bates (Dolores); Jennifer Jason Leigh (Selena); Judy Parfitt (Vera); Christopher Plummer (Det. John Mackey); David Strathairn (Joe); Eric Bogosian (Peter); John C. Reilly (Frank Steemshaw); Ellen Muth (Young Selena)

SYNOPSIS: Dolores Claiborne is a sad, angry, and tired woman. After her husband's death, she fights rumors that she murdered him. When her daughter comes to defend her mother, they both begin to deal with the past they have been avoiding their whole lives.

CINEMATHERAPY: Once in a while, someone will comment, "Dr. Solomon, you include movies in your book that don't have anything to do with the kind of life I've led. I've never been like Dolores, nor do I know anyone like her." Well, it's true. Dolores Claiborne is not your average person. However, the story that is portrayed about her speaks volumes to many people's lives. It is important to feel the content of these movies, not look for perfect parallels to your life. Perhaps you grew up in a violent, alcoholic home. Maybe you've blocked out your past while people around you still retain the burdensome family secret. Do you have a parent whom you've asked repeatedly what was it like growing up in the house and that parent won't tell you the truth? (I know I can relate to that one.) Or maybe you are a Dolores Claiborne, trying to protect your children from a family secret. Did you grow up in an area where there were nasty rumors about you that weren't true? *Dolores Claiborne* is a story about all these issues. One of the things that's most intriguing about the movie is the way that Dolores learned to survive. She fought back and bit the bullet one day at a time. Does that strike a chord within you? How did you feel about the relationship Dolores had with her mean employer? Did you feel the bond these two women had with each other? And what about the way her daughter returns to her hometown filled with resentment and hate? A lot of people who have been trying to jog their childhood memories have come into my office. When they finally realize where they were, they slip into denial and refuse to see the truth. *Dolores Claiborne* will have a tremendous impact on you. You're also going to find yourself making decisions about this violent, vulgar husband. Did you think he should die? Do we have the right to play judge, jury, and executioner? And what about the issue of molestation? Do you have any memories of similar issues? Give *Dolores Claiborne* a try. It will not be an easy journey, but it will be one of enlightenment, rich with long-term awareness and recovery. Put on your safety belts—it could be a bumpy ride.

DOING TIME ON MAPLE DRIVE

(Fox-TV, 1992), color, 100 minutes, PG-rated

HEALING THEMES:
Coming out of the closet about being gay
Dealing with your fears

Trying to live up to your family's expectations
Being deceived by someone
Having to confront your family
Living with someone in the family who drinks

DIRECTOR: Ken Lolin; **TELEPLAY**: James Duff; **CAST**: James B. Sikking (Phil); Bibi Besch (Lisa); William McNamara (Matt); Jayne Brook (Karen); David Byron (Tom); Lori Loughlin (Alicen); Jim Carrey (Tim); George Roth (Dr. Norman)

SYNOPSIS: Home from college, Matt strives to be all that his parents want him to be. This perfect student and fiancé struggles to tell everyone his secret: He's gay. Before the end of the story, Matt deals with the loss of friends and family but emerges triumphant in his own sexual identity.

CINEMATHERAPY: *Doing Time on Maple Drive* is rich in content dealing with issues relating to dysfunctional families and the pain of coming out of the closet. You will immediately be struck by the role of the father. Can you see how he needs to dominate every conversation? No opinion is worth more than his own. He is master and king of his world—his family. Does he remind you of anyone in your household? Notice the way the parents ignore their other two children, focusing their attention on "their perfect son." Did you feel like you were overlooked or abandoned when you were growing up because you had a sibling who got all the attention? Maybe you resented your brothers or sisters because of the special attention that was given to them and not you. How did you feel when you learned that the son, who was gay, used his fiancée to hide his sexual preference and stay in the closet? Can you relate to the pain that comes from keeping a secret from others simply because the world—your family—has a view of who and what you are or should be? Have you ever really felt you were good enough? This is a dysfunctional family, with all the denial, codependency, and emotional upheaval that comes with the label. The family's response to the elders' dysfunction comes out in many ways: an alcoholic son, a daughter who feels worthless, and a son who can't be who he really wants to be in life. Watching this film offers a chance to do healing by seeing what *not* to do as a family. Sit with this one. Really spend the time to get inside the words and body expressions—what I call "body oozing"—being exchanged among the family members. (Most people have experienced "body oozing." That's when you read the feelings of another person by observing their body language.) I think you will kick up some real issues. Just feel the emotions that come with having to deal with your own issues, then get into positive action to make your life the best it can be. We all have closets to escape from. Open the door to the outside now!

DON JUAN DEMARCO

(New Line Cinema, 1995), color, 97 minutes, PG-13-rated

HEALING THEMES:
Losing a parent
Being forced to run away
Searching for your identity
Meeting other people's needs
Learning the simple messages in life

DIRECTOR: Jeremy Leven; **SCREENPLAY**: Jeremy Leven; **CAST**: Marlon Brando (Dr. Jack Mickler); Johnny Depp (Don Juan); Faye Dunaway (Marilyn); Geraldine Pailhas (Dona Ano); Bob Dishy (Dr. Paul Showalter); Rachel Ticotin (Dona Inez); Talisa Soto (Dona Julia); Richard Sarafian (Det. Sy Tobias); Tresa Hughes (Grandmother DeMarco); Franc Luze (Don Antonio)

SYNOPSIS: Don Juan DeMarco is a young man who lives in the past and the present at the same time. He thinks he's the world's greatest lover. He is confronted by Jack, a psychiatrist, who in the end understands Don Juan DeMarco for who he really is, while the psychiatrist sees himself for all the flaws that inhabit his own life.

CINEMATHERAPY: When I first saw *Don Juan DeMarco* I didn't regard it as a very important healing story, but as I began to think about the movie I realized how moved I was, how I had been emotionally touched by this very special man. Isn't it interesting that when we see someone walking down the street with green hair or in an offbeat outfit or doing odd things, we immediately begin to think that they are not normal. Yet they're on their own journey, and they are their own special people. Have there ever been times in your life that you've wanted to do something different, be something a little special? Have you experienced the desire to reach out and break out of life's mold? Think back. Maybe there was a time when you were a child when you were able to dress up like Batman or some other character. Suddenly, when we grow older, we fall into all of life's conformities. As we enter the mundane, everyday work world, we forget about all the richness and colors that are around us, just like the psychiatrist in the film who learned through Don Juan DeMarco the importance and the meaning of love. How did you feel about all the skeptics, the ones who saw Don Juan as being crazy, insane, someone who should go on medication? How many times in your life have you burned out your real feelings by drinking or drugging or gambling or overeating? Don Juan doesn't need that. He sees the richness in life. He offers that richness to each of us when he tries to teach us about how to give and receive love. What a wonderful healing journey Don Juan takes us on. Let yourself reach into this movie; maybe watch it with someone you care about, someone special in your life. There's a bit of Don Juan in all of us, no matter if we're a man or a woman. Go ahead, take this healing journey and enjoy.

DREAM LOVER

(MGM/UA, 1986), color, 105 minutes, R-rated

HEALING THEMES:
Confronting your nightmares
Being haunted by memories
Coping if your dreams are taking over your life
Seeking help and learning to trust
Dealing with repressed memories
Knowing you're not alone with your dreams

DIRECTOR: Alan J. Pakula; SCREENPLAY: Jon Boorstin; CAST: Kristy McNichol (Kathy); Ben Masters (Michael); Paul Shenar (Ben); Justin Deas (Kevin); Joseph Culp (Danny); Gayle Hunnicutt (Claire); John McMartin (Martin)

SYNOPSIS: Kathy survives a brutal attack but starts having nightmares that haunt her and cause her to sleepwalk. She decides to enter into a new kind of therapy. More and more is revealed about her inner thoughts, but she abandons her therapy. The therapist refuses to let her give up and eventually finds the solution to her problem.

CINEMATHERAPY: I don't think a week goes by without one of my clients telling me about a dream he or she had. "So, what do you think, Doc? What's it mean?" "Doc, I have the same dream over and over again. It's beginning to bother me." Well, I wish I had the answer. No matter what you hear or what people tell you, there is no way for someone else to tell you what your dreams truly mean. The person who really knows is you. Do you have wonderful, colorful dreams, or are your dreams scary? Do you envision the same thing over and over again, or do you have different dreams? Do you feel better after your dreams, or are you upset? We dream because we are trying to resolve something in our lives. And that's the main reason I wanted you to watch this movie. Look for yourself in the experiences this young girl has as she struggles with her nightmare. Is there a trauma that you have been unable to resolve in your life? Are your dreams disturbing, but you don't know what they mean? Our young dreamer in this film is on a journey to find out what her dreams are about before they push her over the edge. Notice that she relives her nightmare, and that her father seems to be making his way into her dreams. Is it possible something took place in her childhood that got retriggered by her assailant? Maybe he is her assailant. What experiences from your past have you been avoiding? What is it that you're working so hard to forget that makes its way into your dreams? The point is, if you don't work to resolve your past and put it behind you, it will continue to come back to haunt you. Healing happens when you come clean from your past and allow sweet dreams to fill your present. You don't have to exist in the nightmare of your dreams anymore. Experience freedom by letting go and moving on.

DRUNKS

(Showtime-Cable, 1996), color, 90 minutes, R-rated

HEALING THEMES:

Dealing with an addiction
Learning you are not the only alcoholic struggling to stay sober
Getting support from those who understand you
Staying sober, one day at a time
Being pushed to the point where you feel you can't hold on

DIRECTOR: Peter Cohn; TELEPLAY: Peter Cohn, Gary Lennon; CAST: Richard Lewis (Jim); Faye Dunaway (Becky); Dianne Wiest (Rachel); Parker Posey (Debbie); Amanda Plummer (Shelly); Howard E. Rollins (Joseph); Spalding Gray (Louis); Calista Flockhart (Helen)

SYNOPSIS: A group gathers to discuss their common bond—alcohol. One after another, each tells a story of addiction, loss, and self-destruction. Whereas some hold on and stay sober, one day at a time, others are unable to keep the commitment to sobriety.

CINEMATHERAPY: Most of the movies that deal with alcohol and drugs suggest, as part of the story, that addictions are a problem. Whether it is because of a marriage, bad childhood, or too much partying, these movies tell us stories about other people's lives. Now comes *Drunks*. It cuts right to the chase. If you or someone you know has been dreading the self-confrontation that comes with admitting to an addiction, this movie is going to put you over the top. So you say you can quit anytime? Why not join the rest of the group? You think that sitting with a group of people who tell one another about their past is not for you? Go ahead. Give it a try. This movie reminds each of us that we should not go it alone. Oh, sure, I've known a few people who have gone sober cold turkey and with no support. It's called white knuckling. Believe me, they feel every second of every minute of every day. So why do it alone? There are meetings on addictions to anything: alcohol, cocaine, smoking, gambling, shopping, food, to name a few. These meetings contain people such as yourself, people who need your presence to remind them that they are not alone. Here's an idea: Pick up the phone, call your operator, and get the phone number of the support group you need in your life. Get a list of the support meetings in your area and give them a try. You will find that you are not alone. There are others just like yourself, struggling with the pain of trying to get back on track and lead a better life. As they say in the meetings: "If you don't like what you hear, you can take back your addiction at no charge." By the way, did I mention that these meetings are free?

AN EARLY FROST

(NBC-TV, 1985), color, 100 minutes, not rated

HEALING THEMES:
Having your life turned upside down by AIDS
Coming out of the closet
Learning a family member has a serious physical illness
Having to confront your family
Dealing with death and dying
Living with those who are prejudiced
Feeling overwhelmed with sadness

DIRECTOR: John Erman; TELEPLAY: Ron Cowen; CAST: Gena Rowlands (Katherine); Ben Gazzara (Nick); Aidan Quinn (Michael); Sylvia Sidney (Beatrice); D. W. Moffett (Peter); John Glover (Victor); Sydney Walsh (Susan); Terry O'Quinn (Dr. Redding); Bill Payton (Bob)

SYNOPSIS: A family has their life turned upside down when their adult son tells them that he is gay. Things get worse when he informs them he has terminal AIDS. The family is forced to deal with the reality of his being gay and his gradual decline in health. Confronting the crisis ultimately brings them closer together.

CINEMATHERAPY: It is always my hope that I can reach everyone who is dealing with issues that may create emotional pain in their life. Is there anyone today who has not been touched by AIDS in one way or another? As I was writing this book, my wife learned that yet another friend of ours had died of AIDS. We can't seem to get away from reports of the growing number of AIDS victims. But what of those who are struggling to survive the dreaded desease? How does the family deal with this most difficult situation? Movies such as *An Early Frost* and *Doing Time on Maple Drive* bring these crucial issues to the forefront and beg each of us to heal from the anger and prejudice that spring from this devastating disease. The issue becomes much more sensitive when compounded by the fact that the ailing man is gay. I have dealt with several families with a member who wants to come out of the closet about being gay or lesbian. How difficult this can be for the entire household. We have not yet all come to accept the idea that being gay is an equal lifestyle. As you watch *An Early Frost,* listen and feel the father's pain and denial over his son's being gay.

How would you react? Maybe you're gay and you're afraid to tell your family. It takes a great deal of courage. Give it time. Try and get in touch with your own pain and feelings. What can you do to educate your family about the risk of aquiring AIDS? Are you practicing safer sex? Are you honest with your partner about your past and the level of risk you may be placing on him or her? Try to identify your beliefs about homosexuality, and make the effort to learn more about alternate yet equal lifestyles. There is so much happening in *An Early Frost* that I strongly encourage you and your family to see it. Most important is that we accept people despite their life choices and enjoy one another for the brief time we have on this earth. Self-awareness is yet another way to heal. And remember, AIDS is an equal-opportunity disease. It can touch us all.

EAST OF EDEN

(Warner Bros., 1955), color, 115 minutes, not rated

HEALING THEMES:
Feeling unloved by a parent
Trying to gain attention from those you want to love you
Feeling that nothing you do is good enough for others
Learning the family secret
Dealing with a family crisis

DIRECTOR: Elia Kazan; SCREENPLAY: Paul Osborn; CAST: James Dean (Cal); Julie Harris (Abra); Raymond Massey (Adam); Jo Van Fleet (Kate); Burl Ives (Sam); Richard Davalos (Aron); Albert Dekker (Will); Lois Smith (Ann); Lonny Chapman (Roy); Nick Dennis (Rantone)

SYNOPSIS: The year is 1917. Cal is a young man who can't seem to find his footing in life. Adam, Cal's stoic father, simply tolerates him. Cal can't do anything to make his dad happy. Their world starts to unravel when Cal's brother, Aron, learns what Cal has known for some time—their long-vanished mother, Katie, is very much alive.

CINEMATHERAPY: There is a comedy team named The Smothers Brothers. Maybe you've heard of them. Well, one of the lines Tommy Smothers uses on his brother, Dick, is "Mom always liked you best." It's a simple line that has tremendous meaning in a serious context. Some adults resent the way one parent favored a sibling. One of the things that can result from those negative feelings are extreme differences in the behavior and personality of the children. *East of Eden* begs us to get in touch with those emotions and more. Who were you, Cal or Aron? Were you the one in the family who couldn't do anything to please your parents? Did you send your anger out to the world because you didn't have your needs met at home? Maybe you were like Aron, always getting accolades from everyone as "the good kid," the one who never caused any problems. Did you resent your brother(s) and sister(s) when they got all the attention or they treated you the same way your parents did? The telling scene in the movie comes when Adam's world comes tumbling down around him. He is finally confronted with his lie. Did you grow up in a home where there were long-kept secrets? Have you found out that your father or mother has a secret past that was being hidden all these years? I have worked with people enraged about a parent keeping secrets from them. Have you learned something that your parents were keeping from you? Is there a mystery haunting the family but they won't tell you the truth? I was deeply touched by the scene in this film when Adam became ill, and Cal took on the responsibility of caring for him, not Aron. Yet it was Cal who had been viewed as the irresponsible, worthless child. Is that how you feel? Listen closely to the words used to express this family's dysfunction. Even though it might be a tragedy, it is a time for recovery nevertheless. This movie is special: It provides a different, constructive message for each of us.

EASY RIDER

(Columbia, 1969), color, 94 minutes, R-rated

HEALING THEMES:
Living your life with a moral compass
Crime doesn't pay
Living in a drug culture
Trying to make the big score
Learning to expect the unexpected

DIRECTOR: Dennis Hopper; **SCREENPLAY**: Peter Fonda, Dennis Hopper, Terry Sothern; **CAST**: Peter Fonda (Wyatt); Dennis Hopper (Billy); Jack Nicholson (George); Karen Black (Karen); Toni Basil (Mary); Robert Walker Jr. (Jack); Phil Spector (Connection); Luke Skew (Stranger); Luans Anders (Lisa); Karen Black (Karen)

SYNOPSIS: Two men, biker rebels, decide to make a big score. They put a drug deal together that produces enough money to make them financially comfortable for a long time. They head across the country on their bikes to experience America. They encounter more than they bargained for when redneck truck drivers decide to blow them away.

CINEMATHERAPY: Over the years, *Easy Rider* has become a cult classic. It made the Harley-Davidson motorcycle a symbol of power and rebellion, and it gave us the phrase "easy rider." Most of us have a fantasy of hanging it all up and hitting the road. And many people fantasize about making a big score in the real estate market or a stock transaction and calling it quits forever. Well, this movie reaches that bit of fantasy in all of us. What about you? Would you like to chuck it all for a different life? Would you like to move away, change your name, and start all over again? Maybe you're an executive whose had it with all the pressure. How does a small town and a job in a convenience store sound? You might be a parent living in a big city. Your kids are pulling at you from one side and your spouse is yanking from the other. However, I wouldn't go about it the way these two guys did. An interesting emotional and philosophical journey is taken in *Easy Rider*. Watch the entire movie. Stay focused on the story line. How did you feel when the bikers were killed? Most people felt sad for them. Isn't that odd? These two guys just made a big-money deal by selling drugs, which will ultimately cause other people harm. Why do we experience such feelings for these types of people? I look back on my life and realize how many times I have supported those who should have never received credit for what they did. And there were times I didn't acknowledge those who should have received recognition for a job well done. Try looking at this movie from a different perspective. I think you will discover that healing comes from giving credit where credit is due. Try not to hold back. Congratulate people on a job well done, and don't support those who cheat, lie, and steal for their own gain. Life can be a much easier ride if you live it with a strong moral philosophy.

EDUCATING RITA

(Acorn, 1983), color, 110 minutes, PG-rated

HEALING THEMES:
Making changes in your life
Persevering when someone you care about has given up
Living life in a bottle of booze
Feeling inadequate and doing something about it
Two souls meeting and making a difference in each other's life

DIRECTOR: Lewis Gilbert; SCREENPLAY: Willy Russell; CAST: Michael Caine (Dr. Frank Bryant); Julie Walters (Rita); Michael Williams (Brian); Maureen Lipman (Trish); Jeananne Crowley (Julia); Malcolm Douglas (Denny)

SYNOPSIS: Rita is an uneducated hairdresser who is tired of being perceived as unintelligent. She decides she wants to grow as a person, so she enlists the help of a pompous, alcoholic professor who has had it with the world and spends his days and nights with a bottle. Little by little, teacher and student educate each other as they discover what they need to (re)capture the essence of life.

CINEMATHERAPY: I love the fact that movies send us healing messages in different ways. Some movies knock us over the head and confront us with our beliefs—don't drink, be honest in relationships, life can be difficult, everyone has the right to be loved, et cetera. Other movies, such as *Educating Rita,* help us get the message in a more subtle way. This is a movie for those who have given up on life and need to be reminded that if they want to make a change badly enough, they can. Rita never pictured being anything other than a hairdresser—although there is certainly nothing wrong with being a hairdresser. Bryant, the professor, could never imagine having a new lease on life, so he just gave up. (Boy, have I been there. How about you?) He is drenched in his alcoholism and can't see forces of life beyond the other side of the bottle. I've known some wonderful, loving, and talented people who just quit and turned their life into a bottle, a drug, a deck of cards, a plate of food, or a state of depression. Do you know anyone who has done this? Is that what's happened to you? Are you asking yourself what it's all about? Why you should even go on? Rita's simplicity forces her "teacher" to confront his alcoholism and to see reality. She believes that because he is a professor, life must be perfect for him. People tend to assume that because someone is academically proficient they are automatically happy, normal, moral, and ethical. This is a myth. It's what's inside that counts. What people have you thought had the golden ring, only to find out they were unhappy with their lot in life? Take Rita's challenge and make some changes in your daily ways. Why not take that class in American literature, join a hiking group, learn how to use a computer, or be a part of a political concern. You can do it! All you have to do is take that first step and get started. Sometimes it just happens—that is, it occurs by serendipity. The two main characters in *Educating Rita* needed each other to heal, to help each other reenergize. They met each other's challenge and grew in the process. You've got the power to change—and you may get a boost in the process.

84 CHARING CROSS ROAD

(Columbia, 1986), color, 97 minutes, PG-rated

HEALING THEMES:
Making a unique connection
Having a pen pal
Relationships that grow over the years
Missing the moment
Accepting that someone special has died

DIRECTOR: David Jones; **SCREENPLAY:** Hugh Whitemore; **CAST:** Anne Bancroft (Helene); Anthony Hopkins (Frank); Judi Dench (Nora); Jean DeBaer (Maxine); Maurice Denham (George); Eleanor David (Cecily); Mercedes Ruehl (Kay); Daniel Gerroll (Brian); Wendy Morgan (Megan)

SYNOPSIS: It can be difficult finding some special reading material in the United States. With her limited budget, Helene has no choice but to order her books by mail from a bookstore in London. Mr. Frank Dole, the store manager, and Helene engage in a unique long-distance relationship that spans thirty years.

CINEMATHERAPY: Over the years, I have maintained some beautiful long-distance relationships with people who mean a great deal to me. Some of them have been friends for many years, whereas others are former clients who have moved away or have transitioned out of therapy. I love getting letters from them, and I enjoy taking a few quiet moments to write back. Have you ever had a pen pal, someone with whom you had a unique connection? Did you have feelings of love for someone you were connected to through business dealings? Did they know how you felt about them? Maybe someone who is writing or e-mailing you has deeper feelings than he or she is letting you know. It seems that in our new, fast-paced world, many people don't take the time to nurture that type of relationship. As you watch this film, you will notice that Frank and Helene are falling in love. Cecily gets into the match-making game as she begins to communicate with Helene on the side. Could you feel Frank's wife, Nora, becoming jealous of the relationship? You will appreciate this movie because you will get in touch with your own memories about that special someone from your past. Maybe, like Frank and Helene, you never came right out and said anything but you both knew those special feelings were there. Do you think Frank was having an affair? Are affairs of the mind any different from physical affairs? Here's an idea: Go to that old trunk, box, or suitcase, and pull out the letters you've tucked away. Get in touch with some of those special feelings that you once had for the person. Afterward, sit down and write the person a letter or send an e-mail and let them know how special he or she was in your life. Don't wait as long as Helene to make contact. Reach out and "touch" that person. You will be amazed at the emotions that will come to the surface in the process.

THE ELEPHANT MAN
(Paramount, 1980), B & W, 125 minutes, PG-rated

HEALING THEMES:
Accepting people for who they are
Being a more humane person
Understanding a little more about what it means to condemn someone
Dealing with someone you know who is physically challenged
Mocking others

DIRECTOR: David Lynch; SCREENPLAY: Christopher DeVore, Eric Bergren, David Lynch; CAST: Anthony Hopkins (Dr. Frederick Treves); John Hurt (John); Anne Bancroft (Mrs. Kendall); John Gielgud (Carr); Wendy Hiller (Mothershead); Freddie Jones (Bytes)

SYNOPSIS: Frederick Treves is a prominent doctor who lives in London at the turn of the nineteenth century. John Merrick is the Elephant Man. He is a grotesquely deformed person whom the world sees as a freak. Treves takes an interest in the Elephant Man and decides to help him. Along the way, the Elephant Man emerges as a well-educated person whom society decides to embrace.

CINEMATHERAPY: Life, some would say, is pain—a difficult journey that each of us takes to an indeterminate point in time. (Boy, that was a little weighty, don't you think?) Each of us has a cross to bear, but some of us have a bigger cross to support than others. What makes that burden even larger is a matter of humanity. Rather than accept John, the Elephant Man, for who he is, society treats him as a freak and a misfit. On top of that, he is tortured for his misfortune. Possibly you are someone who has been teased for having a handicap. The handicap does not have to be physical. Maybe you've been taunted for having a learning disorder or simply not being adept at certain activities. I didn't learn to read, write, or spell until I was fifteen. I can still feel the unkind words thrust at me. How do you feel when people treat you for what you are instead of who you are inside? Maybe you have teased someone in the past for being too short or fat or unattractive. How does that make you feel now about yourself? What do you or did you derive from doing that to someone else? Maybe it made you feel "better" about yourself. Also, notice how John becomes a different kind of freak when people suddenly want to be around him to be entertained. And what of the kind Dr. Treves? What were his real motives? If you've seen *The Wild Child*, you may find yourself questioning Frederick's true motives. *The Elephant Man* is a telling movie for us all: Be kind, not cruel. Be giving, not taking. Be understanding, not rejecting. Let your children see this film while they're young. It may help them make the world a more gentle, kinder place in which to live. Maybe they won't make the same mistakes we did. For your information, as is the case with Rocky Dennis in *Mask* (1985), the Elephant Man suffers from a disfiguring condition known as craniodiaphyseal dysplasia. As you will see, this condition causes hideous deformities in parts of the human body.

ELMER GANTRY

United Artists, 1960), color, 145 minutes, not rated

HEALING THEMES:
Understanding addictions
Living a lie
Taking advantage of others
Practicing religion for all the wrong reasons
Paying your dues

DIRECTOR: Richard Brooks; **SCREENPLAY:** Richard Brooks; **CAST:** Burt Lancaster (Elmer Gantry); Jean Simmons (Sister Sharon); Dean Jagger

(William); Arthur Kennedy (Jim); Shirley Jones (Lulu); Patti Page (Sister Rachel); Edward Andrews (George); Hugh Marlowe (Reverend Garrison); John McIntire (Reverend Pengilly) Philip Ober (Reverend Planck)

SYNOPSIS: Elmer Gantry is a man on a mission. He's seeking his true identity in life. When he comes across a traveling religious show, he finds his true calling. He becomes a preacher with extraordinary talents. He pushes those talents way too far when he uses them to take advantage of people.

CINEMATHERAPY: There are very few movies that deal with the issues of religiosity, taking advantage of those who become addicted to religion and what they believe it has to offer. Now I do not suggest that religion and religious leaders are not good things with which to be involved—quite the contrary. Religion and all that it means are individual choices, but when religion consumes your life, takes over everything you have and who you are, you lose sight of your own identity. *Elmer Gantry* is a wonderful portrayal of the kind of charlatans and shysters that emerge in the religious circuit. How do you feel about this guy? How do you react to the way he takes advantage of people? What about the relationship between him and the prostitute? Does he remind you of anybody? Maybe you are someone who is looking for the answers to life and you've found yourself becoming attracted to gurus and soothsayers, or religious leaders, or even therapists. Just like Dorothy in *The Wizard of Oz,* the answer is with you all the time. If you are going to find your way home, it's not through the eyes and the life of someone else. When you watch the way Elmer Gantry behaves, asks yourself "Why is it necessary to turn my life over to someone like him? Why is it that I can't be my own person?" You're going to be quite taken with this movie. The story of this man, and the healing powers he would make you believe he has, is very dynamic. It will ultimately help you realize that *you* are the one who holds all the power you will ever need to heal yourself.

THE END

(United Artists, 1978), color, 100 minutes, R-rated

HEALING THEMES:
Feeling that life is too much
Trying to take your own life
Seeing the lighter side to all of the stress in life
Seeking help when you can't take it anymore
Giving life a second chance

DIRECTOR: Burt Reynolds; **SCREENPLAY:** Jerry Belson; **CAST:** Burt Reynolds (Sonny); Sally Field (Mary); Dom DeLuise (Marlon); Joanne Woodward (Jessica); Kristy McNichol (Julie); Robby Benson (The Priest);

David Steinberg (Marty); Norman Fell (Dr. Krugman); Carl Reiner (Dr. Maneet); Pat O'Brien (Ben); Myrna Loy (Maureen)

SYNOPSIS: Sonny's had it with life. He can't seem to get anything right. He ends up in a sanitarium, but that doesn't help either. He recruits the help of a schizophrenic patient to help him commit suicide. He never quite makes it to the end.

CINEMATHERAPY: Have you ever decided you can't take it anymore? "I can't deal with this life one more day. I'm checkin' out." "Who needs this stuff? Nobody's gonna have the chance to push me around anymore. That's it. This is the end." Do any of these thoughts sound familiar to you? It's important for us to hear healing messages in different ways. *The End* gives us the lighter side of what happens when we've been pushed too far. There are many people who simply give up on life and let it pass right by. Ask yourself, "How much is enough?" Can you relate to our hero when he gives up because nothing is going right for him? Have you ever felt as if you were going crazy? It's normal to feel that way from time to time. Here's something to help you stay grounded: If you can ask yourself if you are going crazy, then you're probably not, since you've got the mental faculties at least to ask yourself the question. Each of us has a time in our life when we feel we can't take it anymore—a moment when we feel we're falling apart. Whom do you have that you can turn to for support? Do you believe your family is there for you? When you share your feelings with your family, do they listen to what you have to say or do they tend to downplay what you're saying to them? It's important to have someone or somewhere that's safe to help you release your feelings. You might consider joining a support group or seeing a therapist or counselor to help you deal with such feelings. Take a look at this movie, have a laugh, then look at yourself. Ask yourself how your life is going and if you need to make changes. If you want to take a more serious look at these issues, try *Falling Down* and *Postcards from the Edge*. If you feel you're too close to the edge, reach out to therapists, support groups, counselors, and religious organizations to help see you through.

EQUUS

(United Artists, 1977), color, 138 minutes, R-rated

HEALING THEMES:
Uncovering the unthinkable
Finding someone to help you on your recovery journey
Trying to put all the pieces together
Confronting yourself and your past
Accepting your past and moving on
Learning about the therapist and therapy

DIRECTOR: Sidney Lumet; SCREENPLAY: Peter Shaffer; CAST: Richard Burton (Dr. Martin Dysart); Peter Firth (Alan); Jenny Agutter (Jill); Joan Plowright (Dora); Colin Blakely (Frank); Harry Andrews (Harry); Kate Reid (Margaret)

SYNOPSIS: Dr. Martin Dysart is a psychiatrist called in to handle a very unusual case. A boy responsible for tending horses blinds one of the animals. As the psychiatrist works to put all the pieces together, he begins to realize that something bizarre in the boy's childhood has set him up to do this horrible act.

CINEMATHERAPY: Some years before *Equus* was made into a movie, I had the opportunity to see the play a few times. In some ways the play may have helped me choose my career as a therapist. I wanted to be a psychological supersleuth just like this investigative psychiatrist, solving the mysteries behind the motivation for our life choices. "I don't know why I did it, Doc. I love her so much. What makes me want to hit her? I can't control myself." "When I get up in the morning, I promise I'm not going to buy anything. Next thing I know, I've got the shopping channel on television, the phone's in my hand, and I'm ordering some stuff I know I'll never use." People come to my office wanting to know why they do what they do. Determining the cause is no easy task. Sometimes I wish my clients understood that there are no pat answers to these questions, and that at best the reasons for a particular behavior are an educated guess. That's really what I would like you to gain from *Equus*. I want you to know that there are no magical answers to explain our behavior. If you spend time with a therapist who says he or she knows these answers for sure, I would suggest you get out of that office as quickly as possible. The best I can do for you as a therapist is help you open some doors in areas of your life that you would like to investigate. Once we reach that point, we can both seek the reasons for what is bothering you and get to a place where there are potential solutions. You see, we must both go on the healing journey together. You cannot be told what the problem is, you must see it for yourself. Together, we uncover the possible reasons for your problems and seek some solutions. It is your job to look at your options and make your own choices. Never let a therapist make those choices for you! *Warning:* There are some very brutal and shocking scenes in this film, so prepare yourself. You're going to have a different kind of growth from viewing this movie. It's another example of the many ways we can experience healing.

E.T.: THE EXTRA-TERRESTRIAL
(Universal, 1982), color, 115 minutes, PG-rated

HEALING THEMES:
Remembering your childhood
Learning lessons about love, trust, and hope

Accepting others for who and what they are
Reaching out to those who are in need
Fighting those who would take advantage of others

DIRECTOR: Steven Spielberg; SCREENPLAY: Melissa Mathison; CAST: Dee Wallace (Mary); Henry Thomas (Elliot); Peter Coyote (Keys); Robert Mac-Naughton (Michael); Drew Barrymore (Gertie); K. C. Martel (Greg); Sean Frye (Steve); C. Thomas Howell (Tyler); Erika Eleniak (pretty girl)

SYNOPSIS: Elliot is an average, fun-loving, ten-year-old boy growing up in your average neighborhood. His life is turned upside down when an extra-terrestrial, E.T., seeks out his help. Elliot's love, trust, and faith is put to the test when his E.T. almost dies. Elliot makes sure his new friend gets home safely.

CINEMATHERAPY: I can recall the first time I saw this movie. I was in a movie theater with a few hundred people, most of whom were on the edge of their seats waiting to see what would happen to E.T. Much to my amazement, the audience was in tears when E.T. said goodbye to Elliot. "What's the big deal?" I thought to myself. "It's just a story." Well, I've experienced my own recovery and I've learned a very important lesson: It's okay that I allow myself to feel emotions like excitement, fear, sadness, and loss. And now you've answered the question Why is *E.T.* in the Movie Doctor's book of healing stories? When we allow ourselves to let go, simply experience the most basic of emotions, we experience a healing, a joyful inner wellness that others work to avoid. Are you someone who feels it's important to show others you aren't emotionally touched when movies like *E.T.* come your way? Maybe you bite your lip or turn away so you don't have to experience the feelings. Do you believe others will think you're weak because you shed a tear of sadness or joy over something like a little boy saying goodbye to his friend? Let it happen. No one is passing judgment on your emotions. You no longer have to be the tough, stoic kid you were when you were growing up. "Stop those tears!" "Don't you dare cry!" "Crying's for babies!" Sound familiar? Learn to be free with your emotions. What did you feel when E.T. was dying? Did you ever experience the loss of someone you cared for, a friend who moved away or a favorite aunt, uncle, or grandparent who died? Here's an idea: Gather your family and watch *E.T.* together. Let your children see your emotions. Teach them that it's all right to show their feelings openly and to enjoy all the colors of their emotions. If your children learn that showing feelings is okay, they won't have to hold themselves back the way you did. What a wonderful, nurturing gift for yourself and your family. Go ahead—do it today!

THE FAN

(TriStar, 1996), color, 117 minutes, R-rated

HEALING THEMES:
Stalking
Being obsessed with someone or something
Losing control of your emotions
Reality and fantasy becoming one
Not being able to see the real danger

DIRECTOR: Tony Scott; SCREENPLAY: Phoef Sutton; CAST: Robert De Niro (Gil); Wesley Snipes (Bobby); Ellen Barkin (Jewel); John Legiuzamo (Manny); Benicio Del Toro (Juan); Patti D'Arbanville-Quinn (Ellen); Chris Mulkey (Tim); Dan Butler (Garrity)

SYNOPSIS: Gil is not just your average baseball fan. He will do *anything* to make sure he gets to each and every game, even if it means losing his job. Gil's interest in baseball turns to obsession when he decides that a baseball star should be obligated to him. Before it's over, Gil's obsession leads to murder.

CINEMATHERAPY: "Doc, I thought this book was supposed to be about self-recovery. What's this movie got to do with healing?" Well, I'm glad you asked. Most people who stalk will scream to the moon that they are, in fact, not stalking—that they are just getting closer to a person who wants them to be close. Many people who stalk actually use the courts to stay in touch with their victims. The reason I wanted you to see *The Fan* is that it is such a great depiction of the pathology—the makeup—of a stalker. This movie gives each of us an excellent opportunity to look at our own behavior and see if possibly we are taking things too far. Having trouble with a fellow employee? Are you doing things to torment that person? You're stalking! Are you angry with someone, calling them and leaving messages, and then hanging up? You are stalking! Have you met someone who has misinterpreted your interest in him or her and now can't seem to let you out of sight? That's a type of stalking. I am hoping you will see *The Fan* to compare what is taking place in the movie with what is happening in your own life. Being obsessed or being the object of an obsession kills. Our prisons contain many people who became obsessed with another person, stalked them, and wound up murdering them. If you or someone you know is caught up in this problem, seek help before it's too late. There are therapists and medications that benefit people with this disorder. Be safe, not embarrassed, to seek assistance and support. Accepting reality is so much more healthy than living in a fantasy at someone else's expense.

FATSO

(Twentieth Century-Fox, 1980), color, 93 minutes, PG-rated

HEALING THEMES:
Persevering when your life becomes unmanageable
Getting help from others
Refusing to see the truth about yourself
Getting a wake-up call
Being confronted with your denial

DIRECTOR: Anne Bancroft; SCREENPLAY: Anne Bancroft; CAST: Dom DeLuise (Dominick); Anne Bancroft (Antoinette); Ron Carey (Frankie); Candice Azzara (Lydia); Michael Lombard (Charlie); Sal Viscuso (Vito); Estelle Reiner (Mrs. Goodman)

SYNOPSIS: A man suffers from morbid obesity. He is grossly overweight and can't stop eating. When his cousin dies, he decides to take a good look at himself. He turns to his sister, Antoinette, in an attempt to stop eating. She struggles at being close with him; his neurotic tendencies badly upset her. He also seeks out a support group to help him deal with his obsessions. Now he knows what he must do—he's simply not sure he wants to do it.

CINEMATHERAPY: Everyone can get healing messages from this movie—not just those with eating issues. Obesity is a devastating emotional problem with roots in early childhood and adolescence. People have a difficult time accepting the idea that food can be addictive. There is a tendency for people to overlook this problem when looking at other addictions, such as addictions to alcohol, drugs, and gambling. They see these troubles as being the basis for the "real" addictions. This is simply not the case. Why is it that we don't tease or joke about the other addictions but feel it is okay to tell fat jokes? I can assure you that people who suffer from obesity are in a great deal of pain, regardless of their ability to shrug off the "humor." Let me dissolve one other myth. I have heard people say things like "Just stop drinking" or "Just stop eating." If it were that simple, we would not be dealing with addiction problems to the degree that we have been in this country. If you are someone, or you know someone, who is dealing with the problem of obesity, give this movie a try. Don't let its funny moments stop you from experiencing your emotions. Humor can be a wonderful healing device as long as the comedy is not at the expense of someone else. Those who suffer from bulimia, anorexia, or compulsive overeating can be cured. It's important to reach out and get help. There are hospitals, clinics, and specialists who are trained to deal with these problems. In addition, there are support groups to see you down your own road to recovery. Gather together friends, sit down, and give this movie a chance. You never know how much healing may come from those you love.

FEVER PITCH

(MGM/UA, 1985), color, 96 minutes, R-rated

HEALING THEMES:

Being addicted to gambling
Taking too much time off from work
Putting your life on hold because of an obsession
Awakening when your performance at work begins to suffer
Being in denial over someone's addiction

DIRECTOR: Richard Brooks; SCREENPLAY: Richard Brooks; CAST: Ryan O'Neal (Taggart); Catherine Hicks (Flo); Giancarlo Giannini (Charley); Bridgette Andersen (Amy); Chad Everett (Dutchman); John Saxon (sports editor); William Smith (Panama Hat); Rafael Campos (Rafael); Patrick Cassidy (soldier)

SYNOPSIS: Taggart, a newspaperman, works hard at his job. Each day this reporter tries to make sure the columns he writes are delivered on time and that they are the best they can be. At least that's the way it used to be. Things change dramatically when he becomes hooked on gambling. He can't seem to stop. He gets the gambling fever, which eventually brings him to his knees.

CINEMATHERAPY: If you think that being addicted to gambling is different from addiction to alcohol, drugs, smoking, or food, addiction, you're going to change your mind when you watch this movie. Many times a family has come to my office asking for help for a father, brother, or sister who is so entangled in their gambling behavior that they no longer are in touch with reality. Like *The Great Sinner* and *The Lady Gambles*, this movie profiles the life of a gambler. As you will see, Taggart reaches a point in his life where he is consumed by gambling. Notice the almost feverlike trance that engulfs him the closer he gets to making a bet. It's the same fever the drug addict, foodaholic, and smoker have when they're on the road to get their fix. Also notice that as with all other addictions, he seems to go through withdrawal whenever he is taken away from his obsession for too long. Can you relate to what he's doing? Have there been times when you or someone you know couldn't stop gambling? I can remember watching a man, still in his oil rig work clothes, standing at a crap table in Las Vegas, cashing his paycheck at the table, and gambling his earnings away right before my eyes. Although I was in my early twenties at the time, even then I could see that gambling was an addiction. Notice the way it becomes, in effect, Taggart's work. Possibly you've gotten to the point where your workday is being hindered by your gambling addiction. I've seen cases where children are not eating properly because their guardians have gambled with the money budgeted for food. Whether it is your problem or that of someone close to you, now is the time to start the journey toward recovery. Call your local chapter of Gamblers Anonymous. Don't put it off until you have lost everything. If you're having trouble getting someone you care about onto the road to recovery, persuade them to watch this movie. There's no need to reach a fever pitch before getting help.

FIRE IN THE DARK

(CBS-TV, 1991), color, 100 minutes, not rated

HEALING THEMES:
Accepting that you're getting older
Facing the fact that someone in the family is getting old
Dealing with memories of years gone by
Feeling as if your family is being turned upside down
Coming to understand that life will never be the same

DIRECTOR: David Jones; TELEPLAY: David J. Hill; CAST: Olympia Dukakis (Emily); Lindsay Wagner (Janet); Jean Stapleton (Henny); Edward Herrmann (Robert); Ray Wise (Richard); George Hearn (Arthur); Joan Leslie (Ruthie); Paul Scherrer (Eric); Amzie Strickland (Gladys)

SYNOPSIS: When Emily, who is getting on in years, has an accident in her home, Janet and Robert, her children, decide she needs to move out of her house. Emily struggles with the fact that she is getting old. She refuses to let go of her past. Memories consume her and rule her everyday life. She eventually learns that all she has is today and the love of her children.

CINEMATHERAPY: How do I handle getting old? What's going to happen when I can't take care of myself? Will I be able to think clearly when I become elderly? Will I outlive my spouse? These are just a few of the questions each of us will ask ourselves as we go through the aging process. When I think of what it might be like to be unable to get around or write my books, I get scared. So I use all the help I can get in trying to better understand how others grow old. *Family Upside Down, A Trip to the Bountiful,* and *The Gathering* are all movies that can help you with your fears of aging. *Fire in the Dark* also examines the way family members handle memories of their childhood and how they treat their aging parents. What did you think of Robert? Did you feel he was taking advantage of Emily? It seemed to me that he was out for her money, and that he was angry over childhood issues and at Janet for being the "favorite." So if that's the case, why is Emily more happy to see Robert? As families go through life's changes, it affects everyone. Notice the stress that's put on Janet's household. They have their own lives, their own routine, and suddenly everything is turned upside down. Emily shares her memories with us. Remembrances are all that many people have. They're so important to help us get through life's difficult transitions. If you're someone who is dealing with fear about aging, or if you're taking care of an aging parent, you will find *Fire in the Dark* a valuable tool to help you and your family take this journey. Try watching this one as a family. It doesn't matter if someone in your family is old or not. Then spend time sharing your feelings with one another. Speak openly about how the movie affected you. You and your loved ones will arrive at a self-awareness that will profoundly nurture your futures.

THE FIRST TIME

(ABC-TV, 1983), color, 100 minutes, PG-rated

HEALING THEMES:
Mother-and-daughter relationships
Feeling pressured to have sex
Finding your own way in life
Trying to control your child's life
Facing up to a bad marriage
Planning to run away from home

DIRECTOR: Noel Nosseck; TELEPLAY: Robie Robinson; CAST: Susan Anspach (Lucy); Jennifer Jason Leigh (Bonnie); Edward Winter (Cpt. Michael McKenzie); Alex Rocco (Jay); John Anderson (Paul); Peter Barton (Steve); Krista Errickson (Karen); Harriet Nelson (Charlotte)

SYNOPSIS: Bonnie is a high school girl who is in love for the first time. Her boyfriend wants to become more intimate than she is ready for. Her mother, Lucy, constantly rides roughshod over Bonnie. When Bonnie's boyfriend moves away, she follows him. The experience ultimately brings both mother and daughter to a greater level of love.

CINEMATHERAPY: Many parents begin to have power struggles with their children right around those high school dating years. "My kid's out of control. She won't do her homework, she's out until all hours of the night, and she's dating a boy who's no good for her." Or how about, "He thinks he's so smart. He thinks he knows everything. He won't listen to us. He comes and goes as he pleases." Any of that sound too familiar to you? Well, for what it's worth, you are not alone. These are difficult transitional times for families. There are some families that don't make it through these battles. Some children rebel and end up living on the streets, turning to violence, or looking to drugs, smoking, and alcohol for "the answer." A healing needs to take place if the family is to emerge triumphant and bonded. Several of the important issues surrounding this healing process are brought out in *The First Time*. Are you a parent who's lost your spouse? As you will see, Bonnie's mother takes a lot of her frustration out on her daughter—frustration built up, in part, from an unsatisfying marriage. Are you overly protective of your children? When they try to show their maturing side, do you take over, making them feel they will never be able to make the right decisions in life? Maybe you can relate to Bonnie. Did you go through times when you felt pressured to have sex and you did not want to? The good news is that, in this movie at least, Steve understands the meaning of *no*. Are you someone who wishes you had said no? Were you in love with someone when you were young, with everything going as planned, only to have him or her leave? Can you feel Bonnie's sense of abandonment, unable to get her life back on track? Can you remember your parents accusing you of doing something you did not do? Why not watch this film with your children. When it's over, discuss what you saw. You will enjoy growth and bonding, and the experience will help prepare them for their first sexual encounter.

FLOWERS IN THE ATTIC

(New World Cinema, 1987), B & W, 95 minutes, PG-13-rated

HEALING THEMES:
Growing up in an abusive home
Being abandoned as a child
Having no one around to protect you
Memories of your past
Learning to let go of the past

DIRECTOR: Jeffrey Bloom; SCREENPLAY: Jeffrey Bloom; CAST: Louise Fletcher (Grandmother); Victoria Tennant (Mother); Kristy Swanson (Cathy); Jeb Stuart Adams (Chris); Ben Granger (Cory); Lindsay Parker (Carrie); Marshall Colt (Father); Nathan Davis (Grandfather)

SYNOPSIS: Four children seem to be doomed even though they live in a mansion. The problem is that they are locked in the spacious home, their grandmother holding them hostage. Acts of incest and sadomasochism are committed against the children. They learn to cope with the experience in a way only children can.

CINEMATHERAPY: Many of you will find this movie very difficult to watch. I know I had trouble dealing with it. I have problems with any movie that explores child abuse. Nevertheless, they remind me how important it is to protect our children. As a therapist, I have encountered many people working at healing the wounds caused by child abuse. Even though I am trained to deal with these difficult issues, I continue to be taken aback by the pain and sadness that children and adults carry in their lives. And I am amazed at the different ways people learn to survive their abuse. Stay in touch with your feelings as your memories come to the surface. Gather your courage and strength to stay focused with this movie. Don't look for the characters' experiences to be exactly the same as yours. Can you relate to feeling powerless with no one to turn to? Did you think you had done something in your life to deserve what was happening? "If I were a good child, then this wouldn't be taking place." "I'll be better and maybe this won't happen again." What things did you do to conceal your shame over the abuse? Did you sit in the closet, hide under your bed, pretend to be sleeping, or escape in your mind, until the abuse was over? What phrases did you hear as a child that reminded you of what you heard in this movie? You can use this film as a springboard to break free of the feelings you have been carrying your whole life. Let yourself feel the rage of what was done to you. If you have not confronted your abuser, empower yourself to do so either through therapy or a support group. As an adult, you do not have to let your abuser—or hostage taker—maintain a hold on you any longer. Prepare yourself for this film, listen and feel, and then move to take back your life. It's time you started healing from the wounds of your childhood. Watching this film requires courage. Hold on tight.

FOOL FOR LOVE

(Cannon Group, 1985), color, 108 minutes, R-rated

HEALING THEMES:
Escaping from an abusive relationship when sex is all there is
Being a little too close to your family
Using alcohol to hide the truth
Becoming obsessed with another person
Refusing to see the truth about someone you are falling in love with
Destructive relationships

DIRECTOR: Robert Altman; SCREENPLAY: Sam Shepard; CAST: Sam Shepard (Eddie); Kim Basinger (May); Randy Quaid (Martin); Harry Dean Stanton (old man); Martha Crawford (May's mother); Louise Egold (Eddie's mother)

SYNOPSIS: May is stuck in a broken-down roadside café and motel in the middle of nowhere. Although she has tried to end her on-again, off-again relationship with Eddie, somehow they always return to each other. He tracks her down and attempts to get her to return home. May fights him, both figuratively and literally, but eventually she succumbs to their obsession for each other.

CINEMATHERAPY: Let's be honest. Have you ever been in a relationship you knew was wrong for you but you simply could not break the tie? When you try to get out of the situation, the other person comes running after you. Conversely, when they try to leave you, you go running after them. Maybe you thought you broke that tie and for some reason you can't seem to let anyone else into your life. This movie gives you a chance to see what's going on with yourself through the lives of Eddie and May. It is clear that May wants to sever the ties. She is working to put physical distance between her ex-boyfriend and herself. But like a magnet, they're drawn back together. Are you someone who is in a relationship you can't break away from? Possibly you feel stuck, and like May, you want to get away but can't. It could be you've tried to help a friend leave a sick relationship, but they just can't seem to make it without the other "sick" part of themselves. It's that joint sickness on which I want you to focus. You see, it's not possible for just one person in the relationship to be ill. If it were just one of you who was ill, there would *not* be a relationship. It simply cannot happen. It is true that it takes two to tango. This is such a difficult reality for people to accept. "It's not me, it's him. He's the one who's doing all the crazy stuff." "She won't leave me alone. She's driving me nuts." And repeatedly they're back together. Did you find yourself being affected by their unhealthy behavior? Did you feel yourself getting sucked into their dysfunction while yours came bobbing to the surface? If you're in denial about your dysfunctional relationship, *A Fool for Love* is going to give you that reality lesson you've always needed. Grab that friend of yours who can't seem to make the break. Set him or her down and watch Eddie and May. Feel your way through the chaos, out the doors of denial, and into a quieter, more satisfying life. You must believe in one basic idea: We all deserve to be at peace in our lives.

FORGET PARIS

(Columbia, 1995), color, 101 minutes, PG-13-rated

HEALING THEMES:
Feeling lonely
Meeting someone special
Relationships that hit brick walls
Being concerned about your friends
Recognizing when your priorities are out of whack

DIRECTOR: Billy Crystal; SCREENPLAY: Billy Crystal, Lowell Ganz, Babaloo Mandel; CAST: Billy Crystal (Mickey); Debra Winger (Ellen); Joe Mantegna (Andy); Cynthia Stevenson (Liz); Richard Masur (Craig); Julie Kavner (Lucy); William Hickey (Arthur); Robert Costazo (Waiter); John Spencer (Jack); Cathy Moriarty (Lois); Tom Wright (Tommy)

SYNOPSIS: When Mickey and Ellen meet, it's love at first sight. And with the exception of an ocean that separates them, they are a perfect match. But when careers, relatives, friends, and babies enter the picture, their love for each other is put to a severe test. The relationship almost falls apart when they cannot compromise about their future.

CINEMATHERAPY: It's safe to say that most relationships go through some of Mickey's and Ellen's machinations. And for many, these emotional roller coasters seem to force one or the other person onto tracks that never allow the relationship to rekindle and grow. Now, the truth is that at first I passed on using *Forget Paris* in this book. I thought it was just a bit too funny to help people see the real issues. But when I took the time to review the movie, I realized that the humor was, in part, an important component of the healing and nurturing process that couples need to experience. Sometimes I think that relationships involve more work than play, making life more full of hardships than joy. Now, I am suggesting that relationships are not "work." To be sure, a lifelong rapport is the most difficult experience we go through, but that doesn't mean we can't have a laugh or two at some of the things we feel are important in our lives. Watch as Mickey and Ellen struggle with just about everything that can happen. Have you ever been torn between your loved one and your job? If your work ever gets in the way, I would suggest you rethink your priorities. Should you ever have relatives come and live with you for extended periods of time? Have you made a child so important that they get in the way of having happy, full relationships? Always work this potential problem out in advance. Children in a marriage can be a real deal-breaker. What's more essential to you: money, looks, power, or love? For some, these ideas and beliefs become so enmeshed that they give up long-term happiness for short-term gain. Please understand: Good, healthy relationships take work. And a result of that effort will be wonderful, joyous, long-term happiness. Here's an idea: Watch *Forget Paris* with friends. When it's over, spend time discussing how the issues presented in this movie made you feel. Look at the topics the movie raises about your relationship and work things out before they are too far gone. And don't forget to have a few chuckles. You deserve to have fun.

FOR KEEPS

(TriStar, 1988), color, 98 minutes, PG-13-rated

HEALING THEMES:
Learning you are pregnant
Putting your hopes and dreams on hold
Starting a family when you're young
Going against the wishes of your parents
Coping when life comes at you from all directions

DIRECTOR: John G. Avildsen; SCREENPLAY: Tim Kazurinsky, Denise DeClue; CAST: Molly Ringwald (Darcy); Randall Batinkoff (Stan); Kenneth Mars (Mr. Bobrucz); Miriam Flynn (Mrs. Elliot); Conchata Ferrell (Mrs. Bobrucz); Sharon Brown (Lila); Jack Ong (Reverend Kim); Sean Frye (Wee Willy); Allison Roth (Ambrosia); Trevor Edmond (Ace)

SYNOPSIS: Darcy and Stan plan to finish high school, go to college, and start a family together. But their plans are put on hold when she becomes pregnant. Against the wishes of their parents, they marry. After life tests them from all directions, they realize they can beat the tough odds as long as they have each other.

CINEMATHERAPY: I would imagine that most of you will relate to this movie in one way or another. I know I did. I can remember being terrified that my girlfriend might be pregnant. We were sixteen and had plans that did not include a baby. How in the world were we going to support ourselves? We were glad that it never happened. This problem and more is offered to us in *For Keeps* in a humorous, yet matter-of-fact way. Maybe you got pregnant at a young age. Did you keep the baby, give it up for adoption, or have an abortion? Observe the way everyone in this movie tries to control Darcy's and Stan's young lives. I understood the feelings of their parents. I simply did not like the unkind way they communicated to their offspring. Is it any surprise that children keep secrets from their parents? Can you remember wanting to talk to your mother or father about a problem but being afraid because of the way they would react and treat you? Were you angry at Darcy's parents? And what about her friends? It is still a bit of a mystery to me why it is necessary to be mean to people. *For Keeps* also gives young people a realistic idea of what it's like out there in the "real world." I have talked to a lot of teens who have decided to live together and start a family. It's not my role to tell people what to do. However, a movie like this can give your children a pretty good idea of what the consequences of that choice are like. Maybe you started a family when you were young. Are you, like Darcy's mother, overly protective? What could someone have said to you when you were young? Nothing, I'll wager. Here's a wonderful chance for the whole family to watch a movie and really open up the doors for discussion. Invite your children to talk about sex, abortion, adoption, and starting a family at a young age. When families communicate and enlighten themselves to one anothers' feelings, hopes, and dreams, they encourage emotional growth and family spirituality. What better healing way is there to bring your family closer together than through the open doors of healthy communication?

THE FOUNTAINHEAD
(Warner Bros., 1949), B & W, 113 minutes, not rated

HEALING THEMES:
Trying to find out who you are
Confronting life's biggest questions
Being held back from achieving life's goals
Standing up for what you believe
Never compromising who you are

DIRECTOR: King Vidor; **SCREENPLAY**: Ayn Rand; **CAST**: Gary Cooper (Howard); Patricia Neal (Dominique); Raymond Massey (Gail Wynand); Ray Collins (Enright); Henry Hull (Henry); Robert Douglas (Ellsworth); Jerome Cowan (Aevoh); Harry Woods (superintendent)

SYNOPSIS: An idealistic architectural student, Howard, refuses to compromise his beliefs, while another student will do anything to get what he wants. The idealist has problems with his career until his true talent is recognized by an influential newspaperman. When the student's design for a housing project is changed without his permission, he dynamites the project. He is arrested, put on trial, and vindicated of the crime.

CINEMATHERAPY: When I look back on my life, I can see things that changed me forever. I read Ayan Rand's *The Fountainhead* when I was attending UCLA, along with *Atlas Shrugged*, her most famous work. My life was changed forever. To truly know who we are on this earth, we must have a philosophy in life. One of the first questions I ask my clients is "What is your philosophy on life?" After a pause, I typically get "Well, I don't know. I guess I never thought about it." When I ask couples to tell me the philosophy of their partner, they look at each other as if they had never met. That's the problem—and why I wanted you to watch this movie. This is a man whose philosophy of life is so strong that he will not compromise himself or his work for anything, be it money, power, or fame. What do you believe in? Are you willing to compromise yourself to get that job, have a relationship, or be with people for whom you don't really care? Have you done things in the past that you regret because they went against what you truly believe? There is no greater force than knowing what is important to you. And from that awareness comes a power that will see you through the most difficult times. *The Fountainhead* is an epiphany—a magnificent journey to understanding yourself. *Warning:* There is one scene in the movie that seems to be inconsistent with a healthy, healing philosophy. Our hero rapes a woman who we are led to believe is in love with him. Please don't accept this scene as part of a moral belief system, and don't ignore the messages the movie offers because of this one obtrusive scene. This is a great movie to watch with friends. Afterward, have a discussion about your beliefs. You will all grow from the experience. If you're in a relationship with someone, this film can be the catalyst for growth to new and greater heights. This picture will be a challenge. Try reading some of Ayn Rand's books. You're in for an incredible experience.

FRESH HORSES

(Weintraub Entertainment Columbia, 1988), color, 90 minutes, PG-13-rated

HEALING THEMES:
Becoming obsessed with another person
Not seeing people for who they really are

Refusing to let others help you through the difficult times
Abandoning someone who loves you
Realizing that happiness comes only from within yourself
Being left behind
Watching someone else go on with their life

DIRECTOR: David Anspaugh; SCREENPLAY: Larry Ketron; CAST: Molly Ringwald (Jewell); Andrew McCarthy (Matt); Patti D'Arbanville (Jean); Ben Stiller (Tipton); Leon Russell (Matt's Dad); Molly Hagen (Ellen); Viggo Mortensen (Green); K .C. Jones (Dr. Price)

SYNOPSIS: Matt Larkin is a college student who is engaged to be married to a local society girl. Life looks like it's going to be pretty comfortable for Matt. While at a party he meets Jewell, a young girl he can't get off his mind. There's something unique about her. He puts everything on hold, including his marital plans, and goes after the girl. Jewell has lots of secrets that begin to emerge as he attempts to develop a relationship with her. Eventually, Matt's life comes crashing down around him while Jewell just moves on.

CINEMATHERAPY: This movie is for those of you who have become obsessed with another person or overfocused on the possibility of having that person in your life. It's for those who are stuck and can't let go. Now, I'm here to tell you that this is a very serious problem and should not be taken lightly. Each year we hear about cases where one lover becomes so obsessed with the other that their lives are turned upside down. Some even turn to murder because they can't let the other go or accept that individual being with someone else. Some of you might say, "To hell with them. There's more fish in the sea." Believe me, when I say that for those who become obsessed with something or someone, there is only one fish out there—and they have to have it, or else. You can open the door to real healing by watching what Matt does to his life. Notice that Matt appears to be mesmerized with Jewell—that he can't think of anything or anyone else but her. Nothing matters except having her in his life. Has anything like this happened to you? Have you or someone you've known been so attached and focused on someone else that the world could come to an end and it wouldn't matter? You can see very clearly that Jewell is lying about who she really is. Why can't Matt see her lies? The answer is denial. He refuses and/or chooses not to see the truth about his new, young love. Matt's in love; he's obsessed with a myth. Have you ever reached the point where you couldn't eat, sleep, or work because of your overwhelming need to have someone else? Use this movie as a way to heal yourself and come out of denial. If you are a friend of someone who has lost touch with reality, sit them down and have them watch this picture. *Fatal Attraction* and *Damage* are two other movies that offer similar messages. And one more thing: Don't be afraid to reach out for help. You need to know that you're not alone.

FRIED GREEN TOMATOES

(Universal, 1991), color, 130 minutes, PG-13-rated

HEALING THEMES:
Surviving when life seems to beat you down
Coping when food is your fix
Meeting someone who has a special impact on you
Getting the courage to stand up for what you believe
Dealing with people who are prejudiced and racist
Feeling life's painful moments

DIRECTOR: Jon Avent; **SCREENPLAY:** Fannie Flagg; **CAST:** Kathy Bates (Evelyn); Jessica Tandy (Ninny); Mary Stuart Masterson (Idgie-Towanda); Mary-Louise Parker (Ruth); Cicely Tyson (Sipsey); Chris O'Donnell (Buddy); Stan Shaw (Big George); Gailard Sartain (Ed); Tim Scott (Smokey); Gary Basaraba (Grady); Grace Zabriskie (Eva); Lois Smith (Mama Threadgoode); Macon McCalman (prosecutor)

SYNOPSIS: Evelyn meets Ninny Threadgoode, an old woman with a whole lot of living behind her. Ninny tells Evelyn the story of the life of Idgie Threadgoode (Towanda), a young woman in 1920's Alabama. As Ninnie shares her memories, Evelyn learns things about herself. In time, they become inseparable friends.

CINEMATHERAPY: When I think back, I can remember a few people who had such an impact on my life that they dramatically changed the way I thought and did things. As a therapist, I can be a role model for the people who I treat. Over the years, clients have told me that one of the things that kept them going was my sharing something about my past and my own healing journey. When I saw *Fried Green Tomatoes* I thought, "What a wonderful way to take people on a life journey." And if there ever was a woman who could take you on that special trip, it was Towanda. After the movie came out, there was a bumper sticker that read TOWANDA! Who is the Towanda in your life? Was there a teacher who took the time to let you know you were special? Did you find someone who showed you how to build a clubhouse, make pottery, fish, et cetera? Maybe you found a spiritual leader, therapist, or philosopher who led you down a positive path that changed your life. As you watch this movie, try to get in touch with that person through Towanda. Evelyn uses food to pacifiy herself the same way an alcoholic or drug addict uses their substance to get through life. Notice how Evelyn grows and emerges through her special bond with Ninny and starts to put food dependency behind her. Maybe you are someone's Towanda and do not even know it. Are you a Towanda to your children, someone who gives them a sense of pride in their own lives? We all need Towandas to see us through the occasional dark moments. They are the people who open the door, illuminate the path, and clear away the debris we have accumulated for so many years. *Fried Green Tomatoes* is a healing movie from start to finish. Have the entire family watch this one. I consider pictures such as this one a special gift. I know you're going to feel the same way.

GEORGIA

(Miramax, 1995), color, 117 minutes, R-rated

HEALING THEMES:
Trying to live up to family expectations
Becoming lost in drugs and alcohol
Living on the edge
Setting boundaries
Living life as you choose to live it

DIRECTOR: Ulu Grosbard; SCREENPLAY: Barbara Turner; CAST: Jennifer Jason Leigh (Sadie); Mare Winningham (Georgia); Ted Levine (Jake); Max Perlich (Axel); John Doe (Bobby); John C. Reilly (Herman); Jimmy Witherspoon (Trucker); Jason Carter (Chasman); Tom Bower (Erwin); Gregory "Smokey" Hormel (Leland); Tony Marisco (Paul)

SYNOPSIS: Whereas Georgia is a successful singer/songwriter with a bright future and a past to match, her sister Sadie can't seem to get on the right track. Nothing ever clicks in her life as she roams from one odd job or strange boyfriend to the next. Although Georgia attempts to get her sister to stop drinking and taking drugs, Sadie remains true to her path of self-destruction.

CINEMATHERAPY: Have you ever wondered why one member of a family can turn out to be so different from another? Why one becomes a teacher, the other a crook? Why one is free from addictions, while the other can be addicted to anything they can get their hands on? To be sure, there a lot of theories: "He was the second of four children." "She was the third of three children." "He grew up in one state and his brother grew up in another." "When she was young, her father worked late." And on and on. The truth is, we really have no way of guaranteeing how a person will turn out or what they will be like in comparison to their siblings. However, many people have a personal experience of growing up with brothers and sisters who were considered better somehow by the rest of the family. Did you have a sister who was always considered the star of the family? Were you the child who had all the pressure to have the best grades, the best career, the best marriage? Are there times when you feel the pride of your siblings' success and at the same time hate them for their achievements? The characters of this movie are going to bring some of those feelings to the surface. For example, Sadie makes no secret that she is an addict with chaos in her life. Can you understand what it is like to live in the shadow of a successful sibling? Sadie uses drugs and alcohol to numb herself from the reality that she is not a success like her sister. Here's a wonderful opportunity to bring the members of your family together and talk about feelings as they relate to personal or career successes and failures. Help your family enjoy the recovery that comes from knowing that each member is cherished for who they are as individuals rather than who they are not.

GIRLS TOWN

(October, 1996), 90 minutes, color, R-rated

HEALING THEMES:
Having close friends
Being raped
Taking your own life
Seeking revenge
Being treated violently
Feeling like you are all alone

DIRECTOR: Jim McKay; SCREENPLAY: Denise Casano, Jim McKay; CAST: Lili Taylor (Patti); Bruklin Harris (Angela); Anna Grace (Emma); Aunjanue Ellis (Nikki); Guillermo Diaz (Dylan); Ernestine Jackson (Nikki's Mom); Ramya Pratt (Tommy); Tara Carnes (Heather); Asia Minor (Marlys); Michael Imperioli (Anthony)

SYNOPSIS: When three high school teenagers find out that their friend Nikki committed suicide, they work to understand why. They discover that she had been raped. The revelation causes each girl to let the others into her life in a way they had not previously experienced. Their new bond becomes stronger as each girl lets down her guard.

CINEMATHERAPY: Many of you will no doubt find this movie to be a bit out of character from most of my other healing movie selections. Normally I have time to watch a movie only once, but there was something about *Girls Town* that haunted me, something with which I could not quite get in touch. When I finally got the message, I began to comprehend the importance of this movie. One of the areas of cinematherapy I enjoy working in is the group process. However, the group process usually applies to movies that are socially palatable—which is not a way to characterize *Girls Town*. Yet this film has so much truth and reality that I believe it is important for young and old to watch it. It may stir up old memories for you, so be prepared. In school were you one of those who lived on the periphery of campus activity? Did you feel you never fit in, and did you attempt to fight the system? Possibly you were part of the crowd who could not understand how "those kids" could be so weird. We all have memories of being part of one group or another. And no matter what group you belonged to, you struggled to get through this most confusing time in your life. This movie will also compel you to look at some more-difficult issues. Did you keep secrets from your friends? Was there someone in your class who ended up taking his or her own life? How did you feel when you learned of the death? Do you miss the person still? Are you angry at them for leaving you? Let your teenagers watch this movie. Yes, I know that it's full of four-letter words. But cruel words are part of our reality. I can assure you, if your children don't feel comfortable enough to share their communication style with you, they certainly will not discuss their innermost secrets. Go one-on-one with this movie. Talk with your friends and children about your feelings and memories. You will become closer than ever, and you will ensure that the paths of communication will always stay clear.

THE GOOD WIFE

(Atlantic, 1986), color, 92 minutes, R-rated

HEALING THEMES:
Becoming obsessed with someone else
Being bored with your life
Betraying your spouse
Losing yourself to the fantasy of someone else
Denying what you are doing to yourself
Losing your self-respect

DIRECTOR: Ken Cameron; SCREENPLAY: Peter Kenna; CAST: Rachel Ward (Marge); Bryan Brown (Sonny); Sam Neill (Neville); Steven Vidler (Sugar); Jennifer Claire (Daisy); Bruce Barry (Archie); Peter Cummens (Ned); Carole Skinner (Mrs. Gibson)

SYNOPSIS: A young woman is isolated in the backcountry of Australia. She is bored with life and even more tired of her husband. When a new man comes to town, she becomes infatuated with him. She can't get him off of her mind and starts to follow him from place to place. In spite of all of her efforts, she can't accomplish having her fantasy relationship. Eventually she is forced to return to an existence that offers little hope and even less happiness.

CINEMATHERAPY: Has there ever been a time in your life when you've had enough and you just had to get out? It doesn't matter what you thought you had to get out of, you just felt like you needed to break away from the routine in your life. *The Good Wife* let's you know that if you don't work through those feelings, if you keep them bottled up inside, they can blindside you in a way you could not imagine. *The Good Wife* offers us a clear example of being so pre-occupied with something or someone that you can't function. Have you ever been so obsessed with someone that you could not think of anything else? If you have seen *Fatal Attraction,* you have a good idea of what it is like when someone becomes obsessed with another human being. There are many cases on record of people being stalked and sometimes killed. We tend to think of such obsessed people as sex fiends who are always on the prowl. However, this is simply not the case. The woman in this film is like you and me. An obsession can happen when your life is not working as you thought it would and you start looking for a way out—a quick fix of something or someone. Can you relate to looking for that quick fix? Do you find yourself compensating for that missing piece of your life by dewlling on a person or bottle or food container or gambling casino, only to find it is the wrong compensation for you? It's all the same; they're just different ways to fix the problem. Marge's friendship with a local man, which is supported by her husband, opens the door to the stranger who comes into town. It's as if she had been drugged. Have you ever felt you were out of control over another person, place, thing, or experience? It can be overwhelming. If you can relate to what she is undergoing—whether you are male or female—seek help. Be kind to yourself and experience freedom from the obsession. There are support groups, therapists, and books that specialize in dealing with this kind of healing. Break the chains that are dragging you down and start living your own life again.

THE GOODBYE GIRL

(Warner Bros., 1977), color, 110 minutes, PG-rated

HEALING THEMES:
Feeling pushed to the limit
Having someone new come into your life
Accepting people for who they are
Helping your parents grow up
Feeling left behind
Falling in love for all the right reasons

DIRECTOR: Herbert Ross; SCREENPLAY: Neil Simon; CAST: Richard Drey-fuss (Elliot); Marsha Mason (Paula); Quinn Cummings (Lucy); Barbara Rhoades (Donna); Marilyn Sokol (Linda); Paul Benedict (Mark); Theresa Merritt (Mrs. Cosby); Nichol Williamson (Oliver)

SYNOPSIS: Paula McFadden is a former actress who has more than a little trouble paying the rent. Elliot Garfield is an aspiring actor who needs a place to stay. When Paula has not moved out of the apartment that Elliot is supposed to occupy, he agrees to share it with her. What began as a business arrangement turns into a rocky personal relationship. Eventually, Elliot and Paula find their way through a maze of intimate turmoil all the way to love.

CINEMATHERAPY: How does love happen? How is it we can spend our whole lives searching for that special someone—only to find them under the strangest of circumstances. I think it's serendipity. Love is all about the right moment, with the right person, at the right time, who is in the right state of mind so they can be connected to your right state of mind. And when all of that happens, you have that serendipitous event. *The Goodbye Girl* gives us a peek at such a moment and much more. It helps us get in touch with ourselves through the world of Paula and Elliot. Watch them and you will see a little bit of yourself in the way they try to deal with a relationship that they don't even know is happening to them. Did you ever find yourself in a relationship with someone you knew but you never imagined it would get to that point? Paula and Elliot do something to each other that I'd like you to *not* do in your relationships. Listen to the way they speak to each other. There are subtle and not so subtle ways that people communicate with one another, and sometimes the way they talk can leave emotional scars. Can you relate to their style of negative, punitive communication? Remarks like these often do permanent damage, eventually undermining a once-happy, nurturing relationship. Communicate in a loving way and your relationship will flourish. Notice the relationship Paula has with her daughter. It is not uncommon for children who live in a household where the adults are childlike to take on the adult role as a compensation for the missing responsible grown-up. This is the case with Lucy, Paula's daughter. *The Goodbye Girl* is worth watching just to see how this couple grows, and in time, bonds. This movie can be fun to watch as a couple. Point out each other's characteristics as depicted in the film, have a laugh, and enjoy the rest of the evening. Most important: For love to prevail, relationships require work and, of course, a little serendipity. Don't you just love it?

THE GREAT IMPOSTOR
(Universal, 1960), B & W, 112 minutes, not rated

HEALING THEMES:
Refusing to see yourself for who you are
Taking responsibility for your behavior
Having trouble being honest with other people
Learning to take the steps in life to get to where you want to go
Being confronted by your own behavior

DIRECTOR: Robert Mulligan; SCREENPLAY: Liam O'Brien; CAST: Tony Curtis (Fredinand Waldo Demara Jr.); Edmond O'Brien (Captain Glover); Arthur O'Connell (Warden Chandler); Gary Merrill (Pa Demara); Raymond Massey (Abbott Donner); Karl Malden (Father Devlin); Mike Kellin (Thompson); Frank Gorshin (Barney); Sue Anne Langdon (Eudalie)

SYNOPSIS: Ferdinand Waldo Demara Jr. is a schoolteacher, a surgeon, a college professor, a prison warden, a monk, a . . . Well, not exactly. He lies so he can get whatever job he wants at the moment. In doing so, Demara stays ahead of the pursuing FBI agents, who eventually arrest him for false representation and impersonation.

CINEMATHERAPY: If you know someone who doesn't like to live in reality, *The Great Impostor* is an excellent movie to use to confront them with their behavior. I had a friend who had a scam for every week of the year. He would do anything to avoid taking the constructive steps needed to accomplish his goals. "School's for suckers. You guys spend four years just to get a piece of paper; I ain't doin' that. I'll just tell everyone I graduated from Yale, or one of those places." Some people do not want to take life's necessary steps. The truth is that life is discipline—lots of self-discipline. Life requires that we all experience discipline to experience growth. Demara simply did not want to take on the responsibility that is part of real life. Think of the number of times you did not want to undertake what was necessary: get a degree, exercise or practice good nutrition to lose weight, stop drinking and go to support meetings, or end a relationship for fear of being alone. These are examples of life events that require discipline. Can you relate to Demara? Do you find yourself embellishing the truth to obtain what you want? Maybe you've dated someone who wasn't honest with you or someone who deceived you for their own ends. Do you have a difficult time telling the truth? Are you afraid people won't accept you for who you are? Life can be so wonderful if you just take it one day at a time. You don't have to tell people you graduated from college when it's not the truth. Start taking classes, and in no time you will be a college grad. Don't tell people you're going to stop drinking or drugging one day. Just do it! Take the self-disciplinary steps today. *The Great Impostor* demonstrates the lengths to which you must go to practice discipline. Do *not* follow in Demara's footsteps. There's a wonderful world out there, one to be lived in truth and honesty. The healing comes when you accept life on its own terms. Why not start living life today!

GROUNDHOG DAY

(Columbia, 1993), color, 103 minutes, PG-rated

HEALING THEMES:
Getting life's big message
If at first you don't succeed . . .
Making amends
Trying to fool others but fooling yourself instead
Falling in love with someone who reciprocates

DIRECTOR: Harold Ramis; SCREENPLAY: Danny Rubin; Harold Ramis; CAST: Bill Murray (Phil); Andie MacDowell (Rita); Chris Elliott (Larry); Stephen Tobolowsky (Ned); Brian Doyle-Murray (Buster); Marita Geraghty (Nancy); Angela Paton (Mrs. Lancaster); Rick Ducommun (Gus); Rick Overton (Ralph); Robin Duke (Doris, the waitress)

SYNOPSIS: Sent to cover a small-town story, Phil arrives with his camera crew, ready to get the inconsequential assignment over with and return to the big city. After spending the night, he runs into trouble when he wakes up and has to relive the previous day over and over again. He finally gets the hang of it and makes well-needed life changes.

CINEMATHERAPY: *Groundhog Day* is about every person's lifelong journey to find personal life answers. For some, the answer comes quickly, but for others . . . well, they never get the answer at all. Those who believe in metaphysics would say that this movie is really about having to come back to earth after you die to live again and again until you learn the true meaning of life and get it right. Others would simply say it's about the concept If at first you don't succeed, try, try again. Whatever your take on this movie, I don't want you to miss the point that this man was going to relive his life repeatedly until he learned to live properly. Can you relate? How many times have you terminated a relationship and promised yourself you would never be with that kind of person again, only to eventually fall madly in love with the same kind of person? Have you ever made an agreement with someone knowing that it was not going to work but went through with it anyway? Did the deal eventually fall apart? Why is it that time after time you are given the message to stop doing what you are doing to your life, yet you persist in your behavior? *Groundhog Day* forces each of us to examine our behavior and our life, and ask: "When am I going to get it right?" I had my Groundhog Day. It started about twenty years ago and took me ten years to move on to the next day. Those were both my worst and the best years. However, now that I've moved on, each day is the best day of my life. If you're someone who is avoiding your Groundhog Day, then here's a little push: Watch this movie. The next day, when you awaken, begin your day by asking, "How long have I been doing the same old things in my life?"

GULLIVER'S TRAVELS

(NBC-TV, 1996), color, 200 minutes, not rated

HEALING THEMES:
Going on life's journey
Responding to people who think that you're lying
Living in a dreamworld
Returning to reality
Seeking life's symbolism

DIRECTOR: Charles Sturridge; TELEPLAY: Simon Moore; CAST: Ted Danson (Gulliver); Mary Steenburgen (Mary); James Fox (Dr. Bates); Edward Fox (General Limtoc); John Gielgud (Professor of Sunlight); Peter O'Toole (Emperor of Lilliput); Omar Sharif (The Sorcerer); Geraldine Chaplin (Empress Munodi); John Standing (Admiral Bolgolam); Alfre Woodard (Queen of Brobdingnag); Edward Woodward (Drunlo); Ned Beatty (Farmer Grultrud); Kristin Scott Thomas (Immortal Gatekeeper)

SYNOPSIS: Gulliver is a young doctor who embarks on an incredible journey. Like Alice in *Alice in Wonderland,* he comes across different worlds and their inhabitants, who take him on fantastic treks. When he returns home, he finds that no one believes him and he must fight to be heard.

CINEMATHERAPY: I'm sure you've read healing stories in my books that kind of surprise you. I know people commented about my use of *Alice in Wonderland* and *The Wizard of Oz* in my first book. They felt I was stretching to include movies of that sense. But every once in a while when I work with people, I find that there are individuals who appreciate examining symbolism and what it all means. Maybe like Alice in *Alice in Wonderland,* Gulliver met those Brobdingnagians—the big people—just as Alice did when she became very small. Or how about when Gulliver finds the Lilliputians when he becomes very large? Then we begin to ask ourselves some questions: What times in your life have you felt like Gulliver? Were there occasions when people did not believe you, didn't trust what you said? Were there moments in your life when you experienced things like what Gulliver did and tried to figure out what caused those moments? Maybe this all came about because Gulliver was using drugs or alcohol. Maybe Gulliver is experiencing what we refer to in psychology as a psychosis, or perhaps he has a physical problem. But whatever the case, we can learn something about Gulliver, and that is he has the right to express the way he sees life and the journey that he goes on. Can you see that Gulliver goes on a life journey, that he sees things that amaze him and cause him to grow, or cause him to shrink in size? We all go on trips of different sorts—and in various symbolic ways. Give *Gulliver's Travels* a try. Watch it as a family. Discuss what it all means. Play with the symbolism. There is no science to what this story means and its implications, it's just a matter of opinion. Regardless, I think you're going to have fun with this film.

THE HAND THAT ROCKS THE CRADLE
(Hollywood, 1992), color, 110 minutes, R-rated

HEALING THEMES:
Being stalked
Being abused by someone you trust
Losing sight in a marriage
Having your morals tested
Being pushed to the limit
Not seeing things as they really are

DIRECTOR: Curtis Hanson; SCREENPLAY: Amanda Silver; CAST: Rebecca De Mornay (Peyton); Annabella Sciorra (Claire); Matt McCoy (Michael); Ernie Hudson (Solomon); Madeline Zima (Emma); Julianne Moore (Marlene); John de Lancie (Dr. Mott); Kevin Skousen (Marty)

SYNOPSIS: Peyton Flanders is the wife of a successful physician. She is also pregnant. Life is good for Peyton until her husband is accused of molesting one of his patients. Her husband is convicted and commits suicide. Peyton loses the baby and then loses touch with reality. She decides to go after the woman who accused her husband. She takes a job as the nanny for their family. Peyton becomes the family's worst nightmare as she methodically plots to destroy them. She almost accomplishes her goal, but ends up succumbing to her own destructive rage.

CINEMATHERAPY: Let's be honest: At one time or another, most of you have wanted to go after someone for what they did—or what you thought they did—to you. I can remember having violent fantasies about another person. The truth is, that's pretty normal. That's an outlet for dealing with our aggressions without acting them out. However, when the fantasy turns to reality, there's trouble. As you will see, Peyton has lost control of her life. She is no longer in touch with reality. There are ways to heal these wounds that seem to overwhelm us. There are counselors, ministers, support groups, and reading material to help you get on the other side of the kind of rage that has consumed Peyton. And the movie brings up other issues. First, many families need nannies and baby-sitters, and it is difficult to find out the complete backgrounds of the people applying for the job. Second, we have had a great many problems relating to professionals molesting their patients. In both of these cases, the movie gives the viewer an opportunity to get in touch with fears about these issues. Unfortunately, the film offers no solutions. Be careful to look at the background of people who might take on the role of a caregiver or provider in your household. And what of the relationship between the husband and wife in the film? Notice how he falls prey to Peyton. Peyton's behavior reminds the viewer that loving relationships can be put to the test. The problem is that this couple did not communicate with each other. They lost touch with what they meant to each other and allowed someone else to take over. This is a scary movie; the fears that it evokes are real. Try to watch the film as a couple, and afterward spend time discussing how it made you feel about your relationship. Keep talking. That's what makes for a solid, safe, and healthy partnership.

THE HEIDI CHRONICLES
(TNT-Cable, 1995), color, 94 minutes, not rated

HEALING THEMES:
Getting started in life
Making life plans
Persevering when things don't go your way
Losing a best friend
Changing directions
Being at peace with yourself

DIRECTOR: Paul Bogart; TELEPLAY: Wendy Wasserstein; CAST: Jamie Lee Curtis (Heidi); Tom Hulce (Peter); Peter Friedman (Scoop); Kim Cattrall (Susan); Sharon Lawrence (Jill); Eve Gordon (Lisa); Shari Belafonte (April); John Saint Ryan (Nick); Roma Maffia (Anrea)

SYNOPSIS: Heidi has lots of goals and aspirations. She is sure she has her life planned out to the last detail. But as time passes, things don't turn out quite the way she thought they would. Between lost loves, passing friendships, and just getting older, Heidi comes to realize that in life nothing is a sure thing.

CINEMATHERAPY: This is my favorite type of cinematherapy movie. When I come across movies such as *The Heidi Chronicles*, I love to share them with as many people as possible. I wasn't one of those kids who had life all planned out, but a lot of my friends sure had it all figured out: finish high school, go to college, get married, have a great job and a couple of kids, and it's retirement time. I was really jealous of them. How were they able to get a handle on their future when I was barely making it from one day to the next? Over the years since high school, I encountered some of my old friends as well as classmates I had looked up to from a distance. Now, let's see, Dana was going to be a lawyer; she died of a drug overdose. John was going into politics; he got married, had two kids, and took a job selling vending machines. My best friend, Larry, the one who quit high school in his senior year, started a computer company of which he is the chief financial officer. I hear the firm is worth in excess of $500 million. And the high school beauty queen? Well, she gained about 150 pounds and still works as a bookkeeper in her father's furniture store. In fact, not one of my pals' lives has turned out the way they had planned. *The Heidi Chronicles* shows us that there is no way to know what tomorrow will bring. And that being the case, Heidi teaches that we are the architects of our own destiny. We have no way of knowing what tomorrow will bring, but we can certainly look forward to each coming day with the promise that everyone has a chance at a satisfying life, not just the prom queen, the football hero, or the class valedictorian. Gather a few friends together, put *The Heidi Chronicles* in the VCR, and let it play. Afterward, have a discussion about your lives: planned versus actual. And if you have ever been down or depressed that you were the only one who has not fulfilled your life plan so far, I can assure you that you will soon realize you're not alone. But remember, it is never too late to fulfill that dream. You are truly the master of your own domain.

HELTER SKELTER

(CBS-TV, 1976), 194 minutes, not rated

HEALING THEMES:
Someone you know being turned into a monster by alcohol and drugs
Knowing someone who has gone off track
Being led down a false path by another person
Taking your life back
Making sure you're not led down a path to destruction

DIRECTOR: Tom Gries; TELEPLAY: J. P. Miller; CAST: George DiCenzo (Vincent Bugliosi); Steve Railsback (Charles Manson); Nancy Wolfe (Susan); Marilyn Burns (Linda); Christina Hart (Patricia); Cathey Paine (Leslie); Alan Oppenheimer (Aaron); David Clennon (Harry); Paul Mantee (Sergeant O'Neal); Ray Middleton (George)

SYNOPSIS: Motivated by the Beatles song "Helter Skelter," Charles Manson and his not so merry band set out to commit murder. They break into two homes over a week's time and commit one senseless murder after another. They are caught for the crime, brought to trial, and sent to prison.

CINEMATHERAPY: Why did I include this in my list of healing stories? Because if I can get people, especially young people, to look at what effects drugs and alcohol have on the mind, I might be able to help them save not only their own lives but also those of other people. Here's a bit of a shocker: In my hippie days, I spent some time on the commune that was next to Manson's. I wonder what my life would have been like had I chosen to be one of his group. I didn't live there long, but I was there long enough to realize that a communal life wouldn't work for me. Have you ever known anyone who seemed levelheaded, the kind of person who might end up being the pillar of the community, only to find out they had turned to drugs and alcohol? Maybe you're that person. When did the change occur? Did you become disenchanted with school, a job, life? Were you pressured to perform when you were young and decided to rebel against those who tried to control your life? As you will see, Manson's behavior is irrational and violent. He is charismatic and leads individuals, who have a need to be led, down a very destructive path. Do you know anyone like Charles—someone who can persuade people to do whatever he wants? I would simply ask that you watch this movie and evaluate who you are, the people you know and hang out with, and where you are going in your life. At vulnerable times in our lives, it is easy to be swayed. If you have any doubt where addictive behavior will lead you, this film should clear up that doubt. The recovery and healing offered by this film benefit not only the individual but also our community and the world around us. If I can confront you with this kind of potential disaster and help you to change your course in life, I will have done my job.

HOME FOR THE HOLIDAYS

(Paramount, 1995), color, 103 minutes, PG-13-rated

HEALING THEMES:
Family dysfunctions
Looking at yourself through your family
Breaking up
Confronting your family
Trying to get on with your life

DIRECTOR: Jodie Foster; SCREENPLAY: W. D. Richter; CAST: Holly Hunter (Claudia); Robert Downey Jr. (Tommy); Anne Bancroft (Adele); Charles Durning (Henry); Dylan McDermott (Leo); Geraldine Chaplin (Aunt Gladys); Cynthia Stevenson (Joannne); Steve Guttenberg (Walter); Claire Danes (Kitt); Austin Pendleton (Peter); David Strathairn (Russell); Amy Yasbeck (Ginny)

SYNOPSIS: It's the Christmas season, a time for the entire family to return home for the holidays. One by one, the clan arrives to once again reenact their dysfunctional behavior. Before the holiday gathering is over, each member of the household will be reminded of the reason why they moved *out* of the house.

CINEMATHERAPY: Every year, right around the second week in November, my appointment book fills beyond capacity. It stays that way until the week following Christmas Day. Why is that, you ask? You need only to watch *Home for the Holidays* for the answer. "Doc, I don't want to go home for the holidays. Every year it's the same thing: Dad gets drunk and passes out on the floor; mom gets in a fight with her sister and they stop talking to each other for six months; and my sister and her husband throw things at each other. It's pure hell." "I hate going home for the holidays. As soon as I arrive, I'm ready to leave." And so the stories continue. One after another, clients and patients stream through my door asking me, begging me, to tell them not to go. I hope by now you know that therapy should be supportive of *your* choices, not an embodiment of the therapist's decisions. But I must say, even though I have been practicing for more than a decade, I am still amazed that people return to these most painful environments without confronting the problem. So what's the solution? The answer is as simple as it is difficult: boundaries, boundaries, boundaries. "Mom, I am willing to come to Thanksgiving dinner. However, if you start drinking, I will leave and I will not return for two years." "Sis, each year you and Dad get in a fight. If you start a war of words this year, I will leave and I will not have contact with you for six months." And so on. If you set a reasonable boundary and the other person crosses that boundary, they are telling you that they don't care about you or your feelings. And since that is true, why be concerned about their feelings? Try this: Bring the whole family together well before the holidays and play this movie, or give each of them an early holiday gift and send them a copy of *Home for the Holidays* with your thoughts on how the family can make the season just a little more functional. Talk about what potential problems may arise before they occur. You will be amazed at the number of calamities that can be avoided if you only set boundaries.

A HOME OF OUR OWN

(Gramercy, 1993), color, 104 minutes, PG-rated

HEALING THEMES:
Following your dream
Realizing you've carried your abusive past with you
Reflecting on the way you grew up
Taking a step back to look at the big picture
Growing up in a home with no money
Meeting someone who is kind to you

DIRECTOR: Tony Bill; SCREENPLAY: Patrick Duncan; CAST: Kathy Bates (Frances); Edward Furlong (Shayne); Soon-Teck Oh (Mr. Munimura); Amy Sakasitz (Annie); Tony Campisi (Norman); Clarissa Lassig (Lynn); Sarah Schaub (Faye); Miles Feulner (Murray); Melvin Ward (Father Tomlin)

SYNOPSIS: A woman loses her factory job which barely supported herself and her five children. She picks up her bags and follows her dream—she wants to own her own home. Life is not easy for this group. It seems they go from one disaster to another. After many false starts and numerous unresolved issues, they finally find peace in a place called home.

CINEMATHERAPY: I doubt many of you will be able to directly relate to this movie and the hardships that it explores. Few people pick up and move across the country, only to live in extreme poverty. But we can all relate to having dreams and hopes. We can recall when times were rough and we didn't know how we could emotionally handle making it beyond the pain of the moment to a point where we might be free of the turmoil we were experiencing. However, somehow, someway, we go inside ourselves and summon the strength we need to get to the other side. In *A Home of Our Own,* we can see the healing that comes from letting go of the past, moving on with our lives, and making it all the way to our dreams. We can embrace those memories of wanting something so bad that we would do whatever it took to get it. And we can also recall simply wanting to give up on life. This movie explores the feelings that come with that special awareness. As you listen to Shayne supply us with his narration and memories of his childhood, do you find yourself relating to his wanting to return home, wanting to go to a place where things are familiar and safe? How about his childhood responsibilities? Did you lose a portion of your youth because you always had to be so responsible for the family that you rarely were allowed to just be a kid? Finally, as an adult, can you relate to the scene where the little girl nails the belt to the tree in an attempt to put her childhood behind her? Can you see that the belt is a metaphor for all the old garbage you've been dragging around with you your whole life? Well, it's time to let go and move on. Watch *A Home of Our Own.* Get in touch with your feelings and memories from your childhood. Work your way through your healing and grow from knowing you do not need to carry your negative past with you any longer. Watch this one with the whole family. You will gain a closeness you've not experienced before.

HOUSE OF CARDS
(Miramax, 1993), color, 109 minutes, PG-13-rated

HEALING THEMES:
Responding when someone you love has lost touch with reality
Looking for the key to the solution
Having to trust someone else to give you the answer
Taking charge and getting into action
Persevering when you feel like giving up
Triumph over adversity

DIRECTOR: Michael Lessac; SCREENPLAY: Michael Lessac; CAST: Kathleen Turner (Ruth); Tommy Lee Jones (Dr. Jake Beerlander); Park Overall (Lillian);

Shiloh Strong (Michael); Asha Menina (Sally); Esther Rolle (Adelle); Michael Horse (Stoker); Anne Pitoniak (Judge); Rick Marshall (Frank)

SYNOPSIS: Ruth Mattews and her two children return to the United States after living among the Mayan ruins of Central America. After their return, the youngest daughter becomes withdrawn. A psychiatrist is asked to work with the child. Ruth and the psychiatrist are in conflict, and she realizes that it's time to use her power as a parent to reach out to her child.

CINEMATHERAPY: What causes emotional changes in the behavior of a person? Why is it that one moment we can be just fine and the next there is an unexplained switch in personality and behavior? This movie deals with these issues. But what's the solution to this complex problem? Does the therapist have the key? Do you have the answers? How about the medical community? There is an underlying message in this film that I would like you to hear loud and clear: The therapeutic community does *not* know everything. If you seek the support of a therapist, counselor, or adviser, please keep that in mind. You are often your own best healer. And like Dorothy in *The Wizard of Oz,* the answer is with you all the time. Don't turn to a therapist for answers and ignore what you feel are the best solutions. Without your involvement, there is no healing. We can see this so clearly as we watch this movie. Notice the child's behavior and the strain it places on the family, especially Ruth. You will see her initially turn the problem over to the therapist, but in short order Ruth becomes personally involved. I want you to look at your own treatment and realize that you must be part of the process. Whether you are dealing with a physical, emotional, or mental illness, you must always keep in mind that you know more of what's going on with you than anyone else does; you are your own best healer. If it involves your children, remember, you are the one who raised them. You know what they've been through. I'm simply saying that you must be constructively involved. As you watch this movie, get in touch with your feelings—probably anger—at the relationship between the therapist and the family. It could be that you or someone you know had a bad experience with a therapist. Maybe you personally don't believe in therapists and won't have anything to do with them. Don't remove yourself from the healing chain: Use cinematherapy to see you through the healing moments. Remember, you are your own physician. Heal yourself. *One final note:* There are groups and organizations to help you deal with a child who is autistic. You don't have to go it alone.

HOW TO MAKE AN AMERICAN QUILT

(Universal, 1995), color, 121 minutes, PG-13-rated

HEALING THEMES:
Trying to find yourself
Listening to your guiding light
Stories that answer life's question
Having an affair
Making the most from every memory
Taking time to learn and listen

DIRECTOR: Jocelyn Moorhouse; SCREENPLAY: Jane Anderson; CAST: Winona Ryder (Finn); Anne Bancroft (Glady Joe); Ellen Burstyn (Hy); Kate Nelligan (Constance); Alfre Woodard (Marianna); Maya Angelou (Anna); Samantha Mathis (young Sophia); Lois Smith (Sophia); Jean Simmons (Em); Kate Capshaw (Sally); Loren Dean (Preston); Johnathon Shaech (Leon); Dermont Mulroney (Sam); Derrick O'Connor (Dean); Rip Torn (Arthur); Mykelti Williamson (Winston); Joanna Going (young Em)

SYNOPSIS: When Finn decides it's time to make a critical life decision, she returns to her childhood home tucked away in the orange groves of sunny California. Surrounded by a group of older women who gather to stitch together memories of love found and lost, Finn comes to understand where love resides.

CINEMATHERAPY: This is one of a few movies that really help put life into perspective. Like *Grand Canyon, Field of Dreams,* and *It's a Wonderful Life, How to Make an American Quilt* begs each of us to take a critical look at life, love, and happiness. We are reminded that we are not the only people who are struggling with painful times and longing memories. Did you fall intensely in love only to be disappointed with the direction your life has taken? Is there someone whom you care for deeply but who can't or won't remain faithful to you? When you finally found the perfect partner, were they already in their own perfect relationship? Are you still feeling resentment toward someone who you feel betrayed you? Was your lover's life cut short, leaving you to live with joy-filled but longing memories? You will be confronted with all these questions and more as you watch these screen characters weave their magic into a mosaic made for Finn. Don't make the mistake of believing this film is just for women. As a man, I am deeply moved by each architect's tale. They remind me that I am not the only one to feel pain from once-happy memories; I'm not the only person with a story to tell. This group teaches us that in life there is death, in good there is evil, in happiness there is sadness, and in love there is hate. And simply because there is a negative side to all things in life, that doesn't mean we need to lock ourselves away in fear to avoid the wide range of feelings that come out when we sew life's colorful quilt. Learn not to fight your destiny. Feel your guiding light and follow the messages. Here's an idea for you and your friends: Rent *How to Make an American Quilt*, gather the group, and watch this movie in a comfortable, emotionally safe place. When you're done, spend time sharing one another's stories. Listen closely. Watch and feel the beautiful healing that takes place. And when you're done, begin to piece together your own quilt of memories.

THE HUSTLER

(Twentieth Century-Fox, 1961), B & W, 134 minutes, not rated

HEALING THEMES:
Being taken advantage of
Being obsessed with one thing in life
Using alcohol to get through life
Selling your soul
Relationships built on convenience
Calling it quits

DIRECTOR: Robert Rossen; **SCREENPLAY:** Sidney Carroll; **CAST:** Paul Newman ("Fast" Eddie Felson); Jackie Gleason (Minnesota Fats); Piper Laurie (Sarah); George C. Scott (Bert); Myron McCormick (Charlie); Murray Hamilton (Findlay); Michael Constantine (Big John); Jake La Motta (bartender)

SYNOPSIS: Fast Eddie Felsen is a pool hustler. His ambition in life is to beat Minnesota Fats, the best pool player alive. Eddie misses his shot with Fats and hangs up his pool cue. He meets a woman who helps him get back on track. Eddie gets another chance at Fats and wins, but not before big trouble comes into his life.

CINEMATHERAPY: When I first saw *The Hustler*, I was so taken by it I never forgot it. I don't know what touched me so deeply, I just knew it affected me in some powerful way. Was it the corruption, the gambling, the abuse, or the fantasy of being so good at something that the world accepts you as the best? What price would you be willing to pay to be the champ at something? Would you give up everything else in your life to have that "success"? Would you sell your best friend down the river just to grab what you want? Perhaps you have experienced someone doing that to you. Do you think Fast Eddie did that to his newfound girlfriend? Notice the needy relationship between the two of them. How do you feel about their situation? Can you relate to feeling as down and out as the two of them when they meet? Have you ever had a relationship built on desperation, only to get back on your feet and regret the involvement? Notice that alcohol and cigarettes play such an important part in everyone's lives. Do you find there are certain environments in which you feel you really need to drink and smoke? Would you be willing to avoid such places to stop your bad habits? Is it difficult to do? Finally, notice the manipulative, crass agent who works for Fats and Eddie. These are the kinds of people who latch on to others to survive. Do you know anyone like the Bert character? Is it time to end the business relationship with him or her? Notice that ending the partnership with the agent is not without its consequences. Prepare yourself if you are going to end a relationship with someone who sees their role as dominating you. What should you do to protect yourself?

I NEVER PROMISED YOU A ROSE GARDEN
(New World, 1977), color, 96 minutes, R-rated

HEALING THEMES:
Staying positive when life gets you down
Learning to live life on its own terms
Looking at schizophrenia
Responding to someone who needs your love and support
Taking time to smell the roses

DIRECTOR: Anthony Page; SCREENPLAY: Lewis John Carlino, Gavin Lambert; CAST: Kathleen Quinlan (Deborah); Bibi Anderson (Dr. Fried); Sylvia Sidney (Miss Coral); Diane Varsi (Sylvia); Ben Piazza (Mr. Blake); Lorraine Gary (Mrs. Blake); Darlene Craviotto (Carlo); Reni Santone (Hobbs); Susan Tyrrell (Lee); Signe Hasso (Helene)

SYNOPSIS: Deborah is not your typical sixteen-year-old. She is a deeply disturbed child. She seeks the help of a psychiatrist, who recognizes her emotional problem: schizophrenia. She shares her innermost thoughts at various stages of her fall into a deeper psychosis.

CINEMATHERAPY: This film's title is a line from a song. I don't think I really knew what it meant until I was a therapist. It's not so much that it took becoming a professional to understand. Rather, it was at that point in my life when I could finally comprehend the meaning of some of the statements I had been hearing my whole life. The truth is, I never thought life was going to be easy. But for some people, life was mapped out to be as simple as one, two, three. All they were going to do was finish school, get a job, and settle into that big house on the hill that they so richly deserved. But sometimes life does not go as planned. And that's why I wanted you to watch this film. It's true that the main character suffers from a serious problem, and I don't want to lead you to believe that if life doesn't go as planned you will end up like her. What I want you to hear is the underlying message: Life has its ups and downs. If you understand that from the beginning, you will be able to handle those sometimes difficult "down" moments. Are there times when you feel you're going over the edge, as if you can't take one more day living in reality? Maybe you want to run away. I've felt that way before. How about you? Some of you may wonder what it's all for: "Why am I working so hard? What's the purpose?" It's so important that each of us accept life on life's terms. If you feel like you're being pushed to the edge, step back, regroup, and start again. When people around you are demanding too much of you, let them know what's happening to you. Ask them to please back off. Take time to have *your* needs met. Be with people who can support you through the difficult times. There is so much healing that comes from learning life's simple lessons. In this telling film, the girl lives in another world, one that protects her from reality. You need not take her course. Learn to live and let live, and life can become pretty simple.

IF THESE WALLS COULD TALK
(HBO-Cable, 1996), color, 100 minutes, R-rated

HEALING THEMES:
Dealing with an unwanted pregnancy
Making informed choices
Having the right to choose
Violence in place of understanding
Standing up for your rights

Directors: Nancy Savoca, Cher; TELEPLAY: Nancy Savoca; CAST: Demi Moore (Claire); Shirley Knight (Mary); Kevin Cooney (Dr. Kramer); CCH Pounder (Jenny); Sissy Spacek (Barbara); Xander Berkeley (John); Joanna Gleason (Julio); Hedy Burress (Linda); Diana Scarwid (Marcia); Lindsay Crouse (Frances); Anne Heche (Christine); Eileen Brennan (Tesse); Jada Pinkett (Patti); Craig T. Nelson (Jim); Cher (Dr. Beth Thompson); Jason London (Kevin)

SYNOPSIS: Over three decades, three women deal with the difficult decision of whether or not to abort their unborn child. Each has a story to tell about a very personal choice and the pressures that come with such choices. In the end, each is left to live and die with her decision.

CINEMATHERAPY: The work of a therapist should always be based on supporting people in their life choices. Some people are adamantly against abortion, whereas others want to have the choice to have a child or abort the fetus. Still others believe that it depends on the circumstances: Is the mother at risk? Will the baby be "healthy and normal"? Was the pregnancy a result of a rape? No matter what your particular feelings on this most volatile issue, you're going to react to this movie. I know that many of you who have children may find this film inappropriate for them. But I would suggest to you that the sooner your children learn the complications and responsibilities that come with having a child, the sooner they can make an informed decision on the subject when the time comes. So often people become frustrated with the lack of awareness on the part of young people. Yet, even in this age of enlightenment, sex and sexual awareness are often learned in a back-of-the-school-yard education. How about you? Did you learn about the issue and idea of abortion when it was too late? Are you someone who could have profited from knowledge about safe sex? Possibly you have a daughter or son who you feel may be putting their future at risk because of their lack of understanding about sex. I know it may be difficult, but try to get the whole family involved in this cinematherapy process. Work to allow your children to have their own opinion about abortion no matter what your beliefs are. While freedom of decision can be a very difficult thing to condone, doing so will help empower your child to make his or her own life choices, *not* yours.

I'M NOT RAPPAPORT
(Gramercy, 1996), color, 135 minutes, PG-13-rated

HEALING THEMES:
Getting old
Living in the past
Telling lies to make yourself feel good
Feeling like you have no purpose
Turning your back on responsibility
Responding when your children try to take over your life

DIRECTOR: Herb Gardner; SCREENPLAY: Herb Gardner; CAST: Walter Matthau (Nat); Ossie Davis (Midge); Amy Irving (Clara); Craig T. Nelson (The Cowboy); Boyd Gaines (Pete); Martha Plimpton (Laurie); Guillermo Diaz (J.C.); Ron Rifkin (Feigenbaum); Irwin Corey (Sol)

SYNOPSIS: Rappaport is an old man who knows how to do one thing very well: lie. Living in a fantasy world, he creates excitement in his life by telling lies to everyone with whom he has contact. When his daughter tries to put him in an old folks' home, Rappaport feels as if his life is over. But not so fast: He has one more trick up his sleeve.

CINEMATHERAPY: Because this movie deals with issues of aging, many of you may not want to spend the time to give it a fair try. We live in a society that sends lots of messages about older people being useless. "Are you kidding me? That guy is over fifty. He's on death's door. Don't hire him." "She was alive before they invented television. What the hell does she know?" "Don't invite them to the party. They bring that old army general of a father-in-law everywhere they go. Before the party is over, he's fighting the war again." And so people who are four—give or take—generations old are pushed away, consistently reminded that they are no longer needed. What does that have to do with those of you who are just getting started with your lives? Unless something happens along life's journey, you will soon be just as old as our Mr. Rappaport. What then? Will you regret having treated those who were older than you with so little regard? Are you going to demand that you are treated with respect because the people around you are ignoring your years of wisdom? Do you think you will just roll over and die because no one will care one way or another whether you stick around? Look, we all have trepidations about getting old. And most of us are not looking forward to reaching the point where people show us little or no regard. So maybe what *I'm Not Rappaport* teaches us is about respect and what life may be like for each of us when we are forced to retire or are pushed aside by someone who is younger, stronger, and quicker. Why not learn this life lesson early and make your own tomorrows just a little bit kinder place to be?

IMAGINARY CRIMES

(Warner Bros., 1995), color, 105 minutes, PG-rated

HEALING THEMES:
Being the child of parents who were never really parents
Memories of a painful childhood
Having to grow up too soon
Never feeling safe and secure
Grieving the loss of a parent
Breaking free from old family patterns

DIRECTOR: Anthony Drazan; SCREENPLAY: Kristine Johnson, David Nelson; CAST: Harvey Keitel (Ray); Fairuza Balk (Sonja); Elisabeth Moss (Greta); Kelly Lynch (Valery); Vincent D'Onofrio (Mr. Webster); Diane Baker (Abigale); Chris Penn (Jarvis); Amber Benson (Margaret); Bill Geisslinger (Bud); Richard Venture (Judge Klein); Seymour Cassel (Eddie)

SYNOPSIS: Ray has been a con man his whole life. He's lied to everyone he's ever known, including his two children, Sonja and Greta. Sonja, the older of the two, does what she can to be a parent to Greta, since Ray has no clue or moral ability to be a parent. Sonja turns her painful childhood into stories that get her and Greta through life.

CINEMATHERAPY: Although stories such as this one are painful to watch, they can be quite healing. What makes films like *Imaginary Crimes* and *This Boy's Life* different from many movies is that they're autobiographical. The characters share their pain, hope, and strength with us to let us know that we're not alone and that there is hope. When you were growing up, did you feel your mother and father were really parents or that they were kids who happen to have gotten pregnant and had children? So many people I see reflect on that awareness. Movies such as this one help you get in touch with some of those old feelings about not having someone in the household you could count on. The first image you will be struck with is Ray and Sonja in the liquor store. Did you have a parent who used alcohol, drugs, or food to avoid living in reality? Maybe they refused to grow up and take responsibility for their actions. What did you think of Mom's fantasy world? Was it that much different from Ray's world? Notice the way Sonja takes charge of being the mature, responsible parent in the home. You're going to experience so much in this movie that it may be overwhelming: grieving the loss of a parent; facing the fact that your mother and father were never really parents; never feeling safe and secure; having to sacrifice your childhood to raise your brothers and sisters; dealing with the embarrassment caused by your childlike mom and dad. My suggestion is that you go this one alone. Sit in a peaceful, quiet room and let this movie help you out of denial and into a recovery that comes from self-awareness and self-confrontation. Afterward, be kind to yourself. You deserve it.

IN & OUT

(Paramount, 1998), color, 90 minutes, PG-13-rated

HEALING THEMES:
Coming out of the closet
Knowing someone better than you know yourself
Homophobia and prejudice
Being yourself
Finding true happiness

DIRECTOR: Frank Oz; SCREENPLAY: Paul Rudnick; CAST: Kevin Kline (Howard); Tom Selleck (Peter); Debbie Reynolds (Bernice); Wilford Brimley (Frank); Matt Dillon (Cameron); Joan Cusack (Emily); Shalom Harlow (Sonja); Gregory Jrara (Walter); Alexandra Holden (Meredith); Shawn Hatosy (Jack); Zak Orth (Mike); Lauren Ambrose (Vicky); Bob Newhart (Tom)

SYNOPSIS: If it were not for the fact that everyone but Howard believes he is gay, his forthcoming wedding might be the event of the year. But, in spite of his personal denial, when confronted with the reality of his sexual identity, Howard soon has to acknowledge his own sexual preference, a decision that makes him a much happier man.

CINEMATHERAPY: Only a few movies are able to combine humor with important therapeutic messages. So when I find such a movie, I look forward to bringing it to your attention. Now, I suppose I should issue a warning: If you are bothered by gay and lesbian issues being presented in movies, *In & Out* is not for you. Here's the big question: Why does it matter whether someone is gay, lesbian, bisexual, or heterosexual as long as one individual does not force his or her personal beliefs or desires on someone else? In spite of all the research that indicates that sexual choice has nothing to do with one's negative or positive behavior in society, many people have little or no tolerance for those who have sexual preferences different from own. Do you know someone who is afraid to disclose their sexual preference? Maybe you're that person. Do you feel threatened by another individual's sexual identity? Possibly you are afraid of your own sexual preferences. Listen closely to the discussion that takes place at the end of this movie. You can't "catch" homosexuality. Because someone is a homosexual does not mean they are any worse or better than a heterosexual. And to be a friend or work with a homosexual does not mean you are going to change your own sexual identity. Here's an idea: Have friends and family over, sit down, and give *In & Out* a try. Have fun with this movie, but spend time to discuss its important issues, primarily the idea of being prejudiced toward someone or something that is different. In life, acceptance is the key.

INHERIT THE WIND
(United Artists, 1960), B & W, 128 minutes, not rated

HEALING THEMES:
Dealing with people who are prejudiced against what you believe
Defending your human rights
Ignorance that stops us from growing
Coping with the closed-mindedness of other people
Dealing with bigotry
Knowing when you have something worth fighting for

DIRECTOR: Stanley Kramer; SCREENPLAY: Nathan Douglas and Harold Smith; CAST: Frederic March (Matthew); Spencer Tracy (Henry); Gene Kelly (E. K. Hombeck); Florence Eldridge (Mrs. Brady); Dick York (Bertram T. Cates); Donna Anderson (Rachel); Harry Morgan (Judge); Elliot Reed (Davenport); Philip Collidge (mayor)

SYNOPSIS: A meek Tennessee schoolteacher is facing criminal charges for teaching Darwin's theory of evolution—the belief that humans evolved from apes instead of being created by God. Henry takes on the job of representing the defendant in what the press calls "The Monkey Trials." The community wants the accused locked up and traditional religion returned to the classroom. By the end of the movie, we learn that the teacher will have a difficult time finding another profession.

CINEMATHERAPY: Ignorance, prejudice, and closed-mindedness are the themes in this movie. But what does this have to do with healing? Think of a time when you were looked down upon simply because you had an idea that was not part of mainstream thinking. Maybe you believed in something with which your friends and family disagreed. It could be as simple as a political candidate or your taste in music or art. "That's a dumb idea!" or "You're crazy!" they might have exclaimed. How did it feel? What was it like to be chastised because of your thoughts? Perhaps you were one of the people who could not accept that new theory or idea. Why were you so quick to judge? Could you have accepted someone's idea and respected them for their individuality without debating with them or putting them down? When we experience the epiphany, the enlightenment, we experience acceptance and healing. But where does this myopic thinking come from? It usually starts in childhood, when many parents begin to direct their children to conform and not make waves. Sometimes when I work with parents I hear, "Now, Johnny, be sure to color inside the lines. Don't go over the lines." Why not? "When you grow up, get a good nine-to-five job." Who says? That's what I'm talking about: being free to be free. Children need to know that it's okay to be different, to be original—that it's all right to be who they are without feeling the fear of reprisal like that seen in *Inherit the Wind*. When we watch a movie such as *To Kill a Mockingbird* or *Inherit the Wind*, we realize how important it is to feel free to believe what we want to believe. The truth is that most of us acquiesce to others out of fear of retaliation or being put down for our thoughts. Next time you are with someone—especially a child—who believes a little differently from you, support the person in the process of free thought and opinion. We can all grow from this movie, because we are all entitled to our own originality. We all have the right to inherit the wind.

INTIMATE CONTACT

(HBO Video, 1987), color, 159 minutes, not rated

HEALING THEMES:
Having an affair
AIDS
Abandonment
Making life choices
Death and dying
Standing up for what you believe

DIRECTOR: Waris Hussen; SCREENPLAY: Alma Cullen; CAST: Claire Bloom (Ruth); Daniel Massey (Clive); Sylvia Syms (Annie); Mark Kingston (Bill); David Phelan (Martin); Abigail Cruttenden (Nell); Maggie Steed (Becca)

SYNOPSIS: When Clive learns that he has contracted AIDS, his family's life is turned inside out. Although he attempts to deny that he is HIV positive, he slowly develops the telltale signs of a dying man. More real-life lessons come when his wife and children are left with his fatal legacy.

CINEMATHERAPY: I came across *Intimate Contact* quite by chance. And although at first I was a little skeptical about it, it didn't take me long to see that this movie sends an important healing message. By now, most people have become used to hearing about AIDS and AIDS-related problems. However, as *Intimate Contact* reveals, many people are still in denial about the devastating effects this currently incurable disease can have on the victim's family and friends, who are just as affected as the individual who contracts the disease. They, too, suffer from loss, abandonment, pain, anger, and so on. In this drama, observe how Clive's children are forced to change their entire lives because of their father's indiscretion. Listen to the way Ruth rationalizes Clive's behavior as being "something men do when they are away from home." Notice that Clive lives in denial about his condition, refusing to acknowledge the full magnitude of his fatal illness. How did you feel about Clive's peers abandoning him when they learned he had AIDS? Why are we surprised when people turn and run when times get tough? And what about his children? Can you understand their anger, their disgust, over their father's behavior? This movie is British-made and thus offers a different communication style. Consequently, for some of us, it may have a greater impact than "just another movie about AIDS." Try to tune in to the very sensitive issues regarding the right to die. What do you believe? Do you think we should have the "right" to take our own lives? Should others govern the time and place our lives should end? Be patient with this movie. I know it may be a bit dry, but you will experience a change in your perspective about AIDS, family, and dying. One last thought: Be honest with your significant other, whose life is in your hands.

INVENTING THE ABBOTTS

(Twentieth Century-Fox, 1997), color, 120 minutes, R-rated

HEALING THEMES:
Memories
Wishing you were somebody else
Being raised by one parent
Living in the wake of rumors
Judging other people for what they have rather than who they are
Trying to be your own person
Forgiveness

DIRECTOR: Pat O'Conner; **SCREENPLAY**: Ken Hixon; **CAST**: Liv Tyler (Pamela); Joaquin Phoenix (Doug); Jennifer Connelly (Eleanor); Billy Crudup (John Jacey); Joanna Going (Alice); Kathy Baker (Helen); Will Patton (Lloyd); Barbara Williams (Joan); Michael Keaton (narrator)

SYNOPSIS: The Abbotts seem to have it all; at least, that's how two young boys, who have very little, view the Abbotts. One boy grows up longing to be part of the Abbott family, and the other turns his back on them and moves on with his life. But nothing turns out the way it's supposed to, does it?

CINEMATHERAPY: I know that we all have about the same life experiences, give or take a relative or two. However, from time to time, I get caught up in the idea that my life is much different from everyone else's. I typically come to that conclusion when I watch movies like *Inventing the Abbotts*. "Surely," I think to myself, "I am the only person who fell in love with someone from the right side of the tracks. No one but me was chased away by someone's mother or father because I was not good enough—not rich enough—for their daughter. And only I felt like I was clawing up life's mountains of sand, having sexual conquests just so I could feel better about myself." And then the psychologist in me kicks in and brings me back to reality. The truth is, most of us have a story from our childhood about the family in the big house on the right side of town. And we all have memories of feeling left out and being inadequate, angry that life has been unfair to us. It really doesn't matter if you're male or female—you're going to find bits and pieces of your life reflected in this movie. And all those chunks of your memory are going to start churning as you try to make sense of it all. Which side of the tracks did you come from? Were you always envious of the family with the big house and the fancy cars? I know I was. Or maybe you grew up in a home where money was no object. Did you have close ties to your brother or sister and now you have little or no contact? This movie is going to make a lot of emotions surface, so hold on, it could be a bumpy ride. Here's what I would like you to do: Watch this film alone, letting your memories flow freely. Afterward, spend as much time as you can by yourself reflecting on your childhood memories. You will be amazed at how unsettling—and eventually centering—the process can be for you.

IT'S MY PARTY

(United Artists Pictures, 1996), color, 109 minutes, R-rated

HEALING THEMES:
AIDS
Death and dying
Saying goodbye

Feeling as if you're not loved
Your family not accepting you for who you are

DIRECTOR: Randal Kleiser; **SCREENPLAY:** Randal Kleiser; **CAST:** Eric Roberts (Nick); Gregory Harrison (Brandon); Margaret Cho (Charlene); Bruce Davison (Rodney); Lee Grant (Amalia); Devon Gummersall (Andrew); Marlee Matlin (Daphne); Roddy McDowall (Damian); Olivia Newton-John (Lina); Bronson Pinchot (Monty); Paul Regina (Tony); George Segal (Paul); Dimitra Arlys (Fanny); Christopher Atkins (Jack); Ron Glass (Dr. David Wahl); Sally Kellerman (Sara); Greg Louganis (Dan)

SYNOPSIS: Nick has AIDS. He knows that he does not have much time left to live. In lieu of a wake after he dies, he decides to throw a party in honor of his upcoming death. He invites his close friends and his family to the celebration. Each says goodbye the only way they know how.

CINEMATHERAPY: It is hard to believe that AIDS has been a part of our culture for two decades. Surprisingly, the stereotyping of the homosexual dying of AIDS still persists. In spite of efforts to educate the public about the fact that AIDS is *not* a homosexual's disease, ignorance remains. And although *It's My Party* helps to perpetuate that misconception, its redeeming cinematherapeutic value far outreaches the skewed on-screen message. If you knew you were going to die, would you want to go out having the best time of your life? Do you want people mourning over you or sharing what time you have left? I don't know about you, but I have always thought it would be wonderful to have a big blowout party while I was still alive. I don't want people standing around crying on my account; I want them having a good time. Nick reminds us that life is for living, so why not enjoy it. He helps all of us understand that it doesn't matter whether you're gay, lesbian, or straight—deep inside we are all the same. He shows us that life is about acceptance, not rejection. Why should we judge people by their sexual preference instead of who they are in their heart, in their soul? Why should families be split apart simply because one member does not like another's lifestyle? Can you see that the relationship between Nick and his gay lover is no different from that of a heterosexual relationship? They have their problems and issues just like anyone. There is nothing unique or different about gay and lesbian issues. Watch *It's My Party* by yourself or with a group of friends. Spend time thinking about the movie. You will grow in the process.

JACK THE BEAR

(Twentieth Century-Fox, 1993), color, 98 minutes, PG-13-rated

HEALING THEMES:

Refusal to take responsibility for raising your children
Losing someone important in your life
Using alcohol to hide from the pain
Being confronted with a family crisis
Trying to get your life together

DIRECTOR: Marshall Herskovitz; **SCREENPLAY:** Steven Zaillian; **CAST:** Danny DeVito (John); Robert J. Steinmiller Jr. (Jack); Miko Hughes (Dylan); Gary Sinise (Norman); Art LaFleur (Mr. Festinger); Stefan Gierasch (Grandpa); Erica Yohn (Grandma); Andrea Maicoricci (Elzabeth); Julia Louis-Dreyfus (Peggy)

SYNOPSIS: John Leary is a single parent trying to raise Jack and Dylan. John has not been himself since his wife deserted them, dying in a car crash. Jack is abducted by a man whom John teased on his weekly horror movie TV show. The incident brings John to his senses and forces him to take responsibility as a single parent.

CINEMATHERAPY: I've had people come to my office who were weary of the battle over raising their children. "I never thought it would be this difficult. I know my parents didn't go through what I'm going through to raise my kids. It couldn't have been this difficult." Being a parent is a tremendous responsibility and a full-time job. That job gets even bigger when you must raise your children alone. Some people see women as responsible for raising the children, especially when they are separated or divorced. *Jack the Bear* lets us know that men can *and* do take on that responsibility. As you will see in this film, John has a difficult time bringing up his children because he is still a child himself. Do you know someone like John? Does he remind you of yourself? No one really ever told you what it was going to entail. You just figured you'd have sex, nine months later a baby pops out, you feed it, and eventually you send it off to college. What a shock, eh? There are lots of reasons why someone might raise a child alone. John's immaturity has caused him to lose his wife. Can you see how he uses alcohol to avoid dealing with the pain? Drinking keeps him numb and stops him from having to grow up. Have you lost someone in your life? Do you find you have a difficult time taking care of your children because you're hiding behind drugs or alcohol? Isn't it interesting how a crisis can get us back on track? Here it took having Jack in harm's way to get John to assume responsibility for himself. You don't have to wait that long. *Jack the Bear* sends a healing message that will enlighten you about yourself, your responsibilities, and what happens when you avoid the grieving process. Give this film a fair try. It's a little different way to absorb some of life's important messages.

JEFFREY

(Orion Classics, 1995), color, 92 minutes, R-rated

HEALING THEMES:

Feeling comfortable with who you are
Being gay
Fear of intimacy
Fear of contracting AIDS
Running away from the one you love
Learning to let people into your life

DIRECTOR: Christopher Ashley; **SCREENPLAY**: Paul Rudnick; **CAST**: Steven Weber (Jeffrey); Patrick Stewart (Sterling); Michael T. Weiss (Steve); Bryan Batt (Darius); Sigourney Weaver (Debra); Nathan Lane (Father Dan); Olympia Dukakis (Mrs. Marcangelo); Christine Baranski (Ann); Robert Klein (Skip); Kathy Najimy (Acolyte); Irma St. Paule (Mother Teresa)

SYNOPSIS: Jeffrey is a young man with a huge fear—he is frightened to death that he may contract AIDS. As a gay man, he is terrified to have contact with other homosexual men. All this fear leads to a another fear—a dread of intimacy. When Jeffrey finally finds a man he can love, he has a difficult time allowing the relationship to develop.

CINEMATHERAPY: The truth is, this movie is not just for gays. Rather, it is for people who are afraid to accept those with a different lifestyle. Now, I have no doubt that I will offend a number of you who believe that same-sex relationships are wrong. And no doubt some of you believe that gays who contract AIDS are merely getting what they deserve. But let's set the record straight: AIDS is a disease that touches each and every one of us. It does not discriminate between heterosexuals and homosexuals. In fact, this disease kills anyone who decides to exchange body fluids with someone who already has the disease. That means blood transfusions or having sex with someone who already has the disease can cause you to contract the virus. So let me really get to the reason why I want each of you to watch this movie. Other than selecting someone of the opposite sex or the same sex with whom to have intimacy, we are all the same. We are all looking for someone to be close to, someone with whom to experience the times of our lives in a loving, caring relationship. And if we are happy and content with that relationship, then why not apply that thinking to those who are looking for same-sex lovers? I challenge each of you to find a difference between the behavior of Jeffrey and his gay companions and that of heterosexuals. Whether Jeffrey was in the gym, at work, or just walking down the block, he experienced nothing different from what heterosexuals experience with other heterosexuals. Try watching this film alone or with friends. Let yourself feel the discomfort of watching two people of the same sex have intimate, loving contact. Then ask yourself: Does it really make a difference as long as the individual is happy?

THE JOKER IS WILD

(Paramount, 1957), B & W, 123 minutes, PG-rated

HEALING THEMES:
Alcoholism
Using an addiction to avoid intimacy
Dealing with someone you love who drinks too much
Being abusive to those who love you
Trying to help someone caught up in an addiction

DIRECTOR: Charles Vidor; SCREENPLAY: Oscar Saul; CAST: Frank Sinatra (Joe E. Lewis); Mitzi Gaynor (Martha); Jeanne Crain (Letty); Eddie Albert (Austin); Beverly Garland (Cassie); Jackie Coogan (Swifty); Sophie Tucker (herself); Barry Kelly (Captain Hugh McCarthy); Ted de Corsia (Georgia); Valeria Alen (Flora)

SYNOPSIS: Joe E. Lewis is a popular nightclub singer. Among other things, he is a ladies' man and more than a bit of a drinker. When he gets himself into a jam, the mob comes after him. His drinking starts to affect his performances. Joe E. eventually loses his fans, friends, and the woman who truly loved him.

CINEMATHERAPY: I'm always on the hunt for movies that can send healing messages in different ways. If we could all hear the same recovery message and have the same positive outcome, my job would be done. However, since that's not the case, how about getting the message the way Joe E. did? Joe E. Lewis was a real-life entertainer who made a good living singing in nightclubs across the country. He coined the phrase "post time," which means "time to drink up." He would stop his performances just to take a drink. The problem is that it eventually affected his voice and his ability to perform. It will become obvious to you that Joe E. has a drinking problem. The way he isolates himself and how he becomes erratic, irrational, and unreliable. Can you relate to his antisocial behavior? Are there times when your drinking has gotten in the way of your work or relationships, or both? Notice the way those who care about him keep coming back for more of his abuse. Do you find yourself in relationships with people who treat you the way that Joe E. treats his friends? The condition of codependency is just as insidious as the alcoholism itself. There are support groups to help you deal with each of these vital issues. Alcoholics Anonymous and Al-Anon meetings are held all over the world. If either of these problems affects your life, take action today. If you have a friend who is in denial about what he or she is doing to themselves and to their friends, sit them down and let them reflect on this movie. You will find films in my books that deal with the insidious nature of alcoholism. Give them all a try. Believe me, it can't hurt and you will grow from the experience. Try watching this movie as a group and see how it affects your friends. Afterward, call one of the many support groups available to see you through your addiction. *Note:* You may find this movie listed under the title *All the Way.*

JONATHAN LIVINGSTON SEAGULL

(Paramount, 1973), color, 99 minutes, G-rated

HEALING THEMES:
Learning about life in the big city
Taking time to smell the roses
Seeing things as they really are
Growing as a person
Breaking free

DIRECTOR: Hall Bartlett; SCREENPLAY: Richard Bach and Hall Bartlett; CAST: The voices of: James Franciscus (Jonathan); Juliet Mills (the girl); Hal Holbrook (the elder); Philip Ahn (Chang); David Ladd (Fletcher); Kelly Harmon (Kimmy); Dorothy McGuire (the mother); Richard Crenna (the father)

SYNOPSIS: Jonathan Livingston Seagull decides there must be more to the world than what he's seen. He leaves the rest of the seagulls to go exploring. The experience leads him to better understand the world around him which, in turn, gives him, a sense of love and hope that he never had before.

CINEMATHERAPY: Did you ever have a light go on in your mind and finally get an idea or concept that you couldn't see before? "I've passed this way many times and have never seen that before." "You know, I've heard that saying a thousand times and have never understood what it meant." Boy, I'll tell you that has happened to me, and I am amazed at the simplicity of the message. I can remember when the Beatles' song "Let It Be" was released. I must have heard it a hundred times. Well, about seven years ago I was driving my car and "Let it Be" came on the radio. *Now I get it.* Just let go. Don't dwell on it. If it's supposed to happen, it will happen. So what's that got to do with *Jonathan Livingston Seagull,* you say? Here's a story about love, understanding, achievement, hope, and individuality offered to us through the eyes of a soaring bird. As the bird takes flight, we can disassociate ourselves from the real world and experience life in a completely different way. We no longer need be confused with life as we know it. We are being given the opportunity to view things through a new pair of glasses. How many times have you been confused by something, wishing you could get the "big picture"? Think back to those moments when you desperately wanted to understand what life was all about but simply did not have a clue. If we learn to appreciate life's larger messages, we can free ourselves from some of the questions that confuse us and send us down false paths. If I can learn to love through the eyes of Jonathan, why not? If I can gain a sense of my own identity in this very different way, why not? Try inviting a group of friends over to watch this film with you. Use the story as a springboard to start a conversation about life and what it means to each of you. Have fun with this movie. Recovery and healing come in many forms. Take every advantage you can get, and like Jonathan you will learn that life is a big and grand place. Enjoy all the colors every moment of every day in every way.

KEEPING SECRETS
(Lifetime, 1991), color, 100 minutes, not rated

HEALING THEMES:
Remembering your past
Living with a parent who abuses alcohol
Life becoming unmanageable
Taking charge of your life
Avoiding the pitfalls of a dysfunctional childhood
Breaking the family cycle
Making a difference in your child's life

DIRECTOR: John Korty; TELEPLAY: Edmond Stevens; CAST: Suzanne Sommers (herself); David Birney (Alan); Ken Kercheval (Frank); Michael Learned (Marion); Kim Zimmer (Maureen); James Sutorius (Kirby); John Scott Clough (Greg); Michael Horton (Danny); Holly Fields (Young); Colleen Casey (Mardi); Susan Krebs (Doris); Rae Allen (Mrs. Wagner); Lynn Llewelyn (young Maureen)

SYNOPSIS: Suzanne Sommers has a past that haunts her. Nothing ever seems to go right for her. When her lies catch up with her, she turns to a therapist for help. She journeys back to her roots and begins to see how her childhood affected her adult life. She works to break the negative cycle of her family upbringing.

CINEMATHERAPY: This movie has its roots in a book of the same title, one of the printed works I recommend most often to my clients. Like the book, the movie is a wonderfully rich portrayal of the effects a dysfunctional upbringing can have on your entire life. There is so much healing to gain from this movie that you may find yourself overwhelmed in the process. You will be confronted with your own behavior as you watch Suzanne live out her life. Can you see how the chaos is always with her? Notice how she reacts when the therapist talks about Suzanne's need to keep her life in constant motion. Can you relate? Do you find that you go from one crisis to the next? If you think back, you will come to realize how you felt when you were not in chaos. You may have felt strange and uneasy, as if it was not okay to be in a calm, safe place. You will realize, as Suzanne did, that the chaos, the crisis, mirrors your own childhood. The alcohol, lying, affairs, pregnancy, yelling, denial, owing money, and so on, keep the chaos going. And it's not just her. Watch how her brothers and sisters fall into the same pattern. And what of the negative thinking about yourself? Notice that no matter what Suzanne does, including meeting someone who loves her, she can't feel good about herself. Any of those old childhood messages ringing in your ears? It doesn't have to be that way. Suzanne Sommers exposes her life, her history, to point the way toward self-awareness and healing in our own journey. She gives you the tools to empower yourself to break free of the family patterns that bind you to your dysfunctional past. *Keeping Secrets* is a great way to come out of denial. When you're finished watching it, show it to the whole family. Recovery is a wonderful gift to take with you into your brand-new future.

KLUTE

(Warner Bros., 1971), color, 114 minutes, R-rated

HEALING THEMES:
Looking at a therapeutic relationship
Uncovering secrets
Taking a course in life that puts you in danger
Losing your identity as a woman

DIRECTOR: Alan J. Pakula; **SCREENPLAY**: Andy Lewins, Dave Lewis; **CAST**: Jane Fonda (Bree); Donald Sutherland (John Klute); Charles Cioffi (Peter); Roy Scheider (Frank); Dorothy Tristan (Arlyn); Rita Gam (Trina); Jean Stapleton (secretary); Richard Shull (Sugerman); Rosalend Cash (Pat)

SYNOPSIS: Klute is a private detective searching for a missing person. Bree is a high-class prostitute who knows her profession very well. She meets Klute and feels trapped into giving him the information he wants. Both of their lives are put in danger as they work to get to the bottom of this missing person's case. Klute saves Bree from being murdered. When it's all over, they both realize their lives will never be the same.

CINEMATHERAPY: Occasionally I screen a movie that offers a few great scenes I want to be sure you see. While some films have wonderful healing messages from start to finish, *Klute* lends you special moments with which to reflect on yourself and help you experience the self-growth you've wanted in your life. Please don't get me wrong: *Klute* is an interesting story with lots of suspense. However, I want you to focus on the relationship between Bree and her therapist, which may help you see yourself in therapy. How long did it take you to realize you never see the therapist on-screen in this movie? When I first saw *Klute*, I found myself listening more intensely to Bree's therapy sessions than I had listened to any other similar scenes in other movies. In time, I began to realize that it was because it felt as if Bree were talking to me. It felt intimate and personal. If you have been in therapy, you will relate to Bree. Really stay with those scenes and ask yourself if that's what it was or is like between you and your therapist. Is your therapist's office environment a safe place to be? Is it comfortable to be in, to talk about what's going on in your life and the issues you want to resolve? How did you feel when you knew Bree was lying? Do you lie to your therapist? Are you afraid of what he or she really thinks of you? I see this problem all the time. Your therapist is there so you can unburden yourself of what's bothering you. The only thing you accomplish from holding back is slowing down your recovery. Use specific scenes from *Klute* to look into your own therapy session. Are you accomplishing what you want in therapy? Is your therapist the right person for you? Working with one therapist for more than two years can be counterproductive except in unusual cases. Check with your therapist from time to time. Ask how they're doing—they should be checking in with you also. To experience healing with a therapist, you must feel sure you're on the correct healing path with the right person.

L.A. STORY

(TriStar, 1991), color, 95 minutes, PG-13-rated

HEALING THEMES:
Getting lost in life
Listening to life's messages
Getting in touch with reality
Falling in love for the first time
Learning to live life on life's terms

DIRECTOR: Mick Jackson; SCREENPLAY: Steve Martin; CAST: Steve Martin (Harris); Victoria Tennant (Sara); Richard E. Grant (Roland); Marilu Henner (Trudi); Sarah Jessica Parker (SanDeE); Sam McMurray (Morris); Patrick Stewart (Maitres); Iman (Cynthia); Kevin Pollack (Frank); Frances Fisher (June); Larry Miller (Tom); Woody Harrelson (station manager)

SYNOPSIS: Harris K. Telemacher is a weatherman living in Los Angeles. He's had it with life's illusions. He's got a materialistic wife who is status conscious. As he looks for the true meaning of life, a road sign offers him direction and resolve. Harris eventually finds the meaning of his existence and gets a handle on the happiness it has to offer.

CINEMATHERAPY: I grew up in the Los Angeles area, so this movie really hit home for me. When I was living there, I got to the point where I started to question what all the running around and chaotic living was truly about. Like Harris, I was all over the place, involved in relationships with people who offered me little in life but more chaos. Then one day I got some messages that were similar to those that Harris receives. Mine were "Slow down," "twenty-minute delay," "Prepare to stop," "Beware. Life ahead." I just always assumed those messages were for someone else, certainly *not* me. You mean you thought the same thing? Well, I don't know about you, but I was definitely ready for those life messages. Are you at a point in your life where you've grown tired of the rat race, the running faster and faster just to keep up with the people next to you? *Well, stop! Enough!* It's time to take stock of life. That's why I included this movie in my healing stories. I wanted you to experience the epiphany that Harris experiences. Listen, I don't expect you to have a freeway sign flashing a loud helpful message. However, I do want you to watch for and listen to the messages that are all around you. Are your mind and body feeling the pain of living life? They're trying to send you the message SLOW DOWN. Is your family falling apart because you're too busy trying to get ahead? That's your life telling you to TAKE A LOOK AT WHAT YOU'RE DOING. You get the idea. Like Harris, some of us must be hit over the head before getting the message. And when we do, we experience a peace and serenity beyond our wildest dreams. How about watching this movie and afterward taking a long walk or drive. Just be with yourself and listen for the message. Open your heart, ears, and eyes and let life in. It will happen. Give it a try—it could benefit you the rest of your life.

THE LADY GAMBLES

(Universal-International, 1949), B & W, 99 minutes, PG-rated

HEALING THEMES:
Life as your addiction
Refusing to see that the person you're with has a problem
Addiction to gambling
Losing everything you have to your obsession
Being emotionally sick in a relationship
Pushing yourself to the point where you don't want to live any longer

DIRECTOR: Michael Gordon; **Screenwriter**: Roy Huggins, Halsted Welles; CAST: Barbara Stanwyck (Joan); Robert Preston (David); Stephen McNally (Corriagan); Edith Barrett (Ruth); John Hoyt (Dr. Rojac); Elliott Sullivan (Barky); Phil Van Vandt (Chuck); Jeif Erickson (Tony); Tony Curtis (Bellboy)

SYNOPSIS: Joan is in love with David, a writer. There's one big problem: She can't say no to gambling. Whenever she has a chance, she gambles away any money she can get her hands on. When confronted with the choice of gambling or David, she chooses her addiction. Although they separate, David comes back into her life just before she hits rock bottom. They both are given a second chance at a future together.

CINEMATHERAPY: *The Lady Gambles* provides solid insight into the addiction of gambling. Despite its 1949 release date, this movie still has much to tell us. Watch how Joan struggles to stay away from gambling. Notice how she becomes excited and out of control the closer she gets to her addiction. This behavior is no different from that of someone who is addicted to drugs, alcohol, or anything else. Take notice of the scene set in Mexico. Listen to the comment made by the couple about "the lady who gambles." "She's just like an alcoholic," he says. They realize that, just like the alcoholic, she is sick and needs help. How about you? Are you aware of how deeply entrenched you've become in gambling? Is it ruling your life and those of your children? She makes promises to stop, but repeatedly she is unable to keep her word. Notice how she places her relationship—with a man who cares deeply for her—second to her addiction. Have you experienced doing that to someone or having that done to you? Watch the husband's behavior. Does it seem that he is both codependent and in denial? Is that what it's like for you? Are you with someone whose "last time" turns out to have a next time and a next time and a next time? Maybe you're someone who can't seem to set boundaries with the addict in your life. There are ways to get on the other side of this insidious disease, and there's a better way to live life than by being self-destructive. Join support groups, go into counseling, and learn how to deal with those feelings you're hiding from. If you're part of a group that is in recovery, why not view this movie together and experience some emotional healing and self-awareness by having a discussion afterward. My guess is you will be surprised at how much of an impact this film has on you and the group.

LEAVING LAS VEGAS
(MGM/UA, 1995), color, III minutes, R-rated

HEALING THEMES:
Alcoholism
Suicide
Escaping from reality
Putting yourself in a dangerous place
Codependency
Looking for love in all the wrong places

DIRECTOR: Mike Figgis; SCREENPLAY: Mike Figgis; CAST: Nicolas Cage (Ben); Elisabeth Shue (Sera); Julian Sands (Yuri); Richard Lewis (Peter);

Steven Weber (Marc); Kim Adams (Sheila); Valeria Golino (Terri); Graham Beckel (bartender)

SYNOPSIS: Since alcohol has consumed his life and destroyed everything he's worked for, Ben decides to drink himself to death. In the process, he meets Sera, a Las Vegas prostitute who is attracted to his anguish. In the end, Sera has only the memory of a man who left her with nothing.

CINEMATHERAPY: How in the world can a movie like *Leaving Las Vegas* be therapeutic? I'm often asked, "Why would I want to watch a dark, depressing movie like this one? You think I'm really going to feel any recovery after you have me watch this movie? You must be crazy, Doc." If that is you reaction, you are not alone in your thinking. Possibly more than any other movie dealing with death and dying, suicide, codependency, and addiction, *Leaving Las Vegas* forces each of us to explore our own true inner feelings, the darkness that exists within each of us. Have you ever just wanted to call it quits? Do you feel as if all you are doing is surviving from day to day with little or no purpose? Are there times when you have wanted to move away, change your name, and start all over again? I think if you are honest, the answer to some or all of these questions will be yes. I have felt all of these things and more. And I admit that I have given some serious thought to calling it quits. *Leaving Las Vegas* is going to force you to take a long look at where you've been in your life and where you are going. Are you practicing self-destructive behavior? Do you put yourself in situations that may cause you harm or injury? Is there someone in your life who is taking advantage of you, always bringing you down so they can feel better about themselves? Have you given up on the future? Make yourself feel every moment of this movie. Don't let yourself drift away to avoid your emotions and reactions. When the movie is over, spend time reflecting on what you've seen. What are your feelings? You must admit to yourself that you're in trouble. Reach out to those who can support you through what appears at this moment to be a long journey of hopelessness. Force yourself to go to support group meetings, see a therapist, tell a friend that you need them. And if you haven't gotten the message, I'll say it another way: Don't go it alone.

THE LEMON SISTERS

(Miramax, 1990), color, 93 minutes, PG-13-rated

HEALING THEMES:
Remembering old friends
Never letting go of your dreams
Keeping a promise
Having trouble letting someone into your heart
Persevering when life is going against you

DIRECTOR: Joyce Chopra; **SCREENPLAY**: Jeremy Pikser; **CAST**: Diane Keaton (Eloise); Carol Kane (Franki); Kathryn Grody (Nola); Ruben Blades (C.W.); Elliott Gould (Fred); Aidan Quinn (Frankie); Estella Parsons (Mrs. Kupchak); Richard Libertine (Nicholas)

SYNOPSIS: Nola, Eloise, and Frankie make a pact to be friends from now to the end of time. They share one another's secrets and dreams. However, life for them is a little more difficult as adults—their dreams haven't quite come true. When all is said and done, they learn that the only sure thing for them is that they have one another.

CINEMATHERAPY: I can recall a time in my life when I had some very close friends. We spent all of our time together. Summer was the best. Each day I would wake up and meet them at our prearranged spot—a secret place only we knew about. I remember promising we would be friends forever. The problem is, now I don't even remember their names. And even as I type these words, I have a sense of sadness about losing those years and not keeping that promise. Movies like *The Lemon Sisters* help me reach back into those memories, those childhood dreams. When did things get so complicated that I lost touch with my special group? Why did I break my promise to them and lose contact? Was it them? Was it me? Here's a chance to get in touch with some of those wonderful memories. Look for yourself in one of the on-screen characters. Were you the one whose parents were always the center of attention? The one with the parent whom everyone loved? Did you fantasize about being a star, flying all over the world to entertain your fans? Maybe you were the individual who didn't have a fantasy and just followed the group. Whoever you were, you're going to be delighted at the feelings that this movie brings forth in you. Here's an idea: After you watch this movie, make an effort to track down one or more of those special friends. It could be that you know where they are and you've "just been too busy" to make contact. You might have an old photograph or school picture. Start simple. Give directory information a call and see if they or their parents are listed. Once you find them, have a special reunion—just you and your old friends. Or invite some current friends over. Watch *The Lemon Sisters* and spend time listening to stories about one another's old friends and life experiences. I'll bet you will find your old memories in one or more of those friends. They've been with you all the time, and you just didn't realize it. And most important, don't forget those dreams.

LENNY

(United Artists, 1974), B & W, 111 minutes, R-rated

HEALING THEMES:
Letting drugs and alcohol rule your life
Looking at the horrors of heroin

Shooting for the stars
Going too far
Trying to buck the system
Going over the edge

DIRECTOR: Bob Fosse; SCREENPLAY: Julian Barry; CAST: Dustin Hoffman (Lenny); Valerie Perrine (Honey); Jan Miner (Sally); Stanley Beck (Artie); Gary Morton (Sherman); Rashel Novikoff (Aunt Mama); Guy Rennie (Jack)

SYNOPSIS: Lenny Bruce is an up-and-coming comedian who works at seedy bars throughout the country. He falls in love with drugs, alcohol, and Honey, a stripper. Lenny is arrested for using profanity on stage. He spends most of his time and money defending himself in courts across the country. His life comes to an end when he overdoses.

CINEMATHERAPY: Occasionally I come across a movie that deals with issues involving actual people—healing stories that hit home because the characters are based on real-life people. Well before I became a therapist, I had an opportunity to see *Lenny* as a stage production. I was stunned. It hit home. I, too, had spent years as an entertainer and seen what drugs and alcohol did to my friends. *Lenny* sends us a clear message: Drugs and alcohol kill. And that is exactly what happened to Lenny Bruce. Recovery happens when you watch movies such as *Lenny* and allow them to pull you out of denial. Notice his consistent and constant deterioration. He becomes more and more incoherent as he uses drugs to struggle through each day. Do you know anyone like Lenny? Are there times when you can't make it through the day without your fix? Maybe you're fixating on something else: food, gambling, work, or sex, for example. Can you see how they're all the same—how they're only different ways of avoiding living in the here and now? What do you use? How do you get through the day? Do you feel you're a victim of someone's addiction? Maybe you're in denial. If you know what this person is doing, why do you continue to be involved with him or her? Could it be that you are codependent in their behavior and believe that you deserve to be treated with disrespect? These are difficult issues to examine. Movies such as *Lenny* help us heal by confronting us with our actions through the characters. It's what I call *paradoxical healing*. If you're having problems in the area of your life that Lenny and Honey are confronting, try Alcoholics Anonymous, Narcotics Anonymous, and Al-Anon to help get you through these times.

LIKE MOM, LIKE ME

(CBS-TV, 1978), color, 100 minutes, not rated

HEALING THEMES:
Losing a spouse or parent to divorce
Dealing with your grief
Growing up way too fast
Trying to set boundaries
Having a child who is more mature than you

DIRECTOR: Michael Pressman; TELEPLAY: Nancy Lynn Schwartz; CAST: Linda Lavin (Althea); Kristy McNichol (Jennifer); Patrick O'Neal (Philip); Max Gail (Henry); Lawrence Pressman (Michael); Stacey Nelkin (Tao); Michael LeClair (Peter)

SYNOPSIS: Philip, a husband and father, decides he's had enough with the responsibilities of life and deserts his family. Althea, the mother, and Jennifer, the daughter, must cope with life without him. Things get complicated when the mother meets another man and the daughter patterns her own behavior on Mom's. Power struggles ensue in a caring but strained relationship.

CINEMATHERAPY: Each year thousands of families are torn apart by a separation. In this case, we see abandonment on the part of the husband/father. Have you ever felt abandoned by a parent or loved one? Have you ever experienced someone simply picking up and leaving without any warning? This can be a very confusing and painful time for any adult or child. The mother in this movie seems to be consumed with herself and satisfying her own emotional needs. But what about her daughter? There is a lot of pain inside her, and she has no one to turn to for support. How does she come to resolve her own issues? Maybe your parents separated when you were young. What memories come rushing back? Did you isolate yourself? Were you angry? Possibly you became an adult overnight and took on responsibilities that were well beyond your years. If you experienced this as a child, you may believe it was your fault this person left, and you may have a sense of guilt as a result. Can you relate? I know I can. In this case, Jennifer decides that one way she can handle her guilt is to grow up fast. Watch as the mother and daughter volley to gain identity and territory in their new, complex relationship. Can you see there are no boundaries? Without boundaries, you never know where you end and another person begins. Notice the way Jennifer almost imitates her mother in an attempt to move into adulthood. This great movie can prompt mothers and daughters of any age to open up and let go of their bad feelings. Talk about what you're experiencing or have experienced, and work to let go of those feelings. Enjoy the closeness that comes from the journey and go on with your lives. Now, isn't that what comes from healing?

LITTLE DARLINGS

(Paramount, 1980), color, 95 minutes, R-rated

HEALING THEMES:

Looking back on your childhood
Remembering your girlfriends
Losing your virginity
Coming down off that high horse
Being friends with someone you never thought you'd be friends with
Leaving home for the first time
Girls just want to have fun

DIRECTOR: Ronald F. Maxwell; **SCREENPLAY**: Kimi Peck, Darlene Young; **CAST**: Tatum O'Neal (Ferris); Kristy McNichol (Angel); Armand Assante (Gary); Matt Dillon (Randy); Maggie Blye (Ms. Bright); Nicolas Coster (Whitney); Krista Erickson (Cinder); Alexa Kenin (Dana); Cynthia Nixon (Sunshine)

SYNOPSIS: It's time for summer camp. Among the girls who attend are Ferris, a rich, pompous girl; Angel, a poor, tough individual; and average neighborhood kids. They struggle at learning to get along and at gaining their own identities. Two of them decide to make a bet over which one will be the first to lose her virginity. By the time camp is over, they have all grown as people and as friends.

CINEMATHERAPY: Movies such as *Little Darlings* take me back to my childhood—those times when life was both overwhelming and exciting. We were all trying to figure out who we were in relation to everyone else in the world. Do you spend time going back to those old photo albums and reminiscing over bygone years? When we get in touch with our past, we can both understand where we've been and how we got to where we are today. Here's a chance to have fun by doing so. *Little Darlings* is especially wonderful for female viewers. As soon as you see the girls get off the bus, try to identify with one of the on-screen characters. Little by little, each child begins to become part of the group. And that's how we all grow, by learning to socialize and communicate through our families and friends. Those who learn few interpersonal skills may end up isolated as adults. Has that happened to you? Do you tend to be by yourself and avoid bonding with others? Follow along as the girls make their bet over losing their virginity. Does this bring back memories for you? Most people can remember a first time. Was it a positive experience for you? What is interesting to me is watching the peer pressure come from the girls instead of the boys. Possibly we have a misconception about who is pressuring whom to have sex. Finally, while the ending seems a little trite, we do see what happens when our guard is let down and we start to listen and communicate with other people in our lives. Parents, how about organizing a slumber party, making this movie the focus of the gathering, and then getting the girls to talk about the movie by themselves? Encourage them to be open and frank in their communication. It could be a good tool for growth. You may consider watching this one with your adult friends, too.

LITTLE MAN TATE
(Orion, 1991), color, 99 minutes, PG-rated

HEALING THEMES:
Being a parent
Trying to raise your child and meet their needs
Remembering lost childhood years
Feeling you don't know how to just have fun
Recognizing when the child's the parent and the parent's the child

DIRECTOR: Jodie Foster; **SCREENPLAY**: Scott Frank; **CAST**: Jodie Foster (Dede); Dianne Wiest (Dr. Jane Grierson); Adam Hann-Byrd (Fred); Harry Connick Jr. (Eddie); David Pierce (Garth); Debi Mazar (Gina); P. J. Ochlan (Damon); George Plimpton (Winston); Michael Shulman (Matt)

SYNOPSIS: Dede has a little boy, Fred, who is smarter than anyone can imagine. Their very special relationship is broken apart when Dr. Grierson, who directs a program for especially gifted children, offers Fred an opportunity to join her school. After some frustration, Fred returns home to Dede, the one who accepts him for who he is.

CINEMATHERAPY: Sometimes parents get confused about their role with their children. I've worked with parents who push their children too hard, forgetting they must first be children before they can become successful adults. If they don't have a chance to be children, as adults they may become removed and distant from everyone, never taking time to have fun, always making business come first. So when I came across *Little Man Tate,* I saw a wonderful opportunity to show you the importance of being a loving parent and letting your children mature at their own pace. Maybe you grew up in a home where you had to perform by getting good grades, being the best on the team, or always being the winner in a beauty contest. Were you pressured into doing things you didn't want to do? Can you remember times when you were punished for not performing up to the standards of your parents? Maybe, like Fred, you felt isolated from everyone else. Notice that Jane doesn't know how to let her hair down. When Fred tries to get close, she doesn't know what to do. I felt sad for her. It seemed to me she never had a childhood herself. However, just because Dede is not smart, rich, or sophisticated doesn't mean she's a bad parent. Notice the way she cares for her child: She listens to him even though she doesn't understand. The reality is that she is a loving, caring mother who is concerned for more than her son's ability to perform to someone else's standards. Let yourself get close to the relationship between Dede and Fred. How do they make you feel? When you watch their rapport, do you sense that something's missing in the situation between you and your own children? Does it bring back memories of your own childhood? When you can appreciate the importance of good parenting, you have the chance to be enlightened in your own life and with your own children. Movies such as *Trading Mom* and *Little Man Tate* can really turn on lights. Watch this film with your whole family. Tell your children about how the movie makes you feel and ask them about their feelings. You may be surprised at some of their comments about this tender movie.

THE LOCKET

(RKO, 1946), B & W, 86 minutes, not rated

HEALING THEMES:
Dealing with a liar
Childhood memories that come back to haunt you
Falling in love with the wrong person
Coming out of denial
Confronting your past

DIRECTOR: John Brahm; **SCREENPLAY:** Sheridan Gibney; **CAST:** Laraine Day (Nancy); Brian Aherne (Dr. Harry Blair); Robert Mitchum (Norman); Gene Raymond (John); Sharyn Moffet (Nancy at ten); Ricardo Cortez (Drew); Henry Stephenson (Lord Wyndham); Katherine Emery (Mrs. Willis)

SYNOPSIS: A young girl has a traumatic experience that causes her to be a liar throughout her life. She meets men and then leaves them, and along the way lives are destroyed. Eventually, she must confront the painful memories of her childhood.

CINEMATHERAPY: *The Locket* is a wonderful depiction of what happens to us when we bury experiences from our childhood. Can you think back to a time in your life when something occurred and you said "That's it. I'll never let that happen to me again" or "I'll never live like that again"? Perhaps there are times in your childhood that you can't recall at all. Why can't you remember? As a therapist, my goal is to help people come out of denial, to kick up some of the memories that people are afraid to recall. *The Locket* is a wonderful portrayal of how that happens. Could you understand how this woman acted? Did you understand her constant lying? In psychology, we refer to that as being a sociopath or a compulsive liar. Do you know anybody like that in your life, someone you can't trust? Or do you know someone who lies but whom other people believe? I've met a few individuals like that, and though I'm reluctant to admit it, there was a time I did it myself. However, that's part of what recovery is about. It's not only physical and it's not only related to the addictions; it's also related to the spiritual self, about being honest, about dealing with one's true feelings. I strongly recommend that you give this movie a try. And after you do, make the commitment to be honest—first to yourself, and then to those around you.

LORENZO'S OIL
(Universal, 1992), color, 135 minutes, PG-13-rated

HEALING THEMES:
Learning that your child has a serious illness
Realizing that sometimes you must find your own answers
Pushing a relationship to the limits
Confronting the fears that your child may die
Never giving up hope

DIRECTOR: George Miller; SCREENPLAY: George Miller, Nick Enright; CAST: Nick Nolte (Augusto); Susan Sarandon (Michaela); Peter Ustinov (Professor Gus Nikolais); Kathleen Wilhoite (Deirdre); Gerry Bamman (Dr. Judalon); Margo Martindale (Wendy); James Rebhorn (Ellard); Ann Hearn (Loretta); Maduka Steady (Omowri)

SYNOPSIS: Augusto and Michaela Odone learn that their newborn son has a rare, degenerative disease called adrenoleukodystrophy. They battle against all odds to find a doctor who can help, but with few results. They grow tired of waiting for the medical community to come up with the answers and look for a cure for their son themselves. They eventually find one.

CINEMATHERAPY: This movie is based on the true-life story of Michaela and Augusto Odone. I included it in the book, in part, because of their son's illness—a devastating but, fortunately, rare disease. However, Michaela and Augusto have something to give us besides a cure for an illness. They also give us courage—courage to fight for what we believe in against all odds. They offer the healing message that if you give up, you can't possibly win. As you watch *Lorenzo's Oil*, work to get in touch with the determination of the parents to find a solution to their son's sickness. Their perseverance is inspirational and spiritually driven. Have you gone to professionals, only to have them tell you there is no solution? Have you felt defeated because you were told you couldn't do something? The Odones got that message everywhere they went. As you will see, they had to deal with the bureaucracy of the medical community and the frustration that comes from everyone saying, "Just accept your child's illness and go on." There is a tendency for us to believe that what a professional tells us is the absolute truth. One of the first things I tell people I am working with is that healing comes only after you believe in yourself. If you try, you will succeed. You must never give up, and you must never listen to those who give you messages of self-defeat. Those negative words are merely a reflection of their own failure and have nothing to do with you. It's about your courage, your challenges, and your successes. And like Michaela and Augusto, if no one has the answer, start working on a solution yourself. You are capable of dealing with and finding many of the solutions to the problems you encounter in your daily life. Trust in yourself. Empower yourself to find your own healing path. And when you do, take it.

LOSING ISAIAH

(Paramount, 1995), color, 108 minutes, R-rated

HEALING THEMES:
Abandoning a child
Growing up with a drug-addicted parent
Trying to adopt a child
Fighting for your rights
Losing someone you love
Surviving the courts

DIRECTOR: Stephen Gyllenhaal; **SCREENPLAY:** Naomi Foner; **CAST:** Jessica Lange (Margaret); Halle Berry (Khaila); David Strathairn (Charles); Cuba Gooding, Jr. (Eddie); Daisy Eagan (Hannah); Marc John Jeffries (Isaiah); Samuel L. Jackson (Kadar); Joie Susannah Lee (Marie); Regina Taylor (Gussie); La Tanya Richardson (Caroline); Jacqueline Brookes (Judge Silbowitz)

SYNOPSIS: When Margaret, a white social worker in Chicago, is put in charge of a case involving a black, crack cocaine–addicted mother and her baby, she gets too involved. She takes custody of the infant and begins to raise him as her own son. Some years later, the child's real mother comes back to retrieve her youngster. The legal battle that ensues changes the lives of all involved.

CINEMATHERAPY: There are several reasons why this movie is important. Should a person who has lost a youngster owing to their own negligence be allowed to retake custody of the child? How soon should an irresponsible parent be allowed back into a child's life? Do we really know who is better suited to raise a child—the birth parents or the adoptive parents? Why does it matter if the adoptive parents and the child they are adopting are of different races? Is it important to allow a child to be part of the process of deciding where and with whom he or she will live? I have some strong feelings about these questions, but I will not present them here. Each of you should watch this movie and come to your own conclusions. Over the years, our courts have been challenged with difficult cases involving custody rights, making decisions on behalf of children, but the truth is we have very little scientific information to help us determine the best course of action in these disputes. Nor do we know if children are psychologically damaged by court battles, or if children in families involved in adoption procedures are damaged in the process. Likewise, little is known about the psychological well-being of children of one race being raised by parents of another race. *Losing Isaiah* forces us to examine these issues closely.

LOVE, LIES AND LULLABIES

(ABC-TV, 1993), color, 100 minutes, PG-rated

HEALING THEMES:

Being addicted to cocaine
Learning you are pregnant
Losing custody of your child
Coming out of denial
Feeling codependent
Digging in your heels to turn your life around

DIRECTOR: Rod Hardy; TELEPLAY: Janet Heaney, Matthew Eisen, Joe S. Landon; CAST: Susan Dey (Christina); Lorraine Toussaint (Florence); D. W. Moffet (Gabriel); Kathleen York (Terry); Guy Boyd (Walter); Andy Romano (Judge Windt); Lawrence Monoson (Simon); Piper Laurie (Margaret)

SYNOPSIS: A young woman, Christina, who likes to have fun with drugs and alcohol, learns she is pregnant. Her baby, Lynn, is born addicted and the state steps in to take Lynn away from Christina. With a great deal of courage, Christina wins a battle to end her addiction and keep her baby.

CINEMATHERAPY: Each year a portion of the population abuses drugs and alcohol. Women are a portion of those abusers. Of the female abusers, a portion become pregnant and give birth to drug-addicted babies. Enter Christina, the newest child abuser on the block. Sound too strong? Good. Let's not kid ourselves. We are sending the message to those who are of childbearing age: If you are going to do drugs, if you're going to drink alcohol, if you're going to smoke, do *not* do it while you're pregnant. So if the message is out, then why is the problem still rampant? Well, that's why it's called an addiction: The body and soul are consumed by the need to have that next line, smoke, drink, or whatever fix the person craves. The fact that a pregnancy is involved doesn't suddenly change the mind and body's need for that next fix. And whether or not a child is involved is irrelevant to the substance abuser. So what do we do? Do you know someone who wants to quit and is thinking of having a baby? Maybe you're pregnant and reading this page while you're under the influence. Or possibly you were born addicted. No matter your background, the bottom line is recovery—self-healing through confrontation of the self or others. I know it's a bit preachy, and I apologize. However, if there is an innocent person in this world, it is an unborn, drug-affected child. Call your doctor. Get physical check-ups. If you are a user, get help at your local twelve-step group. Be around those who will not pass judgment and *will not use*. Be good to your child by being good to yourself.

LOVE STORY

(Paramount, 1970), color, 99 minutes, PG-rated

HEALING THEMES:
Falling in love with the perfect person
Listening to lovers talk
Becoming your own person
Dealing with the pain of saying goodbye to an oppressive parent
Learning that a person you love is ill
Grieving the loss of someone important in your life

DIRECTOR: Arthur Hiller; SCREENPLAY: Erich Segal; CAST: Ali McGraw (Jenny); Ryan O'Neal (Oliver); Ray Milland (Oliver Barrett III); John Marley (Phil); Katherine Balforn (Mrs. Oliver Barrett III); Russell Nype (Dean Thompson); Sydney Walker (Dr. Shapely); Tommy Lee Jones (Hank)

SYNOPSIS: Jenny Cavilleri meets Oliver Barrett IV at Harvard College. Oliver comes from a wealthy upper-class family, whereas Jenny struggles to make it with support from her middle-class, blue-collar father. After a rocky start, Jenny and Oliver decide to marry, much to his father's displeasure. When Oliver's father refuses to financially support them, they struggle to get Oliver through law school. He becomes a successful lawyer and Jenny becomes the proud wife. Then she is diagnosed with a terminal illness. They experience their last days together knowing they will love each other forever.

CINEMATHERAPY: *Love Story* became a cliché in the 1970s. Many people would joke about the line "Love means never having to say you're sorry." Now, I don't know where Erich Segal got the idea, but let me be the first on your block to dispel that myth. Love does mean having to say you're sorry. There is no such thing as the perfect relationship, which means that imperfect things happen. Would you not say you were sorry if you were late? What would you do if you lost your temper and knew you were wrong? Well, some of you may choose to keep your apologies to yourself, but all that will do is stop your relationship from growing. How did you feel about the way these two "very much in love" people spoke to each other? I have worked with numerous couples who were abusive in the same way as Oliver and Jenny. Why is it necessary to be sarcastic and mean-spirited with each other? Are you in a relationship and you're constantly making negative, hurtful remarks to each other? Do you find it difficult to get close to the person you're with because you fear they will make negative remarks in response? Maybe you grew up in a home where very few kind words were spoken. Why not learn to speak with respect for each other? Be kind and loving rather than angry and hurtful. *Love Story* also brings out the pain that comes from losing someone we care about. Do you have a difficult time showing your emotions? There is absolutely no reason to hang tough. Learn to let go of your emotions and open up to those who love you. Watch this film alone or with someone who means a great deal to you. Spend time talking about your feelings and what it would be like to live without the other person in your life. *Love Story* invites us to heal ourselves by witnessing the grief Oliver and Jenny experience.

THE MAN WHO SHOT LIBERTY VALANCE
(Paramount, 1962), B & W, 123 minutes, not rated

HEALING THEMES:
Succeeding when the odds are against you
Standing up for what you believe
Being the new kid on the block
Learning the ropes
Being backed into a corner

DIRECTOR: John Ford; SCREENPLAY: Willis Goldbeck, James Warner Bellah; CAST: James Stewart (Ransom); John Wayne (Tom); Vera Miles (Hallie); Lee Marvin (Liberty Valance); Edmond O'Brien (Dutton); Andy Devine (Link); Woody Strode (Pompey); Jeanette Nolan (Nora); Ken Murray (Doc Willoughby); John Qualen (Peter); Strother Martin (Floyd); Lee Van Cleff (Reese); John Carradine (Maj. Cassius Starbuckle); Carleton Young (Maxwell); Willis Bouchey (Jason)

SYNOPSIS: Liberty Valance is the town tough guy. Everyone stays out of his way for fear of his gun. Tom Ransom comes to town, and Valance gives him a hard time. Although the newcomer is not a gunfighter, he confronts Valance and puts a permanent end to Valance's reign of terror—with a little help.

CINEMATHERAPY: Every school has some tough kids. You know, the ones who walked through the halls pushing and shoving their way from class to class. And if you said something, it would just make matters worse. Sometimes those rough guys make it into adulthood without changing their style. I've come across a few of them in my life, and while I feel sad for them, I would just as soon stay out of their way. What do you remember about those days? Were you teased and harassed by people who just decided to pick on you for no reason at all? Is there a Liberty Valance in your life right now who can't seem to leave you alone? *The Man Who Shot Liberty Valance* is a little different way of getting in touch with some of those old or current fears—with feeling what it's like to be against all odds and gathering the courage to stand up for yourself. How do you feel about our newcomer? Have you ever been in his tough position? Was there a time when you got pushed so far that you could no longer back away from the problem? Isn't it interesting how one man could keep the town in a state of terror? Valance reminds me of some of the families I've seen in my office for whom everything revolves around the mood and temperament of one family member. Like the towns-people, the family simply chooses to adjust and respond to this one person who must have his or her way—or else. Like our lone rider, we must learn to stand up for our rights and what we believe in, or matters will only get worse. We need to learn to take care of ourselves and confront our adversaries to let them know that they can no longer treat us poorly. Sample this movie. Learn to stand up and be counted. Let the world know you can't be pushed around. *Warning!* I do not include this movie to suggest that you use a gun or violence of any type to resolve a dispute.

MARVIN'S ROOM

(Miramax, 1996), color, 98 minutes, PG-13-rated

HEALING THEMES:
Reuniting family
Putting the past behind you
Dealing with a member of the family who is seriously ill
Getting to the bottom of your anger
Learning to laugh
Dealing with family dysfunction

DIRECTOR: Jerry Zaks; SCREENPLAY: Scott McPherson; CAST: Meryl Streep (Lee); Leonardo DiCaprio (Hank); Diane Keaton (Bessie); Robert De Niro (Dr. Wally); Hume Cronyn (Marvin); Gwen Verdon (Ruth); Dan Hedaya (Bob); Hal Scardino (Charlie); Victor Garber (Minister); Margo Martendale (Dr. Charlotte); John Callahan (Lance); Joe Lise (Bruno)

SYNOPSIS: It's been more than twenty years since Lee and Bessie have seen or talked to each other. When Bessie's doctor diagnoses her with leukemia, she calls on her sister to act as a bone marrow donor. While dealing with the family's many dysfunctions, the siblings are reunited.

CINEMATHERAPY: It's rare to come across a movie so rich in messages that enlighten us on our journey to recovery. In fact, there are so many messages in *Marvin's Room* that I cannot discuss all of them here. I grew up in a family similar to the one in this film. Full of dysfunction, we had all stopped talking to one another by the time I was out of high school. Like Hank's family, my family was full of crazy-making comments. The overall message was "Outside world, stay away." Does that thought bring back any old memories? Are there members of your family with whom you no longer have contact? Do you remember why you stopped having that contact? *Marvin's Room* begs us to look at old memories and then confront the emotions conjured by those memories. When Hank, the family troublemaker, sneaks into his grandfather's closet, that's exactly what he is doing—going into a closet of memories. Did you feel the rage in this family? No matter what anyone said, it was consistently taken the wrong way. Is that what happens in your home—no one can talk without an argument surfacing? Are you in charge of caring for someone who is very ill? Maybe you're the person who is dealing with the illness. Do you feel like your are on your own? Perhaps you've wanted to elicit support but feel that no one will listen. Here's a thought: Sit down and write one letter to all the members of your family, inviting them to see *Marvin's Room*. Ask them to look at the similarities between your family and the family in the movie. Sometimes the solutions to life's problems are as simple as cleaning out crowded closets and putting the past behind us. By standing your ground and not running away from your problems, you will discover that life can be rich with joy, freedom, and love.

MARY REILLY

(TriStar, 1996), color, 108 minutes, R-rated

HEALING THEMES:
Growing up with an abusive father
Issues of incest
Living with the devastating effects of alcohol and drugs
Confronting the innerself
Being attracted to choas
Being haunted by old memories

DIRECTOR: Stephen Freas; SCREENPLAY: Christopher Hampton; CAST: Julia Roberts (Mary Reilly); John Malkovich (Dr. Henry Jekyll/Mr. Hyde); Glenn Close (Mrs. Farraday); George Cole (Mr. Poole); Michael Gambon

(Mary's Father); Kathy Staff (Mrs. Kent); Michael Sheen (Bradshaw); Bronagh Gallagher (Annie); Linda Bassett (Mary's Mother); Ciaran Hinds (Sir Danvers Carew)

SYNOPSIS: Mary Reilly is an employee of one Dr. Henry Jekyll, a respected town physician. Quiet and shy, Mary is drawn into participation in Jekyll's experimental transitions to the less desirable Mr. Hyde, the evil, murderous side of Dr. Jekyll. Before Jekyll and Hyde end their demonic, split-personality reign of terror, Mary finds herself torn between her horrible past and futile attempts at establishing a healthy future.

CINEMATHERAPY: How well a movie does at the box office usually has little to do with its healing value. In fact, some of the best cinematherapy movies fared poorly in this regard. *Mary Reilly* is one of those films. However, it is a recovery jewel that will help some of you gain insight into the devastating effects of growing up in a dysfunctional family. Be patient with this film. It's not easy to comprehend, but if you take the time to do so, you will understand how and why you may be attracted to the very nightmares from which you are running. Dr. Jekyll/Mr. Hyde has become synonymous with a person who has two or more sides to their personality, one side being unmanageable: "You know, Ann is sure a different person when she drinks. Sometimes I'm afraid to be around her. She's a real Dr. Jekyll and Mrs. Hyde." "Have you noticed how Eric's personality changes on the weekends? He frightens me. I don't know why I like that Dr. Jekyll and Mr. Hyde so much." Now I ask you this question: If Ann and Eric are such volatile personalities, why do people want to be with them? *Mary Reilly* gives us an answer. Did you notice how Hyde plays out Mary's childhood experiences? Did you see him become her worst nightmare? Could you see and hear how she becomes more entranced in the chaos he creates? This is what Mary is used to. Why? Because the Hyde persona is similar to her father's. She grew up with this kind of deviant behavior and was so familiar with surviving around someone like Jekyll and Hyde. They are the kind of people to whom she grows attached. Do you know anyone like Mary? Perhaps you become involved in relationships with people that re-create those old childhood fears. Do you find yourself feeling comfortable with that behavior? Are you used to those feelings? Is one side of you trying to pull away while the other side wants to be in the middle of all the negative excitement? I warn you, *Mary Reilly* is not an easy movie to watch. Stretch yourself. Make yourself feel the pain and fear that it presents. Then work to remove yourself from all those relationships that have that Dr. Jekyll–and–Mr. Hyde appeal. Life will be so much more peaceful for you. Trust yourself; you do deserve the peace.

MARY SHELLEY'S FRANKENSTEIN

(TriStar, 1994), color, 123 minutes, R-rated

HEALING THEMES:

Being confronted with the consequences of your actions
Living life without life's emotional tools
Looking at the evil side of a person
Creating your destiny
Incest
When you've been abandoned
Passing judgment on someone

DIRECTOR: Kenneth Branagh; SCREENPLAY: Staph Lady, Frank Darabont; CAST: Kenneth Branagh (Dr. Victor Frankenstein); Robert De Niro (the creature); Tom Hulce (Henry); Helena Bonham Carter (Elizabeth); Aidan Quinn (Captain Walton); Ian Holm (Victor's father); Richard Briers (grandfather); John Cleese (Professor Waldman); Robert Hardy (Professor Krempe); Cherie Lunghi (Victor's mother); Trevyn McDowell (Justine)

SYNOPSIS: Dr. Victor Frankenstein has a very creative mind. He decides he can make life out of body parts from the dead. He accomplishes his goal but abandons his creation. Left to survive on its on, his creation comes back to haunt him. Victor's experiments eventually bring about the death of both of them.

CINEMATHERAPY: Okay, Dr. Solomon, now you've really lost it. You're trying to tell us that a monster movie has healing messages. Give this movie a chance. You see there's a little "Dr. Frankenstein" in each of us. We all have some desire to create and control—perhaps not as much as Victor does, but it's there. Think about it: When we raise our children, aren't we trying to create a more perfect human being who reflects all the qualities we believe they are going to need to live in the world? Maybe you're in a relationship where you feel it necessary to control your significant other. And I'm sure you are aware of countries that force their people to do as they want them to do—or else. Aren't all those examples of what Victor Frankenstein does to his creation? And like some parents, friends, and organizations, Victor abandons his project. He decides he doesn't want it anymore, and the creature with no name is left to take care of itself. Victor is like a parent who gives birth to a child but does not give him or her the nurturing and tools needed to survive in the world. Like the creature, that child may turn to violence to survive in a world that expects him or her to perform as others do. If we don't nurture our children and give them the tools they need to survive, we create monsters who roam the world searching for the soul and love they never had. Experience the paradox of love and giving through Victor. See the things in yourself that you no longer want to be part of you, and work to make those changes before it is too late. If in the end *Mary Shelley's Frankenstein* doesn't work for you, move on to another movie. *Note:* There are many versions of this story to choose from. If you can't find this one, try the 1931 or 1973 production. They're both excellent adaptations of the classic novel.

MASK

(Universal, 1985), color, 120 minutes, PG-13-rated

HEALING THEMES:

Being different from everyone else
Getting inside the real person
Helping a child deal with the fact that they are different
Rage over the loss of a child
Letting your child become an adult

DIRECTOR: Peter Bogdanovich; SCREENPLAY: Anna Hamilton Phelan; CAST: Cher (Rusty); Sam Elliott (Gar); Eric Stoltz (Rocky); Estelle Getty (Evelyn); Richard Dysart (Abe); Laura Dern (Diana); Nicole Merceirio (Babe); Harry Carey Jr. (Red); Ben Piazza (Mr. Simms)

SYNOPSIS: Rocky Dennis is a young boy afflicted with a horribly disfiguring condition called craniodiaphyseal dysplasia. His mother, Rusty, loves him for who he is inside *and* out. Together they live one day at a time. Rocky gets a little anxious about life, the world, and women. Rusty makes a difficult decision and lets him spread his wings. Rocky decides he's had enough of life and gives up.

CINEMATHERAPY: Sometimes people can be cruel to those who are different. I remember going to school with a guy who had something wrong with his body. People were very mean to him, teasing and taunting him about his problem. I didn't understand back then why they did that, but now I know it's because they knew instinctively that they could have been the one born with the problem. One of the reasons I want you to watch *Mask* is to experience the healing that comes from getting in touch with your own fears about what life would be like if you had a physical illness. How did Rocky make you feel? Were you grateful you do not have to live life as he does? Maybe you're someone with a condition that makes you stand out from others. Do people seem to be afraid of you, to act as if they could "catch" your infirmity? Do they tend to overcompensate for your problem when they're with you or go out of their way to ignore the problem? *Mask* will help you get in touch with all those feelings and more. Notice the way Rusty deals with her anger and grief over the loss of Rocky. She's been holding her frustrations and fears inside for so long, she now can no longer control herself. But, in truth, it is very healing to let go of so much anger. Can you relate to having that much frustration? Here's an idea: You don't have to tear the house apart to eradicate your anger. Get some old dishes and break them against a wall outside, pound some nails into a board, or scream into a pillow. Just let it all out. Then learn to let go of your anger over time rather than allow it to build up. It will make you feel good. Watch *Mask* with the whole family. If we can teach our children to be compassionate and to accept people for who they are, they will gain self-awareness and undergo personal growth. By the way, *Mask* is based on a true story. *The Elephant Man* looks at the life of a man with the same problem.

MIAMI RHAPSODY

(Hollywood, 1995), color, 95 minutes, PG-13-rated

HEALING THEMES:
Trying to make it in a relationship
Coping when your parents go through a separation
Being honest with yourself
Learning about love
Working with a therapist
Confronting your feelings

DIRECTOR: David Frankel; SCREENPLAY: David Frankel; CAST: Sarah Jessica Parker (Gwyn); Mia Farrow (Nina); Antonio Banderas (Antonio); Gil Bellows (Matt); Paul Mazursky (Vic); Carla Gugino (Leslie); Naomi Campbell (Kaia); Kevin Pollak (Jordan); Mark Blum (Peter); Ben Stein (rabbi); Barbara Garrick (Terri); Bo Eason (Kaia); Jeremy Piven (Mitchell)

SYNOPSIS: A young woman goes to a therapist and tries to work through her feelings over failed relationships, not only her own but those of her loved ones. In time, she begins to realize the life process that we all must go through and the growth that comes from changes in relationships.

CINEMATHERAPY: There aren't a lot of movies that I think depict the relationships between good and bad and right and wrong, but *Miami Rhapsody* does. It reached me and touched me in a way that few films do. It's not just about a relationship between two people and how they come and go or what they do at any given moment in time. Rather, it brings together a number of relationships. We're reminded that we all have times in our lives when not only our own relationships but also those of people we love and care about have problems. When you were young, did your parents separate? Or perhaps the separation came when you were older. That's what happened to me. Maybe you feel very close to your family and that breakup was so devastating you never quite got over it. Perhaps you mimicked that behavior in your own life, going from one relationship to the next, never truly able to bond. What memories do you have? What experiences can you recall? *Miami Rhapsody* covers all that territory. Watch it and allow yourself to feel. If you feel sad, experience the sadness. If you are joyful because a relationship has worked out, then experience the gratefulness that comes from that joy. This is an opportunity to feel on a profound level, so go ahead and feel.

MILDRED PIERCE
(Warner Bros., 1945), B & W, 109 minutes, not rated

HEALING THEMES:
Abandoning a marriage
Having to make it on your own
Following a dream
Dealing with a child who is caught up in money
Dealing with a child who looks down on you
Being betrayed by a lover

DIRECTOR: Michael Curtiz; SCREENPLAY: Ronald MacDougall; CAST: Joan Crawford (Mildred); Jack Carson (Wally); Zachary Scott (Monte); Eve Arden (Ida); Ann Blyth (Veda); Bruce Bennett (Bert); Lee Patrick (Maggie); Butterfly McQueen (Lottie); Moroni Olson (Inspector Peterson); John Compton (Ted); JoAnn Marlowe (Kay)

SYNOPSIS: When Mildred's husband walks out on her, she is left to raise her two children on her own. After struggling just to put food on the table, she follows her dream and opens up a successful restaurant, which eventually becomes a chain of eating establishments. But she can never seem to make enough money to keep her narcissistic daughter, Veda, happy. In the end, Mildred realizes she could never have done enough for her selfish youngster.

CINEMATHERAPY: "What's the problem, Dr. Solomon? It seems that no matter what I do for my children, it's not enough. What am I doing wrong?" "When I was growing up, we didn't have much. I promised I would make sure my children got everything they needed, but it never seems like enough." Sound familiar? I can't tell you the number of parents I have seen who have been frustrated with their children's behavior about material objects. I have never come across a movie that does as good a job as *Mildred Pierce* in dealing with this issue. Let me get the technical stuff out of the way. Mildred's daughter, Veda, suffers from narcissistic personality disorder. Simply stated, "What have you done for me lately?" is her national anthem. You're going to be taken aback by this young woman's bad behavior. You will see bits of yourself in Mildred as she sits passively and accepts sarcasm and abuse from her self-absorbed daughter. Can you relate? Do you have these problems with your children? Can you see how Mildred has become codependent in her daughter's antisocial behavior? Maybe you're a single parent trying to make it on your own. Can you feel Mildred's sense of abandonment? Get in touch with Mildred's courage and tenacity as she struggles to make it in the business world. Is there a part of you that wants to break free from the shackles that keep you down and tied to your job? Do you have dreams of opening your own business but fear giving up a sure thing? Mildred reminds all of us to follow our dreams, to take a chance. *Just Do It! Mildred Pierce* is a wonderful healing story for all of us. It will bring you out of denial and into the brighter lights of awareness about those who love you and those who would use you. Sit back and watch this film alone. You will be astounded at your personal growth.

THE MIRACLE OF KATHY MILLER

(CBS-TV, 1981), color, 100 minutes, not rated

HEALING THEMES:
Running in the race of your life
Coping when someone in your family has been in an accident
Summoning the courage to go on
What a family goes through in coping with a serious illness
Learning to live life all over again
Being the one in the family who feels left out
Triumph over adversity
Having hope where others said there was none

DIRECTOR: Robert Lewis; **TELEPLAY**: Mel Brez and Ethel Brez; **CAST**: Helen Hunt (Kathy); Sharon Gless (Myra Miller); Frank Converse (Larry Miller); Bill Beyers (Larry); John DeLancie (Dr. Christensen); Michele Greene (Sherrie); Bill Forsythe (Mark); Mary Ann Chinn (Nurse Meredith); David Hooks (Dr. Mahan)

SYNOPSIS: Kathy is a teenage girl from Arizona with all the normal interests of someone her age. Life changes dramatically when she is struck by an automobile and sustains horrible physical injuries to her brain and other parts of her body. The doctors tell her parents, Myra and Larry, to expect the worst. With therapy and self-determination, Kathy is able to complete a long-distance race.

CINEMATHERAPY: Like the movies *The Other Side of the Mountain, Mask,* and *My Left Foot, The Miracle of Kathy Miller* offers us hope and gives us courage to go forward in the face of adversity. It is difficult for us to imagine the pain and emotional despair felt by someone who suffers an accident such as this. Somehow it seems even worse when it happens to a person as young as Kathy. Has anyone in your family or someone you've known experienced a debilitating accident? Have you watched the person struggle to gain a physical and emotional foothold on life? Possibly someone you know has been affected by an illness. Whatever the case, Kathy will inspire you to never give up in the face of adversity. Watch as she learns the reality of what has happened to her. It would be easy to simply roll over and die. Focus on how the family deals with the shock, moving from pain and despair to determination, hope, and courage. If you or someone you know is dealing with a tragedy like this, I strongly suggest that you watch this film. I also encourage you to seek therapeutic help in dealing with the many emotions brought about by the accident. As you watch this movie, don't overlook the issues faced by the driver of the car. Sometimes in pictures such as this, the individual who caused the accident gets lost in the shuffle. Have you ever wondered what it would be like to make a split-second error in driving judgment and end up hitting someone? I'm not suggesting it happened that way in this movie. I'm just asking you to view the film in this light.

MISERY

(Columbia, 1990), color, 107 minutes, R-rated

HEALING THEMES:
Dealing with abuse
Being stalked
Getting caught in someone's obsession
Feeling like a prisoner in your own home
Refusing to give up
Being haunted by memories

DIRECTOR: Rob Reiner; **Screenwriter:** William Goldman; CAST: James Caan (Paul); Kathy Bates (Annie); Richard Farnsworth (Buster); Frances Sternhagen (Virginia); Lauren Bacall (Marcia); Graham Jarvis (Libby)

SYNOPSIS: Paul Sheldon is a successful writer. He has an auto accident on a snowy road and is found by Annie Wilkes, one of his biggest fans. She's also psychotic. Annie takes care of him—and holds him hostage in the process. She decides she wants him to write another book—her way. Paul plots to get away from her. In a final act of desperation, Paul kills Annie.

CINEMATHERAPY: Stephen King has certainly become the master of horror stories. If you love strange, scary tales, you can't do much better than his books. However, many of his stories have a message for all of us. He reminds us that there are people who are going over the edge and trying to take us with them. Do you know anyone who appears normal yet does things from time to time that you question? Maybe you have been so overwhelmingly angry and frustrated that you felt like Annie. In Annie, we have a lost, lonely, and desperate woman who seizes—literally—an opportunity to get her way. We experience a sense of total helplessness as we watch Paul being terrorized by this obsessed woman. And maybe that's what we can derive from this movie—a feeling of complete helplessness and fear as she holds her victim hostage. Can you relate to the terror Paul endures? Maybe you are in a relationship where you feel as if you're being held a prisoner with no way out. Now, it's not my goal to have you interpret *Misery* literally. Rather, look for parallels to your life. Are you someone who can't let go of your control over another person? It's a terrible thing when one human being controls another against their will. However, there are constructive ways—therapists, counselors, and treatment centers—to work through these problems. You do not have to give your life over to your sickness, nor do you have to be a person who lives in fear over someone's being obsessed with you. Seek help and enjoy the freedom of coming out of denial over what's being done to you or what you might be doing to someone else. You can embrace the essences of healing when you learn to let go and move on with your life.

MR. MOM

(Twentieth Century-Fox, 1983), color, 91 minutes, PG-rated

HEALING THEMES:

Having to take on a new role in life
Losing your job
Learning to appreciate what your partner does in a relationship
Growing to maturity
The belief that raising kids is a woman's job
Giving the man in your life a reality check

DIRECTOR: Stan Dragoti; SCREENPLAY: John Hughes; CAST: Michael Keaton (Jack); Teri Garr (Caroline); Martin Mull (Ron); Ann Jillian (Joan); Christopher Lloyd (Larry); Frederick Koehler (Alex); Taliesin Jaffe (Kenny); Graham Jarvis (Humphries); Jeffrey Tambor (Jinx); Carolyn Seymour (Eve); Michael Alaims (Bert); Tom Leopold (Stan)

SYNOPSIS: When Jack, a husband and a father, is fired from his job, his wife decides it's time to take charge, so she gets a job. Roles are reversed when Jack is left to do all the housework and take over Mom's bringing-up-the-children job. What he thought was an easy task turns out to be quite an ordeal. He eventually gets things organized and becomes Mr. Mom, a man who has grown to appreciate what it's like to be in a homemaker role.

CINEMATHERAPY: Hey, ladies! Are you tired of being unappreciated around the house? Do you hold down two jobs—one working for a paycheck and the other taking care of the home? Do your kids come running to you for *everything*? Does your significant other make his way from the front door to the couch while you prepare the evening meal? Well, here's a chance for you to show your spouses some of what it's like to be a woman. As a therapist, I see a great many men who do not understand or appreciate what their wives or lovers do in the role of homemaker. "That's their job. What are they complaining about?" "They're trained to do that stuff." "Men's work is on the outside." Guys, does this remind you of anyone you know? I'm talking about you. As you will see, at first Jack is a bit overwhelmed with the whole thing. What he assumed to be true about being a housewife just isn't the case. You will also notice that other people vary in their reactions to his new role. "Did you see that guy? What a wuss." "I wouldn't be caught dead scrubbing toilets." "How come you're not more like her husband? Why don't you lend a hand once in a while?" Is it possible your significant other does not want to get involved in household tasks because of the fear of what other people will think? You can have a lot of fun with *Mr. Mom* and grow emotionally in the process. It can be your first step toward making some constructive changes in your relationship. Try this: Switch roles for a week, a month, a year. See what develops. Afterward, you may see changes in your spouse's attitude and receive cooperation around the house. When you open doors to communication in your relationship, you have a chance to heal a partnership that might have grown weak from long-term resentment.

MOONLIGHT AND VALENTINO
(Gramercy, 1995), color, 104 minutes, R-rated

HEALING THEMES:
Death and dying
Losing the one you love
Learning to grieve
Having the support of your friends
Letting go
Starting over

DIRECTOR: David Anspaugh; SCREENPLAY: Ellen Simon; CAST: Elizabeth Perkins (Rebecca); Whoopi Goldberg (Sylvie); Kathleen Turner (Alberta); Gwyneth Palthrow (Lucy); Jon Bon Jovi (the painter); Jeremy Sisto (Steven); Josef Sommer (Thomas); Peter Coyote (Paul)

SYNOPSIS: It's been a while since Rebecca's husband died, but she is still isolated and uninvolved. Her friends try to get her back into the swing of things, but she can't seem to be bothered with life. Then she is romanced by her unassuming housepainter, who gets her to open up and begin living again.

CINEMATHERAPY: The first time I saw this movie, I passed on using it as a cinematherapeutic tool. But almost every time I did a lecture, someone from the audience would come to me and ask, "Why didn't you include *Moonlight and*

Valentino?" To make a long story short, I gave another look-see and, lo and behold, I finally understood the film. I must have been daydreaming the first time around. Whether you have lost someone to death, or from a breakup, a move, or an argument, *Moonlight and Valentino* will remind you that there is more to life than just living. What do I mean by that? I mean that regardless of what has happened in the past, especially those things you cannot control, you must get on with your life. And that means doing everything you can do to experience all that living has to offer. You cannot sit around grieving the past endlessly; you must embrace the future. You cannot live by the credo "the past did not work out, so why try." You must keep trying—keep on having experiences. Can you relate to Rebecca? Have you closed the doors to others who want to be a part of your life? Are you just surviving without experiencing life as it was intended? Maybe you're a friend of someone who is trying to shut out the world. No matter who you are, you're going to receive an important message from this movie, one that will see you through the tough periods and help you enjoy the good times. Learn to let go. Use this movie as a way to understand that there is more than one person, one job, one space that is good for you. Enjoy all the precious moments you have, and when they're over, grieve, let go, and move on. Life is a journey. Make sure that you experience all of life, the good and the bad, before it's over. By rolling over and letting life pass you by, you merely make meaningless that which once was.

MURPHY'S ROMANCE

(Columbia, 1985), color, 107 minutes, PG-13-rated

HEALING THEMES:
Starting over again
Trying to make it on your own
Disenchantment with the opposite sex
Getting away from a destructive relationship
Falling in love . . . again

DIRECTOR: Martin Ritt; **SCREENPLAY:** Irving Ravetch, Harriet Frank Jr.; **CAST:** Sally Field (Emma); James Garner (Murphy); Brian Kerwin (Bobby Jack); Corey Haim (Jake); Dennis Burkley (Freeman); Georgann Johnson (Margaret); Charles Lane (Amos); Billy Ray Sharkey (Larry); Michael Aabtree (Jim)

SYNOPSIS: Emma's had it with men. She moves to a small town with her son to get a fresh start on life. She meets Murphy, the local drugstore owner. A special chemistry emerges but is interrupted when Bobby, her ex, comes back on the scene. True love wins out, with Emma and Murphy realizing they're made for each other.

CINEMATHERAPY: When I encounter a story that has wonderful messages about love, I make sure to include it with my healing stories. Emma, Murphy, and Bobby all teach us a little bit about life, love, and happiness. Have you given up on finding the right one? Have you gone from one bad relationship to the next, never finding the right one? Could it be that, like Emma, you are attracted to those who couldn't possibly be good for you? I just struck a nerve in myself: I used to love being with people who couldn't meet my needs, would use me, and move on. Now I've struck a nerve in you! Have you ever known anyone like Bobby? He's always got a smile on his face and he's forever looking for the easy way out. You could never depend on this guy to do anything except not be around when you need him. And what about Murphy? Does he seem like a pretty centered guy who knows what he wants? I think so. This is not the kind of guy who just dates to kill time. He is willing to wait for the right one to come along. And he's able to deal with the pain and loneliness that come with the wait. So here's what getting healthy is all about. Before she could find happiness, Emma had to reach a point in her life where she could let Bobby go and let Murphy in. And to do that you must come out of denial, confront yourself and your life patterns, and be willing to change the way you think and do things. You see, that's the healing process. Self-awareness and self-confrontation is the combination of events that must take place to experience wellness and enjoy life as it was intended to be lived. Let Emma and Murphy be absorbed into your soul. Feel the rich colors of their happiness and their true love for each other. Use them as a model for your future relationships and I can assure you that love will find its way into your life.

MY BROTHER'S KEEPER

(CBS-TV, 1995), color, 100 minutes, G-rated

HEALING THEMES:

Keeping secrets
Coping with a serious illness
Gathering the support of your friends and family
Fear that someone is going to die
AIDS and the prejudice that people have
A family's failure to communicate
Confronting your parents about your childhood
Learning to accept people for who they are
Fighting the system that holds you back

DIRECTOR: Gregory Goodell; TELEPLAY: Glenn Jordan; CAST: John Lithgow (Bob and Tom); Annette O'Toole (Joanne); Veronica Cartwright (Pat); Zeljko

Ivanek (Dr. Hill); Richard Magur (Nathan); Brian Doyle Murray (Terry); Amy Aquino (Terry); Peter Michael Goetz (Tabor); Ellen Burstyn (Helen)

SYNOPSIS: Bob and Tom are twins who care a great deal for each other; they have always been the best of friends. Tom learns he is HIV positive. Their insurance company refuses to pay for the treatment. The community rallies to their cause, but it's too late. Tom's family learns to accept his fate as he works to accomplish everything he can in life.

CINEMATHERAPY: I can't imagine that there is anyone who has not been touched in one way or another by AIDS. Some have lost friends and family. Others have lost their favorite entertainers. We have watched our research dollars go toward finding a cure, and the disease has changed the way we talk and think about sex. *My Brother's Keeper* offers a rare opportunity to look at one community's struggle to prevent AIDS from taking someone they love. One of the things that struck me about this movie is how our attitudes have changed with respect to learning someone is HIV positive. Listen to the way the community refers to Ryan White, whose life story, *The Ryan White Story,* is examined in my first book. Tom is certainly regarded differently from the way Ryan was. How did you feel about the insurance company? Have you ever known someone whose treatment was translated into dollars and cents? I was angry at the whole process. Listen to Joanne confront the family about their lack of love and communication. "We were never really close." Did she kick up any memories for you? Do you come from a family in which nothing was talked about? What do you recall about the way you were brought up? Do you still suffer from the effects of a dysfunctional family? Maybe you have problems with intimacy, or you struggle with alcoholism, drug addiction, or workaholism. And don't ignore the relationship between the two brothers. I don't know about you, but I was very touched by their bond. I certainly missed it in my childhood. We can all embrace the healing *My Brother's Keeper* has to offer. Invite your family to watch this movie with you. Your reason doesn't have to concern AIDS; it can be a desire to open the door to dialogue in your family that has never existed before.

MY LEFT FOOT
(Miramax, 1989), color, 103 minutes, R-rated

HEALING THEMES:
Making it in life when you're physically challenged
Giving up on someone
Trying to live life
Parental abandonment
Using alcohol to numb yourself

DIRECTOR: Jim Sheridan; **SCREENPLAY**: Shane Connaughton, Jim Sheridan; **CAST**: Daniel Day-Lewis (Christy); Brenda Fricker (Mrs. Brown); Alison Whelam (Shelia); Declan Aogham (Tom); Ray McAnally (Mr. Brown); Hugh O'Conor (Young Christy); Fiona Shaw (Dr. Eileen Cole); Cyril Cusack (Lord Castlewilland); Adrian Dunbar (Peter); Ruth McCabe (Mary); Marre Commee (Sadie); Eanna MacLiam (Benny)

SYNOPSIS: Christy is a boy born with cerebral palsy. As his parents try to raise him, they struggle with his desire to have a normal life. Christy has both a light and a dark side to him as he grows up in a world that is not built to suit his needs. He finally finds happiness with a woman who truly loves him.

CINEMATHERAPY: You may have someone in your family who is growing up with a physically or mentally challenging problem, or you may be someone who is dealing with the challenge yourself. Whoever you are, *My Left Foot* will beg you to take a second look before turning your back on yourself or anyone who is not like you. When I was growing up, there were several kids at school who were challenged in one way or another. I felt both grateful that I was not like them and embarrassed by my lack of sensitivity toward their conditions. "Hurry up," I thought, "can't you see you're in my way?" Do any of those thoughts go through your mind when a challenged person can't move as fast as you would like? Someone who is physically or mentally impaired often requires the support of others. Watch as Christy's mother reaches out to him and encourages him to grow and be a part of the real world. How about his father's way of handling the situation? I wanted to scream at him, "Hey, how about some love and caring, you old goat!" Maybe Christy's deformity embarrassed him, made him feel like an inadequate parent. Listen to Christy's moments of emotional pain as he expresses his frustration over having to accept his lot in life. You may find yourself dealing with your own feelings if you have been close to someone like Christy or Christy's family. If you haven't, this is a chance for you to gain compassion for those who are dealing with this or a similar condition. Their need for love and caring is no different from that of anyone else. Let your children see this movie and watch them grow from the experience. When we learn compassion and pass it on to our children, we build a foundation for a better world.

MY LIFE

(Columbia, 1993), color, 112 minutes, PG-13-rated

HEALING THEMES:

Dealing with death and dying
Accepting your fate
Saying farewell to those you love
Making the best of every moment

DIRECTOR: Bruce Joel Rubin; SCREENPLAY: Bruce Joel Rubin; CAST: Michael Keaton (Bob); Nicole Kidman (Gail); Haing S. Ngor (Mr. Ho); Bradley Whitford (Paul); Queen Latifah (Theresa); Michael Constantine (Bill); Rebecca Schull (Rose); Mark Lowenthal (Dr. Mills); Lee Garlington (Carol); Toni Sawyer (Doris); Mary Ann Thebus (Miss Morgenstern); Brenda Strong (Laura)

SYNOPSIS: Bob is a happily married public relations executive. He loves life and all its challenges. He has two pieces of news to deal with: He's going to be a father, and he is dying. Bob struggles to accept his fate. He decides to leave his unborn child with a video documentary of the father the child will never know personally. He finds peace, love, and success before he dies.

CINEMATHERAPY: Even as I sit and write, I know there is one course in life that I can never help you change: At one point in your life, each of you will have to deal with the pain of death. Death is life's inevitable reality. And in truth, death is for the living. But how do you learn to cope with the pain of knowing you or someone you care about is going to die soon? How do you accept this harsh reality and still enjoy the time remaining? *My Life* offers answers to these questions and more. Many of you will be afraid to watch this movie. No one is ever prepared for death. You've made it this far without being confronted with this issue, so why must you look at this unpleasant reality now? When it happens, it happens. Others may have lost a parent, spouse, or friend and not want to deal with those feelings—the grief that goes with this kind of loss. However, why not learn to deal with this most difficult life transition? When you do, you will free yourself from the fear and anxiety of wondering what the future will bring. Let our public relations executive in this movie see you to the other side of your fears. Learn to deal with the stages of shock, denial, and depression; leave a gift to those who love you and need to know you were once in their life. Don't turn your back on them. Maybe someone you know won't be around much longer. Have you said a proper goodbye? Have you asked for something by which to remember them? Reach out and express your emotions and listen to their feelings at the same time. And although there can be no physical healing from the inevitability of death, there is spiritual healing for both those who are dying and those who are being left behind. Watch this film alone. Get lots of tissue and let yourself go emotionally. There is an opportunity for self-nurturing here; you simply must be willing to experience pain to enjoy the growth.

MY NAME IS KATE

(Lifetime, 1994), color, 100 minutes, G-rated

HEALING THEMES:
Knowing when alcohol is ruling your life
Growing up in an alcoholic home

Trying to have a family life when someone is an addict
Confronting the addict in your life
Trying to understand the process of recovery
Losing someone you care about to drugs and alcohol

DIRECTOR: Rod Hardy; TELEPLAY: George Eckstein; CAST: Donna Mills (Kate); Daniel J. Travanti (Hal); Eileen Brennan (Barbara); Nia Peeples (Annie); Ryan Reynolds (Kevin); Deanna Milligan (Carrie); Babs Chula (Nora); Linda Darlow (Suzanne); Louie Eli (Pam); Tara Frederick (Jill)

SYNOPSIS: When Kate's family can no longer cope with her drinking, they confront her, and she begrudgingly enrolls at a treatment center. Kate eventually grasps sobriety and her compulsion to help others. Hal, her husband, has a difficult time with her need to attend support group meetings and her working with other alcoholics. Kate's sobriety does not come without losses.

CINEMATHERAPY: If you, or someone you know is in denial about an addiction, *My Name Is Kate* is a useful wake-up call. For as long as I can remember, we have been struggling to find a way to help people kick substance-abuse habits. It doesn't matter if it's smoking, drinking, doping, eating, working, or gambling: When an addiction rules your life and affects the world around you, you've got a serious problem. This movie will unlock the door to the secret of recovery. As you will see, Kate's life is driven by her addiction to alcohol. Notice the way Hal, Kevin, and the rest of the family dance around her behavior. Can you see how codependent they have become? When she acts one way, they adjust to her behavior, and when she acts another, they adjust again. Did you grow up in an alcoholic home? Is that what it was like for you? What feelings were stirred up for you as you watched Kate in this film? Did you become afraid, angry, withdrawn? Maybe you recall a sense of abandonment. Was Kate the mother, father, sister, or brother in your life who had difficulties with an addiction? How are you affected today as a result of growing up in an alcoholic home? Pay special attention to Hal as he has trouble understanding why she needs to go to meetings. He felt abandoned when she was drinking and abandoned when she stopped. People who are in recovery must put their sobriety first, or there won't be any real recovery. That's what happened to Kate's friend in the story line—she forgot to put her sobriety first and it cost her her life. After you watch this picture, make a big step toward healing by getting help for the substance abuser, whether it's yourself or someone else. Remember, there are twelve-step programs of recovery such as Alcoholics Anonymous and Al-Anon to see you through your journey to spiritual health and happiness. There's no need to keep your dependency a secret any longer. Love yourself enough to get well and you will be able to return love to those who love you.

NELL

(Twentieth Century-Fox, 1994), color, 113 minutes, PG-13-rated

HEALING THEMES:
Feeling you're different from everyone else
Coping when your world is turned upside down
Grieving the loss of a loved one
Learning to trust
Teaching those who can hear your wisdom

DIRECTOR: Michael Apted; SCREENPLAY: William Nicholson, Mark Handley; CAST: Jodie Foster (Nell); Liam Neeson (Dr. Jerome Lovell); Natasha Richardson (Dr. Paula Olsen); Richard Libertini (Dr. Alexander Paley); Nick Searcy (Sheriff Todd Peterson); Jeremy Davies (Billy); O'Neal Compton (Don); Jean Bridgers (Mike)

SYNOPSIS: When her mother dies, Nell is left to fend for herself. However, Nell is used to being alone, because she was raised in the woods and has never had contact with the outside world. Once she is discovered, life changes drastically—not only for her but for the world around her.

CINEMATHERAPY: I was deeply touched by this movie. In many ways, it hit home for me. No, I wasn't raised in the woods, but I sure felt I grew up in a world apart from everyone else. I, too, had a language all my own. Since I couldn't read, write, or spell, I was left to live in the fantasies of my own mind. Oh, I tried to act like the rest of the kids around me, but it never worked. So I often lived in isolation, with the world never really knowing who I was or what was going on with me. Like Nell, I was taunted, teased, and made to feel like "a wild child." But I believe that isolation led me to my writing and ultimately made me a better person. I learned to reach people in a way that was different, unique to the world around me. Maybe you have similar feelings. Perhaps you grew up feeling isolated, living with a family secret, one you couldn't tell the world. Nell's mother had a secret—she was raped and had twins from that violent act. What's your secret? What are you hiding from your teachers, spouse, children, and friends? Maybe you had a child you've never told anyone about, or you have a past that embarrasses you today. Yes, you could live like Nell, hidden away in the woods and trying to survive in a world where you don't have to communicate with anyone. However, is that restructured existence what you really want? Is that what you wish for your future or the future of your children? Use *Nell* as a way to begin your healing. Open up and learn to communicate about your experiences, the ones that are holding you back from growing and being a true part of the world. Don't let yourself fall over the edge, pushed to a point where no one can communicate with you. Like Nell, we all have memories, but when you live in the past, you have little chance of experiencing the here and now. Begin the healing by watching this movie. Take it from me: On the other side of the cloud is a rainbow so full of colors that it makes the pain of recovery worthwhile.

NINE MONTHS

(Twentieth Century-Fox, 1995), color, 103 minutes, PG-13-rated

HEALING THEMES:
Married life without children
Learning that you are or a loved one is pregnant
Feeling as if you've lost your freedom
Making bad choices
Taking responsibility for your actions

DIRECTOR: Chris Columbus; SCREENPLAY: Chris Columbus; CAST: Hugh Grant (Samuel); Julianne Moore (Rebecca); Jeff Goldblum (Sean); Tom Amold (Marty); Joan Cusack (Gail); Robin Williams (Dr. Kosevich); Ashley Johnson (Shannon); Emily Yancy (Dr. Thatcher); Kristin Davis (tennis attendant); Charles A. Martinet (Arnie); Joey Simmrin (Truman)

SYNOPSIS: Samuel and Rebecca enjoy their life just about as much as any young couple can. They are footloose and fancy-free. However, when Samuel learns that Rebecca is pregnant, he feels that he is trapped and his life is over. When Rebecca decides to leave and have their child on her own, reality sets in and Samuel learns the true meaning of love.

CINEMATHERAPY: Working as a therapist, I have on numerous occasions counseled couples who did not plan to have children, only to learn that they are pregnant. What then? Is life as they once knew it over? You bet it is. So I try to work with them to help them deal positively with their life transition. Sometimes they stay together, and other times their pregnancy causes them to separate. So how does it get to the point where a pregnancy can cause separation? In most cases, the answer is the same—they did not talk about the issue of having children early on in the relationship. What do I mean? When I was young and single, I spent my days and nights looking for Ms. Right. (The truth is I was seeking physical satisfaction.) Believe it or not, one of the very first messages I would send to someone I had just met was that I did not want to have children. On many occasions, it stopped the conversation cold. Other times, we became friends. And still others, we became lovers with the understanding that the situation was temporary. When people postpone having this discussion, it usually is a recipe for disaster. Denial sets in. "I'll just wait until we get married and then tell her I want children. If she refuses to get pregnant, I'll hide her birth control pills." "Once we're married, I'll forget to use my diaphragm." "When we tell our son-in-law that we will give them a big inheritance, they'll be pregnant in no time." Those tricks are doomed to end in failure. The relationship becomes strained. If the couple does stay together, the children get the brunt of the anger. Use *Nine Months* to learn a lesson in communication. Talk to your lover. Be clear about your desires and life goals. And if they don't meet the other person's expectations, don't trick the person into changing his or her most personal life decisions. To do so is to hate, not love.

NORMA RAE

(Twentieth Century-Fox, 1979), color, 113 minutes, PG-rated

HEALING THEMES:
Being exploited
Standing up for your rights
Gathering your courage and confronting your fears
Realizing that because you're a woman doesn't mean you're not equal
Emerging to be the person you can be

DIRECTOR: Martin Ritt; SCREENPLAY: Irving Ravetch, Harriet Frank Jr.; CAST: Sally Field (Norma Rae); Beau Bridges (Sonny); Ron Leibman (Reuben); Pat Hingle (Vernon); Barara Bauley (Leona); Gail Strickland (Bonnie Mae); Morgan Paul (Wayne); Noble Willingham (Leroy)

SYNOPSIS: Norma Rae spends her days working in a textile mill. She earns barely enough to make ends meet. Reuben, a New York labor organizer, comes to her town in an attempt to unionize the mill workers. He meets with a great deal of resistance until ill-educated Norma joins forces with him. One day, she is pushed too far and all her resolve rises to the surface. Reuben leaves town knowing that the new union is in the capable hands of Norma Rae.

CINEMATHERAPY: Every once in a while, we need to be reminded to stand up for what we believe. That's what Norma Rae does for us: She makes us realize how important our human rights are in this world. Can you recall a time when you thought you could not say how you felt or what you really wanted? Perhaps you grew up in a home where whatever your parents said was the law. There were no questions—you just did what you were told, and fairness had no place in the matter. Later on, when you went to school, you might have had a teacher or professor who treated you or your class poorly. You might have been afraid to say anything against such a dictator. And when you made your way into the workforce, you might have experienced a supervisor who abused his or her power. Perhaps *all* these things are happening to you right now. Well, you do not have to take it. You have every right in the world to demand to be treated with respect and dignity. "But if I do, I could lose my job." That may be true. It might get worse before it gets better. That and more happened to Norma Rae, and when she had endured enough abuse, when she was fed up with being exploited, she let the world know it was no longer acceptable. So have you had enough? Are you tired of taking it? You must take care of *you* before anyone else. Trust that you are a person who is good and deserves to be treated with fairness. *Norma Rae* gives us the chance for some wonderful healing. You will feel Norma's energy and be left with the courage to follow a similar path: Get out of that abusive relationship, and tell the proper authorities of any abuse of power at work or in the home. Let people know that you're someone who will not tolerate anything less than equal and just treatment. If you speak up loudly enough, people will listen. Gather your friends together, watch this movie, and let yourself feel the energy that comes from Norma's Rae's success.

NOW AND THEN

(New Line Cinema, 1995), color, 96 minutes, PG-13-rated

HEALING THEMES:
Reunions
Remembering old friends
The difference between boys and girls
Rumors
Learning about sex
One of life's great lessons
Coming of age

DIRECTOR: Lesli Linka Glatter; SCREENPLAY: I. Marlene King; CAST: Christina Ricci (young Roberta); Thora Birch (young Teeny); Gaby Hoffman (young Samantha); Ashleigh Aston Moore (young Chrissy); Demi Moore (Samantha); Melanie Griffith (Teeny); Rosie O'Donnell (Roberta); Rita Wilson (Chrissy); Willa Glen (Angela); Bonnie Hunt (Mrs. Dewitt); Janeane Garofalo (Wiladene); Lolita Davidovich (Mrs. Albertson); Cloris Leachman (Grandma Albertson); Hank Azaria (Bud); Devon Sawa (Scott); Travis Robertson (Roger)

SYNOPSIS: Four women revisit their childhood during a private reunion in the small town where they once lived. They recall their childhood adventures, curiosities about life and love, and the lessons they learned in the process of growing up. They come to realize that, more than anything, their reunion is about self-healing and fond memories.

CINEMATHERAPY: Where does the time go? Now, there's a familiar phrase. And so are these phrases: Where did all my friends go? Whatever happened to so and so? One of these days, I'm going to call . . . , and so on. For those of you who have fond memories of childhood adventures, *Now and Then* is going to resurrect those forgotten times. You will start recalling those moments when life was more than the next day's work schedule, rushing to a PTA meeting, or struggling to make next month's car payment. Do you remember when life was simple, sweet with the flavors that came from a neighborhood rich with all the life adventures you could ever want? Were you part of a group of friends who were inseparable? How about those secret conversations that you swore no one in the world would ever find out about? You will be both amused and embarrassed as this quartet of young girls explores every subject you have ever denied knowing anything about. Listen as two of the girls learn the answer to one of life's most important questions from a man who gave up on life a long time ago. We must all live in the joy of the present to have any type of positive future. To live in anger over memories of the past is barely survival. Life is more than that; it's about friends and memories of the good times and all that was and all that can be. Here is an idea for you: Take out your old school yearbook and spend time reminiscing. Make an effort to reach some of your old friends and have a special reunion. If there were hard feelings, let the past go. Start the healing process by talking things out. You will be surprised at how wonderful today can be with memories of times spent with old friends. Now, what was that friend's phone number?

THE ODD COUPLE

(Paramount, 1968), color, 105 minutes, not rated

HEALING THEMES:
Living with someone who is your opposite
Working on relationships
Accepting other people's quirks
Reaching out to a friend in need
Moving on in life

DIRECTOR: Gene Saks; SCREENPLAY: Neil Simon; CAST: Jack Lemmon (Felix); Walter Matthau (Oscar); John Fiedler (Vinnie); Herb Edelman (Murray); Monica Evans (Cecily); Carole Shelley (Gwendolyn); Larry Haines (Speed); Kris Adrian (Waitress)

SYNOPSIS: Felix is put out on the streets by his fed-up wife. He turns to his best friend, Oscar, for emotional support and a place to live. Felix and Oscar are exact opposites. Felix is immaculate, whereas Oscar is a complete slob. They fight every inch of the way to survive in the same shared space. It's a battle to the end, but friendship prevails.

CINEMATHERAPY: How many times have you thought, "Now there's an odd couple" or "They just don't seem like they belong together." Well, here's a movie that prompts those thoughts and more. True relationships are built from the inside out, not on superficial needs or attractions. *The Odd Couple* is a great opportunity for a couple of the opposite or same sex to explore some of the more concrete problems in their relationship. What makes this movie unique is we don't expect men to have these concerns. We tend to assume men simply get along no matter what the circumstances. This is not the case, I can assure you. Women are going to enjoy this movie because they will see that, in fact, men have the same problems and issues as women. Notice how Oscar and Felix interact with each other. Does their behavior remind you of anyone you know? The cap left off the toothpaste, the dirty ashtray, being late for dinner, not liking the dinner, and so on. How about the way the duo communicate? Listen to the constant sarcasm and the bickering. Is your relationship similar? Do you feel that no matter what you say, it's not going to be the right thing or it's going to prompt an argument? So, what's the solution to their roadblock? Boundary setting. There are no boundaries in this on-screen relationship, so the two men cross over the line again and again. Without boundaries, it's not possible to have a relationship of any kind, whether it be with a friend or a lover. This is a great movie to watch with your mate or as part of a group. What makes it so surprising is how universal this compatibility problem is for couples. When it's over, explore the problems you see in your own relationship and then discuss the solutions. You can have a lot of fun with this film, and you will mature from the experience.

ON A CLEAR DAY YOU CAN SEE FOREVER
(Paramount, 1970), color, 129 minutes, G-rated

HEALING THEMES:
Remembering past life experiences
Realizing you're not who you thought you were
Finding out what it might be like to be hypnotized
Just letting yourself go
Becoming involved with your therapist

DIRECTOR: Vincente Minnelli; **Screenwiter**: Alan Jay Lerner; **CAST**: Barbra Streisand (Daisy); Yves Montand (Dr. Marc Chabot); Bob Newhart (Dr. Mason Hume); Larry Blyden (Warren Pratt); Simon Oakland (Dr. Conrad Fuller); Jack Nicholson (Tad); John Richardson (John); Pamela Brown (Mrs. Fitzherbert); Irene Handl (Winnie); Mabel Albertson (Mrs. Hatch)

SYNOPSIS: Daisy is more than your average girl. She can read minds and grow flowers where others cannot. Daisy goes to a psychiatrist to get help in dealing with some personal problems. He hypnotizes her and finds out she's had past lives—*many* past lives. In the process of dealing with Daisy's past, doctor and patient fall in love.

CINEMATHERAPY: *On a Clear Day You Can See Forever* gives us the lighter side of the question "Is there such a thing as past lives?" Some people believe it's nonsense. They believe we're on this earth for a certain period and that's it, we're out of here. Others are convinced that we all have had past lives, we simply don't remember them—well . . . *most* of us don't recall them. On occasion, clients have told me they felt that they could remember a past-life experience. They felt awkward about telling me for fear that I would just dismiss such thoughts. And that's one of the points I would like to bring out about this movie: It's your choice to go to a counselor or therapist. You must feel comfortable talking about whatever you want without being intimidated by the person you're seeing. If you're uncomfortable, it is going to be difficult to do the work necessary to surmount the problems that brought you there. As you can see, Daisy allows herself to let go. Do you have a past-life experience that you're afraid to discuss? Are there times when you can remember places you've been, yet you know you have never been there? No one knows for sure if people have past lives, but just because the concept can't be proven doesn't mean it doesn't exist. Let yourself experience Daisy's past lives. As you can see, that's what Daisy needed to do to heal herself. Maybe you could do the same. On a very serious note, by *no* means is it okay for a therapist to have a relationship with his or her client. If that is your situation, report it to the local police or agency so that action can be taken on your behalf. It is not your fault that it happened, but if you continue in such a relationship knowing that it is wrong, you are responsible for the consequences.

ONCE UPON A TIME IN THE WEST

(Paramount, 1969), color, 165 minutes, PG-rated

HEALING THEMES:
Losing someone who is important to you
Trying to get even
Recovering if someone has hurt you
Being obsessed with vengeance
Learning to get on with your life

DIRECTOR: Sergio Leone; SCREENPLAY: Sergio Leone, Bernardo Bertolucci, Dario Argento; CAST: Henry Fonda (Frank); Claudia Cardinale (Jill); Jason Robards (Cheyenne); Charles Bronson ("Harmonica"); Frank Wolff (Brett); Gabriele Ferzetti (Morton); Keenan Wynn (sheriff); Paolo Stoppa (Sam); Lionel Stander (barman); Jack Elam (Knuckles); Woody Strode (Stony)

SYNOPSIS: A railroad is scheduled to go through a small town. Greed takes over and hired guns are brought in to get the land away from someone who is about to profit from the railroad expansion. A stranger throws a monkey wrench in the works when he goes after the hired killers. One by one, the stranger gets rid of the killers. They find out too late that his motive is revenge.

CINEMATHERAPY: Many people have asked me, "Gary, if you're going to include horror movies, futuristic thrillers, and fantasy films, why are you leaving out westerns?" I used to think that westerns were movies that people watched just for all the "shoot 'em-up" action. When I searched for westerns that offered special messages, I came up with *Once Upon a Time in the West* and *The Man Who Shot Liberty Valance*. Now, I can tell you right now that you're going to be uneasy with this movie. It was *made* to make you feel uncomfortable. If you've ever wanted to take revenge, you will experience those feelings through this most unusual reflection of your own inner self. Have there been times in your life when someone has done something to you that you have found unforgivable? Maybe they cheated on you in your relationship or borrowed something from you and never returned it. Perhaps a friend or lover betrayed you behind your back by saying something that wasn't true. "I'm going after you with such a vengeance, you'll never know what hit you." I've been there myself, and the truth is that vengeance destroys lives—not only the life you are seeking revenge against but your own life as well. It takes so much energy and time to seek revenge that it is like a drug: It becomes an obsession that rules your every waking moment. And that's the healing I want you to see in this movie. Watch the lost lives, especially the life of the man seeking revenge. You will grow to understand how he lost his own childhood because of his obsession. Learn to let go, live and let live, and go on with your own life. Keep yourself free of the obsession of getting even. Tell yourself that such concerns are not worth your time and go on with your life. From those thoughts you will experience freedom and self-healing. *Warning!* I do not include this movie to suggest that you use a gun or violence of any type to resolve a conflict or dispute.

THE OTHER SIDE OF THE MOUNTAIN

(Universal, 1975), color, 102 minutes, PG-rated

HEALING THEMES:
Having the courage to go on with life
Persevering when fate has dealt you a low blow
Supporting someone through a difficult time
Gathering your courage to go forward
Living with who you are
Rediscovering the meaning of life

DIRECTOR: Larry Peerce; SCREENPLAY: David Seltzer; CAST: Marilyn Hassett (Jill); Beau Bridges (Dick); Dabney Coleman (Dave); John David Garfield (CRC patient); Griffin Dunne (Herbie); William Rowick (Dr. Pittman);

Dori Brenner (Cookie); Belinda J. Montgomery (Audra-Jo); Nan Maitin (June); William Bryant (Bill)

SYNOPSIS: Jill Kinmont is a young woman on her way to the Olympics. She is a very talented skier who practices her sport on a daily basis. While on a ski outing she has an accident that leaves her paralyzed. Jill gives up on life until a man comes along who helps her pull herself together. She learns there is more to life than a pair of skis.

CINEMATHERAPY: I cannot imagine what it would be like to be confined to a wheelchair, or worse, a bed. And I can't conceive of the amount of courage it would take to make it through each day with the knowledge that there was a time when I was free of the physical or psychological bonds that were now holding me hostage. People like Jill Kinmont confront me with their own courage and remind me of how important it is to go on with life and take action in the face of adversity. I have included *The Other Side of the Mountain* because it gives us such a tremendous inspirational message: Never give up! Maybe you're someone who has been in a debilitating accident or you're a member of a family in which someone suffers from a chronic disease. Maybe you have had problems in school and you're feeling as if you want to give up and drop out. This movie teaches us that there is hope on the other side of adversity. Sometimes it takes the right person to get you to take action. Notice how Jill's friend realizes that she must live life for herself if she is going to make it. Do you find yourself constantly stepping into the role of rescuing people because you think they can't make it on their own? You may be doing it in ways that are so subtle that even you don't know you're doing it. We must not take the journey for people, but we can help them decide which path they should take. And like Jill, we can be an inspiration for those who are struggling to get on that path. After watching this film, you will feel as if anything can be accomplished in life if you simply try hard enough. Tell yourself, "If she can do it, so can I." You can do anything you want. You must not give up. If you know someone like Jill who has given up, show them this movie. It may be just the healing message they've needed to get on constructively with their lives. Reach out and lend a hand to someone who could use your support. There's healing there also. By the way, there is a follow-up to this movie, *The Other Side of the Mountain, Part II.* You certainly can't hurt your healing process by watching that one, too.

OUT ON A LIMB

(ABC-TV, 1987), color, 160 minutes, PG-rated

HEALING THEMES:
Looking for the meaning of life
Being caught up in an affair

Seeking an answer from a higher power
Trying to come to terms with who and what you are
Sharing your knowledge with the world

DIRECTOR: Robert Butler; TELEPLAY: Colin Higgins, Shirley MacLaine; CAST: Shirley MacLaine (Shirley); Charles Dance (Gerry); John Heard (David); Anne Jackson (Bella); Jerry Orbach (Mort); Fabra Drake (bookshop owner); Kathryn Skatula (Katerina)

SYNOPSIS: Shirley is questioning what life is about. She goes on a spiritual journey seeking answers to some of life's questions. On her quest, she meets a man whose mission is to give awareness to her so she can pass on that knowledge to the world.

CINEMATHERAPY: I find that right around forty years of age many people get stuck in a midlife crisis. They start questioning the reason they're on this earth. "What's it all for? Why am I working so hard?" "I don't know what life is all about. You grow up, have children, and die. What for?" Do any of these thoughts sound familiar to you? Do you find yourself wondering why you're here and what your purpose in life is? *Out on a Limb* invites all of us to hear and see Shirley's quest for life's meaning. What is your philosophy of life? What do you believe in? Do you feel you are spiritually grounded? Do you think everything in life happens just the way it should, or do you feel you have control over what happens in your life? Maybe you think there is a purpose for everything in life and you have no say in the process. *Out on a Limb* is a look at one person's vision. I would like to offer one caution about this film: Don't get so lost in the idea of looking for the meaning of life that you overlook the story line. Part of my purpose in having you watch these healing stories is to move you out of denial in the personal areas of your life. Shirley MacLaine is having an affair with a married man. He had two children and a wife that he was cheating on and at the same time trying to represent honesty and truth as a member of his government. How did you feel about that? Shirley is seeking the meaning of life while she is having this affair. Does that seem a little strange to you? The bottom line is that the relationship is built on a lie. Healthy relationships are built on truth. So although *Out on a Limb* takes you on a wonderful healing journey, you should not get caught up in the idea that it is all a healthy experience. Try inviting friends over and watching this movie. Open up the story for discussion and take the time to learn a little more about one another.

THE OUTSIDERS

(Warner Bros, 1983), color, 104 minutes, PG-rated

HEALING THEMES:
Remembering childhood fears
Trying to act tough
Hanging around with the wrong crowd
Getting your life back on track
Staying centered when others pass judgment on you

DIRECTOR: Francis Ford Coppola; **SCREENPLAY**: Kathleen Rowell; **CAST**: Matt Dillon (Dallas); Ralph Macchio (Johnny); Thomas Howell (Ponyboy); Patrick Swayze (Darrel); Rob Lowe (Sodapop); Diane Lane (Cherry); Emilio Estevez (Two-Bit); Tom Cruise (Steve); Leif Garrett (Bob); Tom Waits (Buck); Darren Dalton (Randy); Sofia Coppola (Bit)

SYNOPSIS: It's the mid-1960s. Most teenagers are just trying to make it to the next stage in their lives. But there's a group of boys who have no interest in conforming to the standards of the community—or society, for that matter. They are a tough bunch, even with one another. Some of them are pushed over the edge when life gets too difficult, and, in the process, they learn a valuable lesson.

CINEMATHERAPY: I have included several movies in this book that deal with peer bonding. Growing up, we all had a peer group, friends that we were close to. We did everything with them: talked about our families, complained about doing homework, learned about sex, and so on. Most of us took a pretty safe path with our friends, but some got caught up with the wrong group. *The Outsiders* focuses on a group of kids who push things too far. I didn't like these teenagers very much. They were always causing problems and would fight just to fight. I would be scared to be around them. What kinds of memories does this on-camera group bring up for you? Did you do what you could to avoid such people? Did you walk on the other side of the street? Not go to places where you thought they might be? Or simply stay home out of fear of running into them? It made me angry that they couldn't be controlled. What feelings do you have as you watch this bunch? Listen closely to Ponyboy, the youth whose perspective this story comes from. Try and focus on how he is making changes in his own life. I have pondered problems related to reaching adolescents who are struggling to find themselves. Why is it that we cannot simply tell them the answer? Why must they have to learn it for themselves? Why does each generation refuse to listen to the previous one? Try showing this movie to your children before they get themselves involved with the wrong crowd. Get together with other parents and show this film to your children. Use it to open up the doors of communication between generations. Point out that the adolescents in this movie are actually afraid of the future—they just work hard at covering up their fears by resorting to violence. When you use this approach, you give your children the chance to heal from their fears—and you may begin to examine some of your own fears that have lingered since childhood.

THE PIED PIPER OF HAMELIN

(NBC-TV, 1957), color, 87 minutes, PG-rated

HEALING THEMES:
Recovering when someone backs out of a deal
Making people follow through with their agreement
Remembering the innocence of your childhood
Realizing you may be sending the wrong message to your children

DIRECTOR: Bretaigne Windust; **TELEPLAY:** Hal Stanley and Irving Taylor; **CAST:** Van Johnson (the Pied Piper); Claude Rains (mayor of Hamelin); Jim Backus (king's emissary); Kay Starr (John's mother); Lori Nelson (Maria)

SYNOPSIS: Hamelin is overrun with rats—lots and lots of rats. The town fathers explore every option to get rid of the rats. When all else fails, they employ the Pied Piper. After he gets rid of the rats, the town leaders renege on their agreement. The Pied Piper retaliates by taking all the children to his special hideout. Hamelin has no choice but to pay up.

CINEMATHERAPY: On occasion, I like to examine a movie that is based on a fairy tale or fantasy. Like *The Wizard of Oz* and *Alice in Wonderland, The Pied Piper of Hamelin* offers us a healing story about childhood. There was a time when I was young when I felt I could trust everyone. If someone said they would do something, I believed them. If they borrowed money from me, I trusted they would pay me back. If they said they would phone, I trusted that they would. However, over timeI learned not to trust as much as I did. I gave up believing that people would do what they said they would do. But when did that trust vanish? When did it happen to you? Was it when your parents divorced, or they promised they wouldn't argue, or . . . ? While I was doing my thinking on this movie, I realized how many people have difficulty trusting others. Have you ever made a deal with someone, only to learn you were lied to? Maybe you've been in a relationship with someone who cheated you in one way or another. *The Pied Piper of Hamelin* is just one way of looking at those issues. And what about revenge? Do you think the Pied Piper was taking revenge, or was he protecting the children from the corruption in their town? I think he was trying to let us know that we must live the messages we are trying to teach our children. How can we tell our children not to smoke while we're smoking? How do we teach our children to be honest and at the same time involve them in our "white lies"—like telling them to tell the person who's calling you on the phone that you're not in? There are so many things we have to teach our children, and the Pied Piper forces us to be honest. If it has been years since you've seen this movie, try watching it again. I think you'll find that it's rich in its healing powers. Gather the whole family together. Talk about the film and what it means, and you will grow in the process. Who knows, maybe you will learn to charm the chaos, lying, and negativity right out of your own lives.

PUMP UP THE VOLUME

(New Line Cinema, 1990), color, 100 minutes, R-rated

HEALING THEMES:
Living a double life
Going against the system
Expressing yourself
Growing up
Realizing you're not alone

DIRECTOR: Allan Moyle; **SCREENPLAY**: Allan Moyle; **CAST**: Christian Slater (Mark); Ellen Greene (Jan); Annie Ross (Loretta Cresswood); Samantha Mathis (Nora); Scott Paulin (Brian); Cheryl Pollak (Paige); Mimi Kennedy (Marta); Seth Green (Joey); Ahmet Zappa (Jamie); Betty Morrissette (Mazz)

SYNOPSIS: When a young high school student uses a radio frequency to express his personal thoughts and feelings, the townspeople get upset. No one knows who the mystery broadcaster is, and that's exactly how he wants it. When his teenage following gets too big, the local authorities track him down, but not before he makes a major impact on all his listeners.

CINEMATHERAPY: When I saw this movie, my junior high and high school years came rushing back to me. That was me up there on the screen. I could relate to this "radio flyer." I knew exactly how he felt. There was the "me" that I showed to my family and classmates, and then there was the real "me"—the part I kept hidden away. Certainly no one would accept the way I thought, and for sure no one felt the way I did. Or did they? Maybe everyone had secrets that they kept from the world? Did you lead a double life in school? Was there a diary that held your deepest, most intimate thoughts? Were you the good boy who sat quietly in his seat during the day but was dying inside, working to keep who you really were secret from everyone else? Maybe you were the sweet girl who sat in the front row and kept to herself. No one knew the true you—what you really felt or thought. Did you ever want to just break free from the pretense of what people thought you were supposed to be like and let everyone see the real you? *Pump Up the Volume* sets all of us free through the thoughts and feelings of this introverted character named Mark.

What parts of him were or are in you? Do you work to keep up a front? Are you one self at night and another on the weekends? There is something very healing about seeing what it's like to break free of everyone's preconceived ideas of who you are and how they think you should act. After you watch this film, try letting yourself go and being the person you've kept locked up inside for too many years. Go skydiving, learn to tango, or go to that nude beach you've always wanted to visit. Set the real you free and feel your energy, your life, spring to the surface. Give it a try—you'll love it!

RAGTIME

(Paramount, 1981), color, 156 minutes, PG-rated

HEALING THEMES:
Finding out that you never know where life will lead you
Dealing with bigotry and prejudice
Following your dreams
Breaking away from a controlling parent
Standing up for what you believe in
Being confronted by corruption
Realizing that life is completely unpredictable

DIRECTOR: Milos Forman; SCREENPLAY: Michael Weller; CAST: James Cagney (Police Commissioner Waldo); Brad Dourif (younger brother); Moses Gunn (Booker); Elizabeth McGovern (Evelyn); Kenneth McMillian (Willie); Pat O'Brien (Delmas); James Olson (father); Mandy Patinkin (Tateh); Howard E. Rollins Jr. (Coalhouse Walker Jr.); Mary Steenburgen (mother); Debbie Allen (Sarah); Donald O'Connor (Evelyn's dance teacher); Jeff Dmunn (Houdini); Norman Mailer (Stanford)

SYNOPSIS: The year is 1906. Three groups of people weave in and out of one another's lives. Tateh works very hard to make it in America. Booker T. Washington takes responsibility for his newborn child while being subjected to acts of prejudice and racism. And a family works to help their children and housekeeper stay out of harm's way. Some make it and some don't, and the multistory tale ends with a murder, a separation, and a successful moviemaking career.

CINEMATHERAPY: *Ragtime* offers us healing messages in a very unconventional way. In some ways, it is like *Tales of Manhattan*. In both cases, the healing comes from getting the big picture: Life is incredibly unpredictable. That's it in a nutshell. Now, I know you've heard that message before. You got it when you were growing up, and from time to time you came to that realization yourself. However, something happens when we see this wisdom being played out right in front of our faces. We have an opportunity to see truth in action as the lives of all these characters parade before our eyes. There is no way Tateh could have known he was going to end up becoming a movie producer. How could Booker T. have realized he was going to have to defend his integrity and honor to the point of his death? And what of the wife and mother? She never knew she had the strength to find her independence. Do you see the point? Can you grasp that you must keep moving forward and continue to put out the effort even though you're not sure where life will lead you? You owe it to yourself to reach for the brass ring no matter what happens in the process. You owe it to yourself to look for the proverbial pot of gold at the end of the rainbow in spite of any adversity. If we can hold on to the rich colors that glow all around us, we have a chance to become our own dream. However, if we give up and turn our backs on our potential for success, we have no chance at all. So watch the healing messages and reach out for everything you want in life. There are no promises, but one thing is for sure: If you don't try, you can never get it.

RAPE OF LOVE

(L'Amour Viole, French, 1977), color, 117 minutes, not rated

HEALING THEMES:
Issues you face if you've ever been molested
Trying to recover from being raped
Persevering when you feel like your life is falling apart
Reaching out to those who need your support
Learning how to put the pieces back together

DIRECTOR: Yannick Bellon; SCREENPLAY: Yannich Bellon; CAST: Nathalie Nell (Nicole); Alain Foures (Jacques); Michele Simonnet (Catherine); Pierre Arditi (Julien); Daniel Anteuil (Daniel); Bernard Granger (Patrick)

SYNOPSIS: Nicole is a nurse. She enjoys life and thrives on helping others. She is raped by four drunken men. The ordeal presses Nicole to the limits of her emotional endurance. She continues to experience emotional chaos from her traumatizing ordeal.

CINEMATHERAPY: One of the most difficult issues I deal with as a therapist is molestation of any kind. Those who have been molested carry around the fear, anger, and guilt that comes from being forced to have sex. It's important to know that healing can and does happen, but not without taking the steps to move toward self-recovery. I would like you to focus not only on Nicole but also on her perpetrators. If there is any question in your mind that molestation—rape in this case—is anything but an act of violence, I am sure this story will remove that doubt. Perhaps you're someone who has molested another person. What emotions are brought up for you? Do you find you have difficulty facing up to your violent act? What things have you done in your life to change? You also have some recovering to do. Make no mistake, your recovery is just as difficult, just as painful, as the recovery your victim must go through. For the rest of you: What did you feel when Nicole was being raped? Did you want to kill the rapists? I know I wanted to lash out at them. What motivates people to do such a thing to another human being? I felt fear, rage, and intimidation for Nicole—and I felt helpless. As you watch this movie, notice what happens to the nurse's life. If you have experienced something similar, get support. Don't let your emotions consume you. Keep in mind that the rapist is a sick person, and by allowing your life to be dramatically changed by this act of violence, you are paying homage to his sickness. That's exactly what he wants you to do. Is that what you want to give him? Begin healing today from this unconscionable act. Try some of the other movies I have written about to help you get in touch with this important issue. (By the way, this movie is in French. Please don't let the subtitles stand in the way of your experiencing its healing power.)

REEFER MADNESS

(Road Show Attractions, 1938), B & W, 67 minutes, not rated

HEALING THEMES:
Losing control
Living with drugs
Not seeing things for what they really are
Putting yourself in danger

DIRECTOR: Louis Gasnier; **Sceenplay:** Paul Franklin, Arthur Hoerl; **CAST:** Dorothy Short (Mary); Kenneth Craig (Bill); Lillian Miles (Blanche); Dave O'Brien (Ralph); Carleton Young (Bill); Thelma White (Mae); Josef Forte (Dr. Carroll)

SYNOPSIS: They're wild. They're young. They're over the edge. They meet whenever they can to smoke marijuana and get crazy. Before they smoke, they are just like your next-door neighbor. However, under the influence of marijuana, they're unmanageable and dangerous. Things go from bad to worse as this group gets completely out of hand.

CINEMATHERAPY: Whatever it takes to get the message, right? Yes, I know this is a pretty old movie. And yes, I know you can watch other movies and get the same message: Don't use drugs. But sometimes it helps to get the healing message from different directions. Well, look out! Here comes one now. *Reefer Madness* has become a cult classic. Usually people watch it for the sole purpose of having a few laughs. I didn't find it to be very funny, myself. I can remember attending a party some years ago where *Reefer Madness* was part of the entertainment. To really get in the spirit of things, most of the group was getting high at the same time. Have you ever gone to a driver's education class and used drugs before or after class? Have you ever exercised, then gone to a fast-food drive-thru on the way home? Addictions come in many forms. *Reefer Madness* may be an old movie and you may even get a laugh or two from it, but the bottom line is that this group is pretty sick. Do you know someone who can't stop using marijuana? Maybe you have told yourself a hundred times that you were going to quit and you can't seem to stop. Do you think you have a problem? "No," you say. "I can quit anytime I want—I just don't want to." One of my favorite sayings comes from Mark Twain. Of smoking he said: "I can quit anytime I want. Why, I've done it hundreds of times." Any bells going off? What are you avoiding in your life? Do you use drugs to get away from reality and stew in a fog of fantasy? I once saw a family in my office, three generations of women, all of whom were addicted to marijuana. They wanted to stop. They wanted to see one another living a better, sharper life. What courage and inner strength that took. You or someone you know can find that same inner strength. The healing is right in front of you. Watch *Reefer Madness* and the other movies about addiction that I have recommended. Begin the healing process today. There are support groups, therapists, counselors, and church organizations to help you through the gray to a clear white light of life.

THE RESTLESS YEARS

(Universal-International, 1958), color, 86 minutes, PG-rated

HEALING THEMES:
Having an illegitimate child
Avoiding your past
Trying to help your parents with their problems
Keeping your self-respect when people around you treat you mean
Coping if a bad marriage is all you have
Growing out of the pain of not knowing one of your parents

DIRECTOR: Helmut Kautner; **SCREENPLAY:** Edward Anhalt; **CAST:** John Saxon (Will); Sandra Dee (Melinda); Teresa Wright (Elizabeth); James Whitmore (Ed); Luana Patten (Polly); Margaret Lindsay (Dorothy); Virginia Grey (Miss Robson); Jody McCrea (Bruce); Alan Baxter (Alex); Hayden Rorke (Mr. Booth); Dorothy Green (Laura)

SYNOPSIS: Melinda is a young girl trying to grow up in Libertyville, a small town in Middle America. Her mother is sick with grief over a love she never really had and the fact that her daugher is illegitimate. Will, a newcomer to town, struggles to have a relationship with Melinda. In spite of their many trials and tribulations, true love wins out.

CINEMATHERAPY: I am amazed at the way some of the older movies can cut to the chase as they portray one of a wide range of issues. Like *Come Back, Little Sheba* and *Peyton Place*, *The Restless Years* confronts us with problems dealing with friends and families. There is so much going on in this movie, you may not get the message. Did you notice the way Elizabeth, Melinda's mother, dressed Melinda? She wants to make sure that what happened to her doesn't happen to Melinda, so she attempts to keep her a perpetual little girl. Elizabeth grows tired of this "dirty, little, gossipy town" that she feels has ruined her life. Have you ever been affected by other people's gossip? Maybe you were one of those who were a party to the gossiping? I felt a great deal of pain for Elizabeth. She was trapped in memories that held her life back. And what about Will's family? Did one of your parents constantly berate the other, always making the other feel like a failure? Did they pressure you to be something or somebody you were not? I had friends in school who were constantly trying to meet the tough standards that their parents set for them. You will also notice that teenage Melinda sacrifices her life for her mother. Can you see the codependency? She is so concerned about her mom's feelings that she has no time for her own. Don't turn your back on this film just because of its vintage. Invite friends over and give it a try. Find yourself in one of the characters and work to recall some of your earlier-life experiences. So much healing comes from turning those old memories on and working through the past. You will recall some old secrets and the feelings tied to them. You're going to grow from viewing this movie, of that you can be sure.

THE RIGHT TO REMAIN SILENT

(Chanticleer Films, 1996), color, 97 minutes, not rated

HEALING THEMES:
Taking a look at life
AIDS
Mercy killing
Violence
Stealing

DIRECTOR: Hubert C. de la Bouillerie; SCREENPLAY: Brent Briscoe and Mark Fauser; CAST: Lea Thompson (Christine); Amanda Plummer (Paulina); Christopher Lloyd (Johnny); Judge Reinhold (Buford); Carl Reiner (Norman); LL Cool J (Charles); Patrick Dempsey (Tom); Penelope Branning (Annie); Collen Camp (Mrs. Buford Lowry); Wand-Lee Evans (Tom); Mary Pat Gleason (Doris); Bajorn Johnson (KKK member); Larry Joshua (Sims); Robert Loggia (Lt. Mike Brosloe); Geoffrey Rivas (Pedro); Laura San Giacomo (Nicole); Fisher Stevens (Dale); Jack Shearer (Dr. Koal)

SYNOPSIS: It's just another night at the police station, and a rookie cop gets her indoctrination into the field of law enforcement. Before the evening is through, she sees everything from murder and robbery to cross-dressers and vagrancy—with no end in sight.

CINEMATHERAPY: I think philosophy is a slippery concept. What I believe and what you believe may be the same, but from where do our beliefs come. So when I find a movie like *The Right to Remain Silent,* I enjoy giving you the opportunity to check and test your beliefs. Don't worry, this is not one of those deep, difficult-to-follow movies. On the contrary, it will take you on a bit of a journey, perhaps not unlike your own. And while on this trek, you are going to meet people just like yourself—everyday people dealing with common problems. As you watch this movie, investigate your own feelings. What would you do if someone you were in love with was dying a painful death and wanted to be put out of their misery? Would you help them die? What if you had to make the decision to pull the plug? What a difficult philosophical dilemma this problem presents. What of the teacher who was fired because she had AIDS? Could you understand her rage? Would you allow your child to go to school and be taught by someone who has AIDS? Would you work with someone who has AIDS? Even though we know that AIDS is not transmitted through casual contact, some people feel that those who are HIV positive should be treated with little or no regard for human rights. Do you know someone who has a gender-identity problem—is not sure whether he or she is male or female? Should that person be treated differently simply because his or her lifestyle is different than most people's? Should we live in fear of those who have a way of life different from our own? Try watching this movie with friends. Afterward, discuss how your individial beliefs and philosophies were affected by this film. You will be amazed at the growth that occurs when you open the doors of philosophical thought.

THE ROSE

(Twentieth, 1979), color, 134 minutes, R-rated

HEALING THEMES:
Trying to fill the emptiness inside you
Making it all the way to the top
Learning that fame and fortune isn't all it is cracked up to be
Being used by your friends
Alcoholism
Losing sight of what is really important
Trying to find love inside sexual relationships

DIRECTOR: Mark Rydell; **SCREENPLAY:** William Kerby, Bo Goldman; **CAST:** Bette Midler (Rose); Alan Bates (Rudge); Frederic Forrest (Dyer); Harry Dean Stanton (Billy); Barry Primus (Dennis); David Keith (Mal); Sandra McCabe (Sarah); Doris Roberts (Rose's mother); Sandy Ward (Rose's father); Michael Greer (emcee)

SYNOPSIS: Rock singer Rose has really made it. She's popular with her fans, and her concerts are always sold out. However, there is a problem: Rose doesn't like herself very much. She has trouble making it through performances because she spends most of her time drinking and drugging herself into oblivion. Her self-abusive lifestyle catches up with her. She fatally overdoses on drugs and alcohol.

CINEMATHERAPY: How many times have you heard "Money and fame won't bring you happiness" or "Money can't buy you love"? When I was growing up, I certainly didn't accept that idea, not for one minute. Why, there were people living up on the hill in big houses driving fancy cars, the names of which I could not pronounce. The last thing I wanted to believe was that money couldn't bring me happiness. Whoever came up with that phrase is someone who must have had a lot of money and learned that lesson first-hand. And when that lesson is learned, we experience one more level of healing—the healing that comes from knowing you must feel your wealth from inside or you can never enjoy love or material wealth. Rose teaches us that lesson when she makes a desperate attempt to find the love that has always eluded her. Watch as she escapes the routine of her concerts and returns to the bar scene on the journey back to her roots. Try to feel her pain as she searches for some relief to her loneliness. Do you ever feel like returning to those happier, simpler times when money and power were not the focus of your life? Notice how she uses alcohol to dull her feelings. Is this what you do in your life? Do you drink to hide from your emotions? What is it you're really looking for? Do you want a relationship? Would you like people to care for you simply because of who you are inside, not what you can give them? Take a few moments after watching this movie to ask yourself if you are on a crash course with disaster. Get involved in support groups that can help you get back on track. Start working through the issues that are eating away at your sense of self. Taking some time for a journey back to your old high school, your first job, or the place where you used to play games as a child may bring back old memories. It will reenergize and help you get in touch with the person who's screaming to get out. If you take all of these steps, you won't have to worry about crashing the way Rose did. There's no need to feel the pain one more day. Start to plan your healing journey *today*!

RUSH

(MGM, 1991), color, 120 minutes, R-rated

HEALING THEMES:

Being blindsided
Doing the very thing you were against doing
Realizing that every action has its consequences
Being betrayed by those whom you trust
Getting caught up in the world of drugs
Refusing to see what you are doing to yourself

DIRECTOR: Lili Fini Zanuck; SCREENPLAY: Pete Dexter; CAST: Jason Patric (Jim); Jennifer Jason Leigh (Kristen); Sam Elliott (Larry); Max Perlich (Walker); Gregg Allman (Gaines); William Sadler (Monroe); Tony Frank (Nettle)

SYNOPSIS: Kristen Cates is a cop fresh out of the police academy. She is teamed up with Jim Raynor, a seasoned law enforcer who knows the ropes. In the process of doing their job undercover, Jim becomes drug addicted. Kristen falls in love with him and slips into the addiction herself. As they attempt to cope with what is happening, they continue to put their lives at risk for their agency, which has only one agenda: Get the bad guys at any cost. They succeed, but Jim dies in the line of duty.

CINEMATHERAPY: It's a little overwhelming knowing how many people out there are dealing with the pain that comes from being addicted. It doesn't matter whether the addiction is sex, smoking, drugs, gambling, or working— each addiction is based in pain. However, sometimes even I forget that no one—absolutely no one—is immune from the disease of addiction. It can happen to the big-time lawyer, the famous surgeon, or the couple next door. It can even happen to those who make their living by trying to stop other people from getting the latest drug of choice. Such is the case with Kristen and Jim. I'd like you to watch *Rush* and get the message loud and clear: It can happen to anyone, including you. If family members of those who are hooked on drugs will take the time to watch this movie, they will see that the disease of addiction does not discriminate: man or woman, young or old. Each and every one of us needs to know that we can heal from the pain and emptiness that may cause and perpetuate the addiction. Stay with Kristen and Jim's slide into their disease. Don't be fooled by the idea that they get hooked in the line of duty. This is nonsense. They get hooked because they find an answer to dealing with their own emotional pain. Do you know someone who has lots of excuses for why he or she is hooked? Maybe you're having trouble taking responsibility for your actions. I have no doubt it is difficult, but now it's time to do something about it. It's time to move on with your life. And that's the big message hidden inside of *Rush*: Get in touch with how you got started, take responsibility for what you're doing to your life, and take charge of putting a stop to your self-destructive behavior. You can do it. You can take that first healing step and admit you need help. Call any of the support groups available in your area, like Alcoholics Anonymous or Narcotics Anonymous. Make contact with counselors and therapists who are trained to see you to the other side of your addiction. Rent movies like *Rush, The Boost, Drug Store Cowboy,* and *Sid and Nancy,* and follow the path out of denial to a safer place on the other side of the disease we call addiction.

SAFE PASSAGE

(New Line Cinema, 1994), color, 98 minutes, PG-13-rated

HEALING THEMES:
Looking at family issues
Living in chaos
Surviving a crisis
Weakened family bonds
Living with your memories
Getting a second chance at having a healthy family

DIRECTOR: Robert Allan Ackerman; **SCREENPLAY:** Deena Goldstone; **CAST:** Susan Sarandon (Maggie); Sam Shepard (Patrick); Robert Sean Leonard (Alfred); Nick Stahl (Simon); Philip Basco (Mort); Jason London (Gideon); Sean Astin (Izzy); Philip Arthur Ross (Merle); Steven Robert Ross (Darren); Marcia Gay Harden (Cynthia)

SYNOPSIS: Patrick and Maggie are separated. She lives with her children, "all the boys," and he lives in his workshop. The dysfunctional family falls into a deeper crisis when they learn that one of them may have been killed in a bombing. The crisis opens the doors to communication and brings back old, buried memories.

CINEMATHERAPY: Whenever I come across a movie that focuses on family life, I try to make sure I work it into my cinematherapy discussions. *Safe Passage* is the soft side of *Curse of the Starving Class,* so hold on to yourself when you watch this movie. What memories do you have of growing up with your family? When you look back, do you see your childhood and adolescent years as being hectic and unpredictable? Was there always chaos in the family, and did you feel that a crisis would arise at any moment? Maybe one of your parents was always coming or going. As you watch *Safe Passage,* some old feelings are going to crop up, some of which you may not be able to identify. You might find yourself becoming nervous and upset. You may experience physical pain. Or you might have trouble concentrating on staying in the moment. Do any of the feelings that you experience remind you of what you felt when you were living with your family? Which family member were you? The perfect kid who did everything right? The one who gave up and decided not to try? Maybe you were the one who just blended into the background—no one knew if you were there or if you were missing. Perhaps you can relate to the parents. Watch as Maggie finally lets go of what's been bothering her, only to find out that her husband Patrick never even had a clue. So where's the healing? It occurs when we emerge from denial and embrace self-awareness. We confront our past so we can live in the moment and enjoy our future. Like Patrick, there is no need to be blind to what's going on around you. Try inviting the whole family to watch this movie. Open the doors to healthy communication and start taking more steps to be the family you always wanted. By watching this film, you've already taken the first step to safer passages.

THE SEARCH FOR SIGNS OF INTELLIGENT LIFE IN THE UNIVERSE

(Orion Classics, 1991), color, 120 minutes, PG-13-rated

HEALING THEMES:
Taking a look at yourself
Making a journey through your past
Asking some of life's big questions
Being confronted with who you are in the world
Accepting your imperfections

DIRECTOR: John Bailey; **SCREENPLAY**: Jane Wagner; **CAST**: Lily Tomlin (all charaters)

SYNOPSIS: Trudy is not just your average street person. She is a woman who is in touch with life and with life-forms outside of our universe. She shares her worldly experience and philosophy. Trudy takes us on a journey through her mind to help us understand who she is and, more important, who we all are in this big world.

CINEMATHERAPY: This is a rare opportunity to get in touch with yourself and your own life experience. Don't be deceived by Trudy's appearance, because she is all of us. She is everything we've thought, think, and believe. She is a reflection of every color that we enjoy or hate on our journey through life. Listen carefully to her words. Doesn't her philosophy cut to the bare truth about life? She is taking each of us on a trip through life and forcing us to see things as they really are: "Okay, let's try it one more time. This is soup and this is art. Got it?" Listen to the characters and feel yourself getting in touch with one or more of them. Look at the different directions we have all taken in our lives. Who are you? The housewife? The businesswoman? The streetwalker? The tough guy? Notice how things that were once important seem to go by the wayside. Can you remember being part of a group that you once felt strongly about? What happened to those times? Where are all those people with whom you spent your life? How many times have you been in denial about life, only to be confronted by someone or a truth that you've worked hard to avoid? Make no mistake about Trudy: She may have found an answer to getting through life that you may never have thought about. She may have found signs of life that you have been overlooking. At the very least, she will confront you with your own life and ask you to examine your motives—your real reason for being on this planet. This is a great movie to watch with friends. You may find yourself looking into corners of your life that otherwise you would have left untouched.

SHATTERED DREAMS

(CBS-TV, 1990), 100 minutes, PG-rated

HEALING THEMES:
Meeting that special someone
Having an abusive spouse
Realizing you have no control over your anger
Feeling as if you deserve the violence
Violence that reaches the whole family
Refusing to see what is really happening to you
Taking charge of your own life

DIRECTOR: Robert Iscove; TELEPLAY: David Hill; CAST: Lindsay Wagner (Charlotte); Michael Nouri (John); Georgeann Johnson (Helen); James Karen (Charles); Ken Jenkins (Hal); Irene Miracle (Elaine); Stan Ivar (Bryan); Bryan Clark (Martin); Tom Dahlgren (Judge McAuliffe); Jay Ferguson (fifth Luke); Patricia Heaton (second Dotte); Marilyn Rockafellow (Ellen)

SYNOPSIS: When Charlotte marries John, she feels she has found the man of her dreams. Over the twenty years of her marriage, Charlotte struggles with John's abusive nature and questions if she and the children deserve his unwarranted attacks. Eventually she gathers the courage to leave him and reaches out to help others.

CINEMATHERAPY: As long as I have been working with people and dealing with a wide range of emotional issues, I am still baffled by why people remain in abusive relationships. Maybe that's because I grew up in a home that closely mirrors the abuse portrayed in movies such as *Shattered Dreams*. And when I get in touch with my own feelings, I realize how difficult it is to come out of denial, see things as they really are, and take steps to lead a healthy, self-nurturing life. So if you or someone you know is living in an abusive relationship, you're going to be stunned by the behavior of this on-camera family. Notice some of John's characteristics. Everything has to be his way. He's controlling, moody, and unpredictable. Being with him is like being on a roller coaster: You never know what's going to happen next . Can you see how John needs to put Charlotte down so he can feel better about himself? Does this remind you of your own relationship? As you watch the movie, do you find yourself becoming angry, hurt, embarrassed? How about just pure fear—the fear of what will happen tomorrow and what you need to do to stop the abuse? Maybe you think you deserve to be mistreated. Why? What messages did you get as a child that told you that this is what your life is supposed to be like? Maybe you're like John. How do you feel about seeing yourself? Do you feel as if you're out of control and can't stop your abusive behavior? Can you see the message the children on-screen are getting? What they're learning today they will take with them tomorrow. I was very angry at the message the church sent Charlotte. What about you? Don't be too hard on yourself after you watch this movie. Pulling out of an abusive relationship can be a long, painful journey. But it is well worth taking. I encourage you, whether you are the abused or the abuser, to find help. I promise there is a much better life ahead, full of love and free of this type of emotional pain.

SHE'S HAVING A BABY

(Paramount, 1988), color, 106 minutes, PG-13-rated

HEALING THEMES:
Meeting that "special someone"
Losing your independence
Getting married
Learning to deal with relatives
Being tempted to have an affair
Trying to get ahead in life
Being afraid to lose the love of your life

DIRECTOR: John Hughes; SCREENPLAY: John Hughes; CAST: Kevin Bacon (Jake); Elizabeth McGovern (Kristy); Alec Baldwin (Davis); James Ray (Jim); Holland Taylor (Sarah); William Windom (Russ); Cathryn Damon (Gayle); Reba McKinney (grandmother); Bill Erwin (grandfather); Dennis Dugan (Bill); John Ashton (Ken); Edie McClurg (Lynn); Paul Gleason (Howard); Isabel Lorca (fantasy girl)

SYNOPSIS: Jake and Kristy fall in love the moment they see each other at a high school party. They decide to get married and take a journey through life, which leads them to having a baby. Their marriage is put to the test more than once as they experience many of life's tough challenges.

CINEMATHERAPY: I remember when I met the person I thought was going to be that "special someone"—the one I would be with for the rest of my life. Surely no one felt the way I did. No one else was going through what I was going through. If you have ever thought you were going it alone, see *She's Having a Baby*. It takes you on a comical/serious journey through the thoughts and feelings of one couple's life experiences. What was it like when you thought you were about to lose your independence? Did you feel trapped, as if you couldn't breathe? Maybe you felt pushed into your marriage, unable to get away from the obligations and responsibilities that came with the marriage certificate. Were you afraid and overwhelmed? "I can't even support myself, let alone a wife. What am I going to do?" "I can't imagine what it will be like to sleep with the same person for the rest of my life." "He's still a child. I spend most of my time picking up after him. I can't deal with this forever." And that's just the first day's worth of thoughts. There's the first apartment, meals that end up in the trash, pointless jobs, nights on the couch, temptations of affairs, relatives and relatives and relatives. Perhaps, as with Kristy and Jake, getting pregnant took the romance out of the relationship and turned lovemaking into work. At the end of the movie, let yourself get in touch with Jake's pain and fear over the possibility of losing Kristy. You may find that your laughter turns to tears when you realize how short and quick life can be. I know that when I think about losing my wife to an illness or time, I can become overwhelmed with sadness and fear. That's why I work to live every day in happiness and joy, with her by my side. This movie reminds me that life with that "special someone" is a journey. And how grateful I am to have someone special on the trip with me. Care to take your own journey?

SHINE

(Fine Line, 1996), color, 105 minutes, PG-13-rated

HEALING THEMES:
Growing up in an abusive home
Trying to please a parent
Being controlled
Feeling like you're going over the edge
Trying to hold on to reality

DIRECTOR: Scott Hicks; SCREENPLAY: Scott Hicks, Jan Sardi; CAST: Geoffrey Rush (David, as an adult); Armin Mueller-Stahl (Peter); Noah Taylor (David, as an adolescent); Alex Rafalowicz (David, as a child); Sonia Todd (Sylvia); Lynn Redgrave (Gillian); John Gielgud (Cecil); Nicholas Bell (Ben); Googie Withers (Katharine); Rebecca Gooden (Margaret); Danielle

Cox (Suzie, as a child); Mareanne Doherty (Suzie, as a teenager); Joey Kennedy (Suzie, as an adult)

SYNOPSIS: David is a brilliant pianist, a genius with a bright future. But his father has a tight grip on David—he will not allow him to make his own decisions about life or his musical career. David has an emotional breakdown and is unable to continue living a normal life until a woman is able to reach him, freeing him from his father's negative childhood messages.

CINEMATHERAPY: I doubt that many of you can watch *Shine* without recognizing the abuse Peter, David's father, places on his son. The abuse is physical, mental, and emotional. Phrases like "No one will ever love you like I do" and "You can't trust anyone but me" have left scars deeply embedded in David. Make no mistake, Peter is an ill man, sick with his obsession and his need to control everyone in his family, most of all his son. So here's my question for you: Are there times that you push your children too hard? Maybe you think they should get all As and that a B is totally unacceptable. Perhaps you believe they must be nothing but the best at any sport they play. Did you grow up in a home where you were constantly pressured to perform to the expectations and will of your demanding parents? How has it affected you as an adult? Do you have trouble trusting yourself? Are you drinking or using drugs? Like David, do you smoke? We must learn to love and nurture our children through their images of themselves, not through the image of ourselves or our parents. "When you grow up, you're going to be a great surgeon." "You're going to take over the family business when you grow up." What do *they* want? What would make *them* happy? Help your children to find their own way in life. Never send them messages that suggest they will be nothing without you. Listen to the way David's father used guilt to control his family. Notice the way Margaret and Suzie, his sister, were shoved to the background. Watch as his mother takes a passive role in David's life. How incredibly inappropriate. *Shine* is a perfect example of what can happen when a family fails to work as a unit. David's recovery starts when he ends the relationship with his dad. Like it or not, sometimes that's the solution to the problem of living with a dysfunctional family.

A SIMPLE TWIST OF FATE

(Touchstone, 1994), color, 106 minutes, PG-13-rated

HEALING THEMES:
Seeing life as unpredictable
Making the choice to not fight fate and serendipity
Having your world fall down around you

Turning your back on life
Feeling that you have no purpose
Being a single parent
People using power to get what they want

DIRECTOR: Gillies MacKinnon; SCREENPLAY: Steve Martin; CAST: Steve Martin (Michael); Gabriel Byrne (John); Laura Linney (Nancy); Catherine O'Hara (April); Alana Austin (Mathilda, at age ten); Stephen Baldwin (Tanny); Byron Jennings (Keating); Amelia Campbell (Marsha); Michael Des Barres (Bryce); Tim Ware (Rob)

SYNOPSIS: Michael McCann's wife leaves him after she becomes pregnant by another man. When he is robbed, Michael goes into a shell until a little girl wanders into his life. His world becomes brighter until John, the child's real father, decides he wants her back. Michael appears to be lost again until fate steps in with a helping hand.

CINEMATHERAPY: I was an adult before I learned to believe in fate. Oh, I had heard all the wonderful clichés: "What goes around comes around," "You reap what you sow," and so on. However, I was beyond all that nonsense. Well, I've changed my mind-set. *A Simple Twist of Fate* reminds us that things do happen for a reason. It shows us that there is a much larger plan in store for us—something I prefer to call serendipity. There's simply too much in this movie to give you all of its healing messages here. Try to focus on the full landscape. Think back to times in your life when you took a particular life direction, only to find that it didn't work. "I was going to go to law school, and then the girl I was dating got pregnant. That's why I'm working in this convenience store now." "When I was going to school, I was nothing but trouble. They told me I would spend my life in jail. After I opened my third hobby store, I realized they had no way of knowing my future." We all hear those tales; we simply don't believe that it's serendipity that guides us through life. The truth is we don't know what tomorrow will bring. However, if we keep our conscience clear of negative memories, we have a much better chance of letting the fates take us in positive directions. Let yourself feel the sensations in your body after you watch this movie. Get in touch with the calm—or lack of it—that settles in when you come to grips with the fact that life, after all, is unpredictable. We must all learn to let go and let what happens happen. Learn to live life honestly and in good faith. Make your time on this planet the best it can be. You can't control fate, so why not let life in and enjoy the moments? And don't worry, whatever comes around *does* go around. You need not be concerned about those who are evil; the fates and serendipity will have their day.

SINGLE BARS, SINGLE WOMEN

(ABC-TV, 1984), color, 100 minutes, not rated

HEALING THEMES:
Trying to find a relationship
Learning to be honest
Looking for love in all the wrong places
Understanding that men and women really have the same needs
Letting intimacy grow
Accepting that not every relationship will work

DIRECTOR: Harry Winer; **TELEPLAY:** Michael Bortman; **CAST:** Tony Danza (Dennis); Paul Michael Glaser (Gabe); Keith Gordon (Lionel); Shelley Hack (Frankie); Christine Lahti (Elsie); Frances Lee McCain (Patti); Kathleen Wilhoite (Dee Dee); Mare Winningham (Bootsie); Rick Rosovich (Dolph); Jean Smart (Virge)

SYNOPSIS: Some men and women spend their days and nights trying to find happiness in the local singles bars. The women group together and use their "feminine techniques" to get the men, and the men use their "masculine techniques" to get the women. They struggle to get what they want out of their newfound relationships. Some win and some lose.

CINEMATHERAPY: I saw this TV movie when it debuted in 1984. By coincidence, the movie aired again while I was researching this book. It really hit home. I can remember those days when I was working, going to school full-time, and hitting the club scene until two in the morning. And it was all about one thing—meeting women and having sex. You remember what it was like, don't you? They said their favorite color was blue, and lo and behold, that was your favorite shade, too. They said they loved a particular kind of music, and wouldn't you know it, that was your favorite also. Let's tell the truth: You sold yourself short to have a relationship with someone you knew was not the right person. And being able to own up to that is a big part of the healing process. It's about maturing, emerging to be who you are, and learning to wait for the right person to come into your life. Look for the on-screen character who most closely represents you, your behavior, and how you think. Do you really like what you see? Are you happy with how you are acting? Watch what all the characters go through to "get their mate." When people work this hard at finding a partner, they set themselves up for disappointment. Can you relate to their feelings of frustration, hurt, and disenchantment? Can you remember finding someone, having an intense relationship you thought would last forever, only to have it end as quickly as it began? Do you see that your pattern of looking for love may be a setup for failure? Watch this movie with friends. It's okay to laugh a little. When the laughter is out of your system, get down to serious feelings about what you have gone through in your efforts to find that special someone. Maybe it's time to do a reality check regarding your behavior and the kind of people you are attracting.

SLING BLADE

(Miramax, 1996), color, 134 minutes, R-rated

HEALING THEMES:
Being pushed too far
Growing up in an abusive family
Feeling as if your parents were not there to protect you
Reaching out to those who need your help
Accepting people for who they are
Making the ultimate sacrifice

DIRECTOR: Billy Bob Thornton; SCREENPLAY: Billy Bob Thornton; CAST: Billy Bob Thornton (Karl); Dwight Yoakam (Doyle); J. T. Walsh (Charles); John Ritter (Vaughan); Lucas Black (Frank); Natalie Canerday (Linda); James Hampton (Jerry); Robert Duvall (Karl's Father); Rick Dial (Bill); Jim Jarmusch (Frostee Cream)

SYNOPSIS: After years of being confined to a mental institution, Karl is released to go it on his own. He finds a companion in a young boy who accepts him for who he is. The boy and his mother are abused by her live-in boyfriend. Karl decides that the man needs to be punished, but carrying out this punishment puts Karl back in a mental institution.

CINEMATHERAPY: Why do we turn out the way we do? What events in our lives cast the die for our future? In this book, I talk about many movies that give us examples of what a dysfunctional childhood might do to your future. However, no movie goes about making this point the way *Sling Blade* does. Don't make the mistake of overlooking the tie between yourself and Karl simply because Karl is mildly mentally handicapped. "I can't relate to him. The guy's slow." "Doc, what are you talking about? I wasn't like that guy. I'm not mentally challenged." By seeing yourself through Karl's life, you may have an opportunity to feel your own experiences with nothing getting in the way. You will not be in denial, because you can put yourself in Karl's place without trying to live up to the character. For instance, listen to the scene between Karl and his father. Watch as he returns to confront his father, who abandoned him. His dad was never a parent, because he did not want to take responsibility for his son. Can you relate? Did you grow up in a home with a parent who had little or nothing to do with you? Perhaps you were put up for adoption because your parents were irresponsible. Or maybe you were left to raise yourself because your parents had "better things to do." Feel Karl's anger, his disappointment in his father. Look at the pathetic excuse for a parent living in his own filth. And what of the stepdad? Were you raised by a parent who brought an abusive partner into the house? Were you always afraid of the next wave of violence, never knowing from where it would spring?

THE SNAKE PIT
(Twentieth Century-Fox, 1948), B & W, 108 minutes, not rated

HEALING THEMES:
Feeling like you are losing your mind
Putting your life in someone else's hands
Coming back from the depths of mental illness
Struggling to stay alive

DIRECTOR: Anatole Litvak; SCREENPLAY: Frank Partos, Millen Brand; CAST: Olivia de Havilland (Virginia); Mark Stevens (Robert); Leo Genn (Dr. Mark Kirk); Celeste Holm (Grace); Glenn Lanagan (Dr. Terry); Helen Graig (Miss Davis); Leif Erickson (Gordon); Beulah Bondi (Mrs. Greer); Lee Patrick (asylum inmate); Isabel Jewell (asylum inmate), Victoris Horne (asylum inmate); Natalie Schafer (Mrs. Stuart); Ruth Donnelly (Ruth); Frank Conroy (Dr. Jonathan Gifford); Minna Gombell (Miss Hart); Ann Doran (Valerie); Betsy Blair (Hester)

SYNOPSIS: Virgina slips into mental illness. People around her have no choice but to place her in a mental institution. As she struggles to regain her sanity, she deals with doctors who don't know how to reach her.

CINEMATHERAPY: If ever a movie was a wake-up call, this one's it. Although *The Snake Pit* is an older movie, it has messages that are still valid today. From time to time we've all felt that we might be "losing it"—that we cannot go on one more day, that we should be taken away and locked up. Sometimes I feel that way myself. Simply because I'm a therapist doesn't mean I'm beyond feeling that life at times is too much, that I can't take it anymore. I am bothered by the same stresses you are: too much traffic, people who are sarcastic and mean, friendships that go astray for no apparent reason. It's how each of us copes with the stress that makes us different. Some may take drugs, others may gamble or use food as an escape, some will turn to violence, and still others may simply give up and check out. It's this mentally "checking out" that many people fear the most. How did you react when you saw Virginia slipping away? Were you afraid for her, or were you afraid for yourself? Were you angry at the doctors for the way she was treated? Did you want to shake her and tell her to get a grip—to get a life? Watch as the people around her seem to be uninterested in her feelings and thoughts, almost as if she were being left to die in her emotional upheaval. Get in touch with what's happening in your life that makes you feel you're slipping from reality. Accept that you don't have to hang tough or hold on for dear life. One part of the healing process is knowing when you require help—knowing when it's time to get support for yourself. There are therapists, counselors, support groups, and friends you can turn to when you are in need. Part of a strong self-enrichment program is staying in touch with whatever stress you're undergoing and finding a healthy, safe release before it's too late. Give *Dialogues with Madwomen* a try, as well. It's another incredible eye-opener.

SOUL FOOD
(Twentieth Century-Fox, 1997), color, 114 minutes, R-rated

HEALING THEMES:
Family feuds
Trying to understand life
Having an affair
Death of a family member
Feeling like an outcast
Bringing the people you love together

DIRECTOR: George Fillman Jr.; SCREENPLAY: George Fillman Jr.; CAST: Vanessa L. Williams (Teri); Vivica A. Fox (Maxine); Nia Long (Bird); Michael Beach (Miles); Mekhi Phifer (Lem); Jeffrey D. Sams (Kenny); Irma P. Hall (Mother Joe [Big Mama]); Carl Wright (Reverend Williams); Gina Ravera (Faith); Brandon Hammond (Ahmad); Mel Jackson (Simuel)

SYNOPSIS: If Big Mama believes in one thing, it's family. No matter what happens in this world, blood relations have to stick together. That's why Mama makes sure the whole family comes together every Sunday to have a home-cooked soul food dinner. And before Mama dies, she makes sure the tradition will continue.

CINEMATHERAPY: Sometimes I'm surprised at the number of people who come to my office and talk about their disappointment over the lack of family bonding in the world today. "It seems that everyone I know is spending time with their family. Hell, I've got five brothers and sisters. We never talk!" "When I was young, we used to get together for family dinners. Not anymore. These days everybody's fighting with one another." It seems that people nowadays have grown isolated from their families. And with the pressure exerted by righteous politicians and religious groups, the guilt over not being with family makes matters much worse. So when movies like *Soul Food* come along, I view them as a wonderful opportunity to celebrate the family. "But wait a minute,

Doc. This family is always fighting. If it's not one thing, it's another." You're right—it *is* always something, just as in real life. And part of being a family is knowing that no matter what, you have a place to return to in good times and bad. Now, I'm not suggesting you should feel obligated to return to an abusive environment. And to be sure, there is a lot of unacceptable boundary crossing in this on-camera household. I am suggesting that if relatives work together to make their family safe and supportive, that family can be a joyous place through which to experience life's transitions. Perhaps you are someone who resents a particular family member. Maybe you have not talked to them in some time. Do you miss the family but feel too angry to make contact? Are you using one family member as an information source to learn about another? Why not ask the family to meet and work things out? Use a mediator if necessary, someone who has no bias and whose sole purpose is to support the family in coming together. Use this move as a way to open the doors to discussion and to help the family experience the recovery they have needed for so long. Start the healing today and make plans for future gatherings tomorrow.

STAND AND DELIVER

(Warner Bros., 1987), color, 105 minutes, PG-rated

HEALING THEMES:

Having someone come into your life who inspires you
Seeing your friends make changes in their lives
Needing your family when it is time to make changes
Getting a break
Finding the courage to endure

DIRECTOR: Ramon Menendez; SCREENPLAY: Ramon Menendez, Tom Musca; CAST: Edward James Olmos (Jaime Escalante); Lou Diamond Phillips (Angel); Rosana De Soto (Fabiola); Andy Garcia (Ramirez); Will Gotay (Pancho); Ingrid Oliu (Lupe); Virginia Paris (Raquel); Mark Elliot (Tito); Adelaide Alvarez (Pancho); Patrick Baca (Javier); Danile Villarreal (Chuco)

SYNOPSIS: Jaime Escalante, a Hispanic teacher, is assigned to teach in a tough East Los Angeles barrio high school. He challenges his students to pass a college entrance exam. One by one, they confront him as they attempt to get him to back off. He meets them head-on and continues to push to make them all that they can become. They all pass the test, but they're accused of cheating. They emerge triumphant when they retake the test and pass with flying colors.

CINEMATHERAPY: I could relate to this group of students. I wasn't a very good student myself. The way the schools handled my education was to put me in a classroom full of other students who were like me, close the door, and "throw away the key" until the bell rang. Not until I was in tenth grade, when I met someone like Jaime Escalante, did I get a chance to break away from my impoverished schooling. That's why I like to discuss movies that offer inspiration and hope. When you watch this film, ask yourself if you could make it through school under the circumstances in which these teenagers exist. Sometimes I hear people say things like "Well, it's their fault they didn't make it through school," or "The problem is they're just not very bright," or "Those kids don't try hard enough." Maybe you can recall hearing such negative messages when you were growing up. I know I can. How did they make you feel? I felt increasingly stupid as the years went by. The truth is, most students' accomplishments are attributable not to intelligence but rather to their environment and the support they receive. Often students such as those in this film come from homes where abandonment, divorce, and abuse take place. Consequently, it takes a very special person to break through and make a difference. Can you recall a person in your life who changed the way you believed or felt? Who was in your life long enough to help you take a different direction? Jaime gives his students the opportunity to change their life's path. Perhaps you are a person who could make a positive difference in someone's life. Try volunteering your time. Contact your local chapter of Big Brothers or Big Sisters, call your local school, or help the elderly. In doing so, you will also feel better about yourself. Who knows what kind of an impact it will have on your life and someone else's future? Don't wait. Get started now.

A STAR IS BORN

(First Artists, 1976), color, 140 minutes, R-rated

HEALING THEMES:
Getting your big break in life
Falling in love with someone who is your exact opposite
Refusing to see people for who they really are
Putting people on a pedestal
The destructive effects of drugs and alcohol
Accepting death and moving on
Watching someone destroy themselves

DIRECTOR: Frank Pierson; SCREENPLAY: John Dunne, Joan Didion, Frank Pierson; CAST: Barbra Streisand (Esther); Kris Kristofferson (John); Paul Mazursky (Brian); Gary Busey (Bobby); Oliver Clark (Gary); Marta Helflin (Quentin); M. G. Kelly (Bebe Jesus); Sally Kirkland (photographer); Joanne Linville (Freddie)

SYNOPSIS: John Norman Howard, a rock superstar, is bored with his fame. He decides he wants to help a young singer, Esther Hoffman, with her career.

They begin a relationship and marry. In the process of pushing her to the top, he gradually slips to the bottom. People become more interested in Esther and less interested in John. He begins to lose his identity in his alcohol and depression. When he can no longer cope with his own reality anymore, he ends his life. Esther is forced to go on with her fame and her life alone.

CINEMATHERAPY: *A Star Is Born* has been produced three times to date: once in 1937, again in 1954, and then in 1976. All three versions are available to rent. I think all are excellent, but this is the one I prefer. Have you ever wondered why someone who has made it to the top would do something to destroy themselves? As a therapist, I have had people come to my office who have lost it all. Others have been on the verge of losing everything. And the questions are always the same: "Why did this happen to me?" "How could I have destroyed everything I have worked for?" There are no simple answers. Perhaps that is what they believed they deserved. Or perhaps they saw themselves as more powerful than they really were. As you watch *A Star Is Born*, you will see some of the reasons that brought this man to his knees. Clearly an overuse of alcohol was the main path to John's destruction as an entertainer and the disintegration of his relationship with Esther. Notice how he is never really coherent, always living on the edge. Watch how he methodically destroys his life and his relationships with those around him. Is there a bit of John in you? Are you someone who is drinking, doping, gambling, or spending to such an extent that it is adversely affecting your life and your relationships with those who love you? How do you feel about yourself when you watch John destroy himself? Does it remind you of a problem in your own life? You cannot help but feel sorry for John, and yet he is the one who decided to take this path. He is constantly searching for an inner peace through other people and substances. And therein lies the key: We cannot find ourselves through other people, places, or things. If you do not live in the here and now, you will forever be searching to fill the hole in your life. If you can learn from John's mistakes, you will experience self-enrichment in knowing that you alone make your destiny, and you will have a chance at a full life. This is a great movie for those who are on the road to self-destruction or are associated with someone who is. If you have friends who are on this path, sit them down and make them watch this movie.

STUART SAVES HIS FAMILY

(Paramount, 1995), color, 95 minutes, PG-13-rated

HEALING THEMES:
Looking at the lighter side of recovery
Dealing with a member of the family who drinks

Growing up in a dysfunctional family
Learning to take care of yourself
Getting on with your own life

DIRECTOR: Harold Ramis; SCREENPLAY: Al Franken; CAST: Al Franken (Stuart); Laura San Giacomo (Julia); Vincent D'Onofrio (Donnie); Shirley Knight (Stuart's mom); Harris Yulin (Stuart's dad); Lesley Boone (Jodie); John Lark Graney (Kyle); Majorie Lovett (Aunt Paula)

SYNOPSIS: Stuart is a man on a mission. He is a member of numerous twelve-step support groups, and he has his own television show. While on the road to recovery, he tries to help his dysfunctional family see the light. In the end, Stuart saves himself and supports his family in their recovery process.

CINEMATHERAPY: I remember when I started on my own recovery. It was a journey that I took very seriously. Years later, after I realized that part of the process of recovery was laughter, I came across *Stuart Saves His Family*. Stuart is all of us. He seeks to find the answers to life's many questions. And isn't that what we are trying to do? This is one of those wonderful films that can make us laugh and smile at ourselves while in the process of our own recovery. Like *The Wizard of Oz* and *Drop Dead Fred*, *Stuart Saves His Family* reminds us that the process of recovery is that kind of a journey. Just listen to Stuart's clichés, which have helped millions of people deal with their personal issues: "Do the steps," "Work your program," "Drop the rock," "One step at a time," and "Live and let live." Like the Serenity Prayer, these phrases are the things that keep people going in their own healing process. As you watch Stuart, you will see him confronted by many issues that may be like yours. Are you someone who is terrified to confront your employer? Maybe you grew up in a family dysfunction that is so ingrained that when you return to that household you revert to being a dependent child. Do you have a brother or a sister who is still dealing with old emotional issues that are keeping them tied to their dysfunctional behavior? I thought the way the film portrays the obese mother and sister and the alcoholic father and brother is wonderful. What a perfect scenario for a dysfunctional family. Notice the way the family history comes out. Do you have a similar history of dysfunction? Are you someone who struggles with years of family imprinting? Watch *Stuart Saves His Family* and get in touch with your own feelings and memories. Like Stuart, start a family of your own if your efforts to see your family out of their dysfunction don't work. Join support groups such as Overeaters Anonymous, Alcoholics Anonymous, Gamblers Anonymous, and Debtors Anonymous to support you in your recovery. Remember, shared laughter, smiling, and joy are valuable parts of any journey to recovery.

SULLIVAN'S TRAVELS

(Paramount, 1941), B & W, 91 minutes, not rated

HEALING THEMES:

Learning about life
Losing your appreciation for what you have
Being wrongly accused
Losing the power that comes with being free
Realizing the power of laughter

DIRECTOR: Preston Sturges; **SCREENPLAY**: Preston Sturges; **CAST**: Joel McCrea (John); Veronica Lake (the girl); Robert Warwick (Mr. Lebrand); William Demarest (Mr. Jones); Franklin Pangborn (Mr. Casalais); Byron Foulger (Mr. Valdelle); Robert Greig (Sullivan's butler); Eric Blore (Sullivan's valet); Torbin Meyer (the doctor); Jimmy Conlin (Trusty); Porter Hall (Mr. Hadrian); Alan Bridge (the mister); Almisa Sessions (Ursula)

SYNOPSIS: Sullivan is a big-time Hollywood movie director who's had it with all the trite, silly movies he's been forced to make by his studio. He disguises himself as a bum to get a real taste of life. His life lessons on the road take a big turn when he is mistakenly convicted of murder and sentenced to work on a chain gang. His employers eventually find him, but not before Sullivan gets an important life message.

CINEMATHERAPY: *Sullivan's Travels* is a classic movie that often airs at two in the morning on weekdays, so you might not have seen it unless you had a bad case of insomnia. This is one of those films that all of us could benefit from by watching. Sullivan teaches us a lesson: We learn about ourselves and the world around us as we take the road less traveled. Let's be honest: When you go to work, don't you take the same path every day? Is there a certain part of town that you rarely venture beyond? Is there a small list of restaurants that you go to repeatedly? Sullivan reminds us that there is a big world out there, some of which we may want to avoid because we don't want to see "the other side of the tracks." How can you grow as a person and how do we mature as a society if we don't take the time to see what's happening in the world around us? How do you feel when Sullivan leaves his ivory tower to live among those with whom he would normally never have contact? Did you think, "Who cares? That's their problem" or "I don't have to live like that, so I don't have to worry"? Can you see that this is all part of life's healing lessons? Sullivan needed to learn more about the world at large before he could truly love and be loved. He needed to see the healing power of laughter and what it does to mend the human mind and spirit. The gift he gave to himself is a present he could pass along to everyone. This is a terrific movie for the entire family to watch. When it's over, sit with your children and ask them what they thought of reaching out to others who need a helping hand. Make an effort to show them the "other side of the tracks." Ask them to reach out to those who are less fortunate, and watch your whole family expand to new spiritual heights. What an adventurous way to travel the healing path.

THE SUMMER MY FATHER GREW UP

(NBC-TV, 1991), color, 100 minutes, G-rated

HEALING THEMES:

Having parents who are divorced
Spending time with each parent in different cities
Trying to understand what caused a breakup with your spouse
Telling your parents what you really think about them
Working to survive as a stepparent
Having trouble accepting the truth about who you are

DIRECTOR: Michael Tuchner; **TELEPLAY:** Sandra Jennings; **CAST:** John Ritter (Paul); Margaret Whitton (Naomi); Karen Young (Chandelle); Matthew Lawrence (Timmy); Joe Spano (Louis); Anne Betancourt (Alita)

SYNOPSIS: It is summer, which means it's time for Timmy to be with Paul, his father. Timmy is tired of his father's self-centered ways and decides to spend his summer with Naomi, his mother, and Louis, his stepfather. This creates trouble, but it also forces Paul to see what he's done and grow up.

CINEMATHERAPY: When I was growing up, I had my hands full taking care of me. I couldn't imagine taking on the responsibility of raising another human being. As a therapist, I know something today about raising kids that I didn't know when I was younger: What I thought was a big responsibility is, in fact, an *unbelievably* big responsibility. I have seen so many couples come to my office in pain over issues related to raising their children. When divorce and immaturity are added to the problem, well . . . you have a real mess on your hands. *The Summer My Father Grew Up* invites us to look at what happens when parents fail to take responsibility for themselves. Becoming an adult is a painful process, and simply because you are a professional and make money, as is the case with Paul and Naomi, doesn't necessarily mean you are responsible parents. Can you relate to the petty arguing that goes on between them? Do you see that they are dragging Timmy into their unresolved issues, forcing him to take sides and to grow up too quickly? Maybe you grew up in a home like Timmy's. Did you feel divided and torn between your parents? How about Timmy? Could you feel him being abandoned and ignored by a father who was always too busy to spend quality time with him? To truly be a family, we must let down the barriers of anger and resentment that prevent healthy, nurturing communication. Without this type of communication, there can be no real healing. Children need to know that their parents are there for them; they need to know that their parents can be trusted and will love them unconditionally. Make this a family viewing experience. Ask your children to share their feelings about what they're seeing. Let them know you're there to support them, and that you will not put them between the two of you. And if they tell you something you don't like, listen to them—don't cut them off as Paul did in the film. Go for it. You'll get the hang of it.

SWEET NOTHING

(Warner Bros., 1996), color, 90 minutes , R-rated

HEALING THEMES:
Trying to make ends meet
Raising a family
Getting hooked on drugs
Losing sight of what you are doing
Putting your family in danger
Forsaking your friends and family for crack cocaine

DIRECTOR: Gary Winick; SCREENPLAY: Lee Drysdale; CAST: Michael Imperioli (Angelo); Mira Sorvino (Monika); Paul Calderon (Raymond); Patrick Breen (Greg); Richard Bright (Jack the cop); Billie Neal (Rio); Brian Tarantina (Dee Dee); Lisa Langford (Edna); Maria Tucci (Monika's mother)

SYNOPSIS: Like most young married couples, Angelo and Monika work hard to make a life for their two children. However, it's difficult because everything they earn just goes to pay bills. Angelo realizes he can make a better living by selling drugs. And for a while he makes a lot of money—until he starts using more drugs than he sells. The inevitable disaster occurs when he can't rescue his family or himself from the clutches of the dragon called crack cocaine.

CINEMATHERAPY: Like *The Boost*, **The Basketball Diaries**, *The Days of Wine and Roses,* and *Clean and Sober, Sweet Nothing* reminds us of the devastating effect drugs have on the human race. So what's healing about that, you ask? I know of no better way to help people out of denial and onto the road to recovery than to confront them with a movie like this. If you or someone you know is losing everything to an addiction, this is an important movie to watch carefully. Angelo tells you in his own words how drugs took away his life, his self-respect, and his humanity. Some people think it just happens—one day you are clean, and the next day you are hooked. However, it's more complicated than that. There are so many variables that direct the mind and body to take the step-by-step descent into addiction. Watch how Angelo goes from his day job to making a full-time career of being an addict. "I used to have a day job, but it got in the way of getting high," he admits. Have you lost your sense of reality because your addiction is consuming you? Are you living with someone who can't see the difference between sense and insanity? Is your family taking second place to your need to get your next fix? Maybe you can relate to Monika trying to hold on to the hope that her husband will be able to find his way home. Perhaps you feel a sense of guilt knowing that your children are profiting from something that is hurting others. Make no mistake, this is an evil, cruel force that can consume anyone, anytime, anywhere. Did you notice how Angelo's friends turned him on to the drugs? With friends like that, Angelo certainly didn't need enemies. If you have not tried drugs, don't. If you have, don't do it again. If you are hooked, get help before you end up like Angelo. And one more thing: Be sure to pass the word.

TABLE FOR FIVE

(Warner Bros., 1983), color, 122 minutes, PG-rated

HEALING THEMES:
Being abandoned by a parent
Dealing with feelings of abandonment
Having a relationship with children with whom you've lost touch
Opening up the doors of communication
Trying to make a family whole again

DIRECTOR: Robert Lieberman; SCREENPLAY: David Seltzer; CAST: Jon Voight (J. P.); Richard Crenna (Mitchell); Marie-Christine Barrault (Marie); Millie Perkins (Kathleen); Roxana Zal (Tilde); Robby Kiger (Truman-Paul); Son Hoang Bui (Trung); Kevin Costner (newlywed husband); Cynthia Kania (newlywed); Mara O'Brian (Mandy)

SYNOPSIS: A divorced man wants to have a relationship with the children he abandoned. He takes the children on a cruise to Europe—what he sees as a perfect opportunity to spend quality time together. It all backfires as the children act out and protest his attempts at retroactive love. As time passes, the cruise brings the family together.

CINEMATHERAPY: Each of us has experienced feelings of abandonment—the sense that you're being left out or behind. I can remember times when I lost a relationship and it wasn't my choice. It was devastating. The kind of abandonment that comes from feeling a parent's rejection can be overwhelming. I work with adults in their mid-fifties who still carry around the pain of being left by a parent years before. *Table for Five*, like *A Face on the Milk Carton*, reaches out to those who are trying to heal from wounds such as these. It also shows us what happens when a parent tries to rekindle an abandoned relationship with a child. Men who are working at having a relationship with children they haven't seen in some time will gain a lot from this movie. Can you sense J.P.'s uncomfortable-ness? You can almost feel him trying too hard. Are you struggling for a connection with children you haven't seen in some time? Are you experiencing some of the same emotions that J.P. does? What about the youngsters? Oftentimes they see themselves as the cause of a parent's leaving. This may turn to guilt that can stay with the child throughout life. How did you act when your parent came back and wanted to take charge of your life? Were you angry, hurt, scared? Watch as each of these youths handles that issue in a different way. Try to put yourself in their place. You will no doubt find yourself getting quite emotional. Here's an idea. Ask those with whom you're trying to rebond to watch the movie with you. Use it as a means of opening the doors of communication. If you are a parent who is dealing with this issue, learn to be patient—both with your children and with yourself. This kind of healing takes a long time and a lot of work.

TALES OF ORDINARY MADNESS

(Station, 1983), color, 107 minutes, not rated

HEALING THEMES:
Going from one bad relationship to the next
Avoiding intimacy
Drinking as a way of life
Living life all the way to a dead end
Trying to understand when and where it all went wrong

DIRECTOR: Marco Ferreri; SCREENPLAY: Sergio Amidei, Anthony Foritz, Marco Ferreri; CAST: Ben Gazzara (Charles); Ornella Muti (Cass); Susan Tyrrell (Vera); Tanya Lopert (Vicky); Roy Brocksmith (bartender); Hope Cmeron (landlady); Jay Julian (publisher)

SYNOPSIS: When a poet begins to drink twenty-four hours a day, his life gets complicated. He meets one woman after another who offers more confusion than he can handle. Nothing can stop his philandering or his drinking.

CINEMATHERAPY: Here's a movie everyone can relate to. *Tales of Ordinary Madness* gives you an opportunity to look at relationships between women and men that have alcohol as a catalyst. Most people go through a period in their lives when they're on the hunt for fun—they want to party. It usually starts in the high school years and continues through the late twenties. Some people get caught in the lifestyle and it becomes who and what they are. For them, there doesn't seem to be any other purpose in life than to go from one meaningless relationship to another. Do you know anyone who lives that way? How old are they? Thirty-five? Forty? Fifty? Add alcohol to the equation and life can get very complicated. How do you feel about Charles's behavior and the women he meets? Can you relate to one of these characters? What is it you like and dislike about yourself that you see in these characters? I hated the manipulation and lies Charles used to get whatever he wanted. It reminded me of some of my old traits that caused me personal embarrassment. Once you can identify those qualities, work to make changes for the better in yourself. That's what these stories of self-recovery are really all about. Remember paradoxical healing? You learn and heal by seeing what *not* to do. Also, focus on Charles's drinking. Watch as he hides inside the bottle, never letting anyone really know him. He probably doesn't know himself. Do you know anyone who uses alcohol the way he does? Are you attracted or repelled by such behavior? Take the time to watch this movie and absorb what you're seeing. Don't get lost in the story; rather, look for the healing messages within the plot line. Most important, don't let yourself become a lost soul with memories and tales of ordinary madness.

TALKING WITH
(Lifetime Studios, 1995), color, 90 minutes, not rated

HEALING THEMES:
Thinking you're alone
Feeling as if you're on the edge
Telling someone who you really are
From birth to death, listening to other people's stories
Learning not to make the mistakes that others have made

DIRECTOR: Kathy Bates; SCREENPLAY: Jane Martin; CAST: Kathy Bates; Frances McDormand; Marcia Gay Harden; Mary Kay Place; Beverly D'Angelo; Celeste Holm

SYNOPSIS: Caro, Laurie, Big Eight, April March, Alain, and Lila are all women with a story to tell. One by one, they expose their inner feelings and thoughts as they attempt to explain who and what they are. Each one is at a different stage in her attempt to answer her own life questions.

CINEMATHERAPY: Here's the honest truth: This movie is beyond me. I used to be intimidated when I didn't understand the meaning of a movie, so I would just go with the conversation and hope people believed I knew what the heck I was talking about. Well, after spending the better part of my life in school, achieving academic success, I figure I can afford to say, "I didn't get the whole message." So why is *Talking With* in the book? Because what I did see tells me that this is an important movie, especially for women. We are given the opportunity to get inside the souls of six women who are willing to pour their hearts out to us. As the six vignettes unfold, Caro, 'the Handler," shares her religious fanaticism with us. She reminds us that "crazy people do crazy things." Do you know someone who is so entranced in religious beliefs that they no longer have a life of their own? Laurie, in the part of the movie called "Clear Glass Marble," remembers in detail that each of us has thoughts of death and dying. It's how and when we say goodbye that separates us from one another. Did someone shut you out before you could help them? Big Eight tells us in "Rodeo," in the midst of her drunkenness, that life can pass you by and that you better be prepared, because the process can be cruel. Are you afraid it's too late to have your dream? April March is caught in yesterday and can't let go. She's having a bit of a difficult time growing up. She looks like an adult, but she is really a little girl. Alain, in "Marks," is a woman who was a goody-goody, but no more. She just lives from social taboo to taboo. Maybe you can relate to being branded for what you do or think, or wanting to break out of the mold of the way people see you. And finally, Lila, who glows brightly in "Lamps," gives us her wisdom on life and love. Her existence is buried in her philosophy. She's getting old and is able to look back with quiet reserve. Find yourself in these six women. I've just scratched the surface of what they're trying to tell us. Take it the rest of the way. At the end of this journey is wellness and healthy introspection.

A THOUSAND ACRES

(Touchstone, 1997), color, 101 minutes, R-rated

HEALING THEMES:
Dealing with molestation issues
Losing someone you love
Having an affair
Being called a liar
Confronting your past
Getting on with your life

DIRECTOR: Jocelyn Moorhouse; SCREENPLAY: Laura Jones; CAST: Jessica Lange (Ginny); Michelle Pfeiffer (Rose); Jason Robards (Larry [Dad]); Jennifer Jason Leigh (Caroline); Keith Carradine (Ty); Kevin Anderson (Peter); Pat Hingle (Harold); John Carroll Lynch (Ken); Anne Pitoniak (Mary); Vyto Ruginis (Charles); Michelle Williams (Pammy)

SYNOPSIS: You would think that life on a midwestern farm would be about as simple as life can get. However, for Rose and Ginny, memories of life with Larry, their abusive, tyrannical father, are anything but pleasant. Now their anger and sadness leave little time for healthy relationships. In the end, Ginny is left with Rose's sister's children to remind her that she is not alone.

CINEMATHERAPY: I review hundreds of movies each year. Few make their way into my work as a cinematherapist. And of the small group of films that meet my criteria for therapeutic content, only a handful have touched me as deeply as *A Thousand Acres*. If you come from a home where molestation was the order of the day, or if both of your parents intimidated you, or you lived in fear of being battered, this movie is going to touch you in ways you could never have imagined. Watch and listen as Ginny works to dance around her father's domination. Feel the anger that comes from Rose every time she tries to please her father, only to be rejected again. Notice the way their dad manipulates the family all the way to the end. Can you see how these two sisters never had a real chance to have an emotinally secure life? Do you understand how Caroline was sucked into believing in her father, seeing him as the rest of the town saw him, as a victim? I could not help but think that the cornfields are the opposite of a field of dreams; this is a field of nightmares. It is difficult to imagine the horrific emotional experience of being raised in a house such as the one in which Ginny and Rose were raised. So often, people work to deny what has happened to them in an attempt to get on with their lives. But, as with these two women, growing up in a dysfunctional home stunts emotional growth and can lead its victims to a life of mistrust, drug abuse, inappropriate behavior, unfulfilling relationships, alcoholism, and so on, unless issues of abuse and molestation are resolved. If you feel caught or stunted in your life, call a therapist, join a support group, or use cinematherapy to bring your feelings to the surface. Once you work through those troublesome issues, you will be free to live the life you desire. Don't avoid the recovery process any longer. Start today.

THREE MEN AND A BABY

(Touchstone, 1987), color, 102 minutes, PG-rated

HEALING THEMES:
Remembering the days when you were single
Taking on adult responsibility
Learning to be a parent
Abandoning a child
Losing somebody you love
Finding yourself through a child

DIRECTOR: Leonard Nimoy; SCREENPLAY: James Orr, Jim Cruickshank; CAST: Tom Selleck (Peter); Steve Guttenberg (Michael); Ted Danson (Jack); Nancy Travis (Sylvia); Margaret Colin (Rebecca); Philip Bosco (Detective Melkowitz); Alexandra Amini (Patty); Celeste Holm (Mrs. Holden); Derek deLint (Jan); Cynthia Harris (Mrs. Hathaway); Lisa Blair, Michelle Blair (Mary)

SYNOPSIS: When three bachelors, whose lives are anything but family oriented, end up taking care of a newborn baby, their world is turned upside down. Clueless about the needs of an infant, they flounder until, little by little, they realize how rich their lives have become through caring for this baby.

CINEMATHERAPY: Both men and women come into my office and tell me that they do not want children in their life; they just don't want to be responsible for another person, no matter the age. "You know, Doc, I just don't want to take on the responsibility of having a child. I'm having too much fun." "I'll tell you what: All my friends are laden down with two or three children, and I don't want to have anything to do with it. I like the freedom." "I feel guilty that I don't want to have children. All my friends have them. Is there something wrong with me?" The truth is that everybody has different feelings about having children. It's okay if you prefer to live without children in your life. So don't let this movie sway your decision—unless, of course, it can't be helped. *Three Men and a Baby* reminds some people of the special joy that comes from having youngsters in their lives. Maybe you are someone who felt lost—someone who had no purpose in life. Suddenly, when a child came into your life, your world changed for the better. Of course, the reverse can happen: Your life can get worse, too. Be sure of your choice before you make it.) Watch as the lives of the men in this movie alter because of this tiny person. It looks like the men on-screen are growing along with the baby. Can you relate? Are you and your significant other struggling with the idea of having a child? Will it be a good or a bad choice? There's a special lesson that comes from this movie that I'd like you all to see: We tend to think that men can't take care of children as well as women. However, in reality, men and women can both be good caretakers, provided they have equivalent amounts of training. You may be a man who feels incapable of taking care of a child. As this group of men does, give yourself time. There's a special joy that comes from watching the way these guys work together and reminds us of how important it is to love our children. *Three Men and a Baby* is a wonderful, uplifting movie. I suggest watching it as a couple. If you've been struggling with the decision of whether or not to have a baby, it may help you.

TO GILLIAN ON HER 37TH BIRTHDAY
(Triumph, 1996), color, 92 minutes, PG-13-rated

HEALING THEMES:
Death and dying
Losing the most important person in your life

Letting go
Learning that life goes on
Making room for someone new in your life
Memories

DIRECTOR: Michael Pressman; SCREENPLAY: David E. Kelley; CAST: Peter Gallagher (David); Michelle Pfeiffer (Gillian); Claire Danes (Rachel); Laurie Fortier (Cindy); Wendy Crewson (Kevin); Bruce Altman (Paul); Kathy Baker (Esther); Freddie Prinze Jr. (Joey)

SYNOPSIS: It has been some time since Gillian, David's wife, died. And although time is supposed to heal all wounds, David is having a very difficult time letting go of his time with her. Now, even the ghost of Gillian won't allow David to restore his emotional equilibrium. Eventually, however, David is able to let another woman into his life.

CINEMATHERAPY: Losing Robin, my significant other, is the most painful scenario I can think of. I cannot imagine what life would be like without her. Even though I am a therapist, even though I know that death is inevitable, I do not want to deal with the possibility that one day I'll be without her. I have no doubt that those of you who have found the love of your life can relate to such feelings. And I believe those of you who are looking for this kind of extraordinary relationship can imagine the pain of this thought. This movie invites each of us to get in touch with our feelings about losing someone special. Have you lost someone special and are having trouble moving on with your life? Are there people around you who are a constant memory of that person? Do you feel pressured to get on with things by those who don't seem to understand your pain? Make no mistake: Grieving is an important part of emotional healing. However, when you do not allow yourself to grieve, you may, like David, deny the reality that your loved one is gone. Whether this person has died, moved away, or simply ended the relationship with you, it is important to let go of the past and move on. Try watching this movie on your own. Get in touch with David's pain. Feel your loss through his. Maybe there are children involved. Do you know how they are handling the loss? Have you asked them how your denial makes them feel? If, after watching the movie, you are still having trouble letting go, seek the support of a therapist, counselor, or religious leader. Reach out to others who are going through the same experience. Nurture yourself into a new life with wonderful memories of the past, buoyed by the knowledge that your lost loved one would not want you to be unhappy. That is what loving them and yourself is really all about.

TORCH SONG TRILOGY

(New Line Cinema, 1988), color, 117 minute, R-rated

HEALING THEMES:

Falling in love
Accepting that you are gay
Living with the death of a loved one
Learning that one of your children is a homosexual
Enjoying life to its fullest

DIRECTOR: Paul Bogart; SCREENPLAY: Harvey Fierstein; CAST: Anne Bancroft (Ma); Matthew Broderick (Alan); Harvey Fierstein (Arnold); Brian Kerwin (Ed); Karen Young (Laurel); Charles Pierce (Bertha); Eddie Castrodad (David); Kim Page (Murray Rey); Edgar Small (Arnold's father); Bob Minor (Roz)

SYNOPSIS: Two gay men, Arnold and Alan, have a chance meeting. Arnold is quite openly gay; Alan is somewhat reserved in demonstrating his sexual identity. In time, they realize that they have a great affection for each other. But their union is destroyed when Alan dies in a senseless murder. Arnold's life seems all but over.

CINEMATHERAPY: For those of you who struggle with your sexual identity, this movie offers support in your freedom to be who you want to be. However, it is not just for those who are gay or are questioning their sexual identity. *Torch Song Trilogy* is for anyone who has been in a relationship of any sort. It shows us the importance of being loved for who we are. You may recall being in a relationship with someone of whom your family did not approve. What emotions did you experience as you tried to get them to accept your lover? Anger? Rage? Hurt? Pressure? Notice the mother-and-son relationship in this story line. How did you feel about the way they spoke to each other? I felt strained, as if I wanted him to get out of there. It didn't feel like a very healthy relationship. How did you feel when you saw the two men being intimate on-camera? Did viewing this portion of the movie make you uncomfortable? Why is it not okay for people of the same sex to be intimate? It seems that most people believe that same-sex relationships are wrong, and it is important for us to ask where we got those negative messages. If you look into your past, you will realize that your understanding of homosexuality is founded mainly on rumor. How did you feel when Alan was murdered? Let yourself feel the pain and anger associated with his death. I am still amazed when people face violence for not agreeing with another person's point of view or lifestyle. If you are a homosexual, you will grow from seeing this couple's on-screen relationship. If you are heterosexual and intolerant of other sexual orientations, you will grow by taking a step closer to accepting people for who and what they are. Therapy is always aimed toward supporting people in their life choices and directions. How much more at peace our world would be if we simply practiced acceptance of others' way of life.

TRADING MOM

(Trimark, 1994), color, 82 minutes, G-rated

HEALING THEMES:
Unhappiness with your parents or family
Looking at only the bad things
Living in a fantasy
Having to make a choice
Realizing that what you have is the best of all

DIRECTOR: Tia Brelis; SCREENPLAY: Tia Brelis; CAST: Sissy Spacek (Mama/Natasha); Nancy Chlumsky (Dr. Richardson); Anna Chlumsky (Elizabeth); Aaron Michael Metchik (Jeremy); Asher Metchik (Harry); Merritt Yohoka (Mr. Leeby); Andre the Giant (giant); Maureen Stapleton (Mrs. Cavour)

SYNOPSIS: Three young children, Harry, Jeremy, and Elizabeth, are fed up with their mom. An old woman teaches them how to wish their mother away. They can go to the "Mommy Market" to obtain a new parent. They learn that finding the perfect mom is no easy task. Life becomes much more settled when they eventually agree to take their own mother back.

CINEMATHERAPY: When I was growing up, I always wanted to be a part of someone else's family. It seemed to me that my friends had it much better than I did. Their fathers made more money, their mothers were more involved with the family, and for sure my friends had better brothers and sisters than I did. What if you could have wished yourself a new parent? Well, Harry, Jeremy, and Elizabeth take you on that journey. How do you feel about their mom, who has nothing nice to say to her children? Does she remind you of one of your parents? Maybe you are the parent and she reminds you of yourself. What could you do to change after seeing a reflection of yourself through this on-camera mom? And what of their choices in a new mom? Can you see there is no such thing as the perfect parent? The lesson is to make the best of the family we have rather than wishing for a new one. But there is something else going on here. It's about living in a dreamworld, trying to survive in a fantasy that things will get better if you just choose to ignore life around you. When you were growing up, was it easier to exist in a fantasy world? Did you grow up in a home where everything around you was scary and unpredictable? Did you want to run away? And when you realized you had no place to go, did you live in a fantasy just to get through the day? *Trading Mom* forces us to look at our own reality. Why not watch this movie with your family? Afterward, spend time discussing how the film made each of you feel. Listen to your children rather than question their feelings about the movie. Work to make your family better by seeing and avoiding the mistakes the three children in the movie go through. Healing takes place when we have the courage to look at ourselves and make changes for the better.

TRAINSPOTTING

(Channel Four Films, 1996) color, 94 minutes, R-rated

HEALING THEMES:
Being hooked on heroin
Living for your next fix
Going nowhere fast
Taking steps to change your life
Finding friends who are more than just junkies

DIRECTOR: Danny Boyle; SCREENPLAY: John Hodge; CAST: Ewan McGregor (Mark ["Rents"]); Ewen Bremner (Daneil ["Spud"]); Jonny Lee Miller (Simon David ["Sick Boy"]); Kevin McKidd (Tommy); Robert Carlyle (Begbie); Kelly Macdonald (Diane); James Cosmo (Mr. Renton); Eileen Nicholas (Mrs. Renton); Susan Vidler (Allison)

SYNOPSIS: A group of society dropouts make a career out of being hooked on heroin. Irresponsible and untrustworthy, they spend their days getting money any way they can and their nights strung out on drugs. There is no end to their bad behavior, and nothing works out for the best because nothing ever could.

CINEMATHERAPY: I suppose I should warn you that this movie consists primarily of four-letter words. And for that reason, much to my dismay, parents and schools will see to it that children do not watch this film. However, I will tell you that in this writer's opinion, *Trainspotting* can do more to prevent people from using drugs than most drug-education programs can. The hell with worrying about the profanity in this film. If that is what it takes to get people to see the vulgar truth behind drug use, then so be it. If you or anyone you know is on the verge of turning to heroin or another drug, try watching this movie. Like *The Basketball Diaries* and *Sweet Nothing*, *Trainspotting* forces you to take a hard look at the effects that drugs have on the individual and society. Listen to the narrator share his thoughts with you. He gets right to the truth: "Being addicted is a full-time job." "The problem is not getting straight, it's staying straight." "It's never enough and it's never the last time; there always seems to be one more high before you quit—for good." Do any of those thoughts sound familiar? Have you tried kicking the smoking, drinking, gambling, overeating, or drug habit, but can't seem to keep your promise to remain clean? The real trick is to learn to live with the boredom and depression that come from getting clean. For many, it is those by-products of getting drug-free that make staying clean and sober an overwhelming one-day-at-a-time challenge. The good news is, that unlike the rough crew in this movie, you or someone you care about does not have to go it alone. There are support groups that can help you make it from one day to the next for the rest of your life. Counselors, teachers, and religious leaders may also be able to point you in the right direction. If, after watching this movie, you don't get the message, watch it again. Parents and teachers, let the language be part of the lesson. Better a few harsh words than a lifelong harsh existence.

A TREE GROWS IN BROOKLYN

(Twentieth, 1945), B & W, 128 minutes, not rated

HEALING THEMES:
Never letting go of your dream
Dealing with someone in your family who drinks
Struggling to make ends meet
Losing someone in your family
Trying to make your life better
Believing tomorrow will be a better day

DIRECTOR: Elia Kazan; **SCREENPLAY:** Tess Slesinger, Frank Davis; **CAST:** Dorothy McGuire (Katie); Joan Blondell (Aunt Sissy); James Dunn (Johnny); Lloyd Nolan (McShane); Peggy Ann Garner (Franny); Ted Donaldson (Neeley); James Gleason (McGarrity); Ruth Nelson (Miss McDonough); John Alexander (Steve); B. S. Pulky (Christmas tree salesman)

SYNOPSIS: It's the beginning of the twentieth century. Times are tough for the Nolan family. Johnny drinks too much and has a difficult time supporting his wife and two children. Katie works at being both parents to her children. Tragedy strikes when Johnny dies, leaving his loved ones to fend for themselves. The family learns to make it on their own.

CINEMATHERAPY: When I find movies such as *A Tree Grows in Brooklyn*, I see them as very special gifts—treasures that we can take out of hiding whenever we want. So much of going forward in our lives means letting go of the past. If we walk around angry or regretting things that happened or never occurred, it's very difficult to live in the here and now. Was there a time in your life that was very difficult? Can you recall not having enough money to buy food and clothes, or pay the rent? Maybe you came from a family with a parent who had a problem with alcohol or drugs. Or possibly you lost a loved one and were never able to properly grieve their loss. These issues and so much more are brought to the surface in this movie. Johnny is a wonderful man and everybody loves him, but he drinks excessively. He can't hold down a job, and he spends most of his time dreaming about what could or will be. What did you feel toward him? Did you get lost in his being a good guy, or were you angry at his irresponsible behavior? Katie becomes both parents at the risk of her looking like the taskmaster. It is difficult to feel close to her. Yet she did what she thought was in the best interests of the family. Pay close attention to Franny. Does she remind you of anyone? Maybe you were more like an adult than your own parents. Were there times when all you wanted to do was be a carefree kid, but you didn't feel or know how to be one? Notice the way Franny works at avoiding her inner feelings. She acts tough to let everyone know she can take it. Do you feel her anger toward her mother? What are your own experiences related to the loss of someone you care about? This is a great film for the whole family to watch. You will find yourself wanting to nurture your family relationships and draw your family members closer to you. If I can leave you with one strong message that this movie wants you to hear, it is that there can be a brighter tomorrow but you must get through today to get there. And when you do, you'll find a strong, sturdy tree within your grasp.

TREES LOUNGE

(Orion Classics, 1996), color, 94 minutes, R-rated

HEALING THEMES:
Looking at going nowhere
Alcohol, alcohol, alcohol
Refusing to let go
Losing a friend
Sexual abuse

DIRECTOR: Steve Buscemi; SCREENPLAY: Steve Buscemi; CAST: Steve Buscemi (Tommy); Chloe Sevigny (Debbie); Mark Boone Jr. (Mike); Michael Buscemi (Raymond); Anthony LaPaglia (Rob); Elizabeth Bracco (Theresa); Daniel Baldwin (Jerry); Carol Kane (Connie); Bronson Dudley (Bill); Debi Mazar (Crystal); Michael Imperioli (George)

SYNOPSIS: Going nowhere and being nobody is the focus of Tommy's life. He is incapable of keeping it together long enough to accomplish good for anyone, including himself. But that's not terribly surprising, since alcohol and smoking represent the sum total of his existence. If necessary, he'll even screw over his best friend.

CINEMATHERAPY: For decades, therapists, educators, politicians, and religious counselors have attempted to convey the message that alcohol and drugs will get you nowhere. They have tried, with increasing repetition, to tell the world that while you are under the influence and even in between binges, the world will pass you by and leave you with nothing but bad memories. Do you know someone who can't get his or her life started because much of their day is spent in and out of a drug stupor? Do you feel as if your life is slipping away from you while you go from one drink, one toke, one line to the next? Have you entered a fantasy world by checking out of the real world? If you can't tell the truth from fantasy, the lead character in this film is going to shake you up and straighten you out. Watch as nothing ever comes together for him. Listen as his immaturity rules his life, taking him from one go-no-place adventure to the next. Like many movies dealing with the issue of addictions, *Trees Lounge* is not a fun tale to watch. It takes what little joy you get from the movie and tosses it out the window. It's not my intent to get preachy, and the last thing I want to do is turn you away from great movies like this one that have so much paradoxical healing value. However, if you can help yourself or a friend see what addiction is doing to your or their life, then the discomfort that this film makes you feel is worth it. Try watching the film alone. When it is over, sit with your feelings. Confront yourself with these forgotten issues: What am I doing to myself? When will I have had enough? Ladies and gentlemen, boys and girls, it's time to rejoin the human race.

THE TURNING POINT

(Twentieth, 1977), color, 119 minutes, PG-rated

HEALING THEMES:
Recalling old friendships
Dealing with feelings of jealousy and envy
Accepting yourself
Looking for the courage to step beyond yourself
Confronting your anger

DIRECTOR: Herbert Ross; SCREENPLAY: Arthur Laurents; CAST: Anne Bancroft (Emma); Shirley MacLaine (Deedee); Mikhail Baryshnikov (Kopeikine); Leslie Browne (Emilia); Tom Skerritt (Wayne); Martha Scott (Adelaide); Marshall Thompson (Carter); James Mitchell (Michael); Anthony Zerbe (Rosie); Donald Petrie (Barney)

SYNOPSIS: Emma and Deedee were best pals when they were young ballerinas. Their friendship is put to the test when Deedee's daughter Emilia is invited into an elite ballet circle. The two veteran dancers confront each other with their individual feelings, which they've kept suppressed over the years. In the process, they become closer friends.

CINEMATHERAPY: Here's a little-known fact about me: When I was in high school, I was in a rock-and-roll band called the Marauders. We were the popular band around town. The Crossfires were a rival band from across town. We were always in competition with each other. We got a movie contract and changed our name to The U.S. Males. They changed their name to the Turtles. Need I say more? I have always had mixed feelings of envy and resentment over their tremendous success. However, I've come to learn that what is more important is the friendship I had with members of both bands—friendships that got lost in the competition between us. You will be able to relate to some of your own hidden resentments when you're watching *Turning Point*. Which one are you? Emma, the successful ballerina who put everything else on hold for a career? Or Deedee, the successful wife and mother who put her career on hold for her daughter? Do you have regrets because you did not follow your dream, while your best friend did exactly what he or she planned to do? Have you severed that friendship because of your anger and disappointment over your own life choices? What you probably don't know is that your friend is envious and jealous of your life course. You have just assumed that they have the more attractive life because they have power or money or fame. Can you see that at the same time Deedee was envious of Emma's career, Emma was jealous of Deedee's family life? What really matters is that you are happy with yourself, not that you compare well with someone else. You can do whatever you want, but you must do it for yourself. That's the loving, spiritually healing thing to do. And when you've taken those courageous moves in your life, you will have reached your turning point. Now just *make* the turn. Here's another thought: Why not give that old friend a call and share your feelings? Invite them to share their feelings and work to rekindle that old friendship. You'll be glad you did.

THE VANISHING

(Twentieth, 1993), color, 110 minutes, R-rated

HEALING THEMES:
Losing somebody you love
Inability to let go
Understanding that someone is mentally ill
Trying to get on with your life
Getting help from the most unexpected places
Dealing with feelings of guilt and abandonment

DIRECTOR: George Sluizer; SCREENPLAY: Todd Graff; CAST: Jeff Bridges (Barney); Kiefer Sutherland (Jeff); Nancy Travis (Rita); Sandra Bullock (Diane); Park Overall (Lynn); Maggie Linderman (Denise); Lisa Eichhorn

(Helene); George Hearn (Arthur); Lynn Hamilton (Miss Carmichael); Rich Hawkins (Stan)

SYNOPSIS: A young couple, Jeff and Rita, take a road trip. While they are en route, the young woman is abducted. The police try to find her, but fail. Over the years, Jeff refuses to give up searching for her. Barney, the man who abducted Rita, decides to go after Jeff. Barney is stopped in his attempts to kill Jeff, and questions about the past are answered.

CINEMATHERAPY: I must say, even I had a difficult time watching this one. The issues here are abduction and obsession. Whether it is a lost child or adult, we need to know what happened to that person. Each year, loved ones are lost to abductors. Families and friends spend days, weeks, months—in some cases their whole lives—searching for them, usually at considerable risk. This movie offers an example of that risk. First, the abductor is a well-respected man who appears to be above suspicion. The point is that the abductor can be anyone—a neighbor, a friend, or an ex-spouse. He is mentally ill and no one knows it. Second, he has the ability to track, stalk, and lure victims with a great deal of effectiveness. Third, he is able to use the emotional pain of those who are on the hunt to get them to do what he wants them to. How did you feel about this man? I wanted him hung by his toes, I was so angry. Did you note that he is a product of a sick childhood? His obsessiveness is just one of many character traits that could have developed in his attempt to cope with his painful upbringing. For example, he might have become an alcoholic, a workaholic, or a gambler. He also could have sought help and worked through his problems instead of taking them out savagely on the world. If you have lost someone, take precautions and attempt to understand the nature of individuals who perpetrate such evil acts. Don't take them for granted. Also, work on dealing with your loss and the loss of those around you. And remember: As devastating as the ordeal is, you have your own life to live. You must go on. Reach out and help others who have suffered similar tragedies.

THE VERDICT
(Twentieth, 1982), color, 112 minutes, R-rated

HEALING THEMES:
Getting a second chance in life
Taking steps to prevent alcohol from destroying your world
Standing up for what you believe in
Trusting your morals
Never letting go of what you truly believe in

DIRECTOR: Sidney Lumet; **SCREENPLAY**: David Mamet; **CAST**: Paul Newman (Frank); James Mason (Ed); Charlotte Rampling (Laura); Jack Warden (Mickey); Milo O'Shea (Judge Hoyle); Lindsay Crouse (Kaitlin); Edward Binns (Bishop Brophy); Julie Bovasso (Marvien); Roxanne Hart (Sally); Weslay Addy (Dr. Towler)

SYNOPSIS: Frank Gavin is a down-and-out attorney. He spends most of his days in the local bar telling stories and bumming drinks. His friend Mickey, a man who still believes in him, offers him a case that can put him back on top. Frank stays sober long enough to win the case against all odds.

CINEMATHERAPY: *The Verdict* sends us important messages. First and foremost, alcohol can bring anyone to their knees. There is a tendency for us to believe that addicted people are poorly educated, or that people with an education are above such problems. Here's a big wake-up call: This once-upon-a-time, top-notch lawyer is a falling-down drunk. Addictions can hit anybody, from any family, in any way. There are high rates of alcoholism among the well-educated. I once read a report that suggested that the highest rate of alcoholism is among Nobel Prize winners. It puts all alcoholics in good company, don't you think? Sometimes an event occurs that brings a person back to reality—an event that sends the individual on a healing journey. The lawyer in this story is ready for that journey even though he appears incapable of accomplishing anything. It helps to have a friend or a support group that believes in you. Friends and groups like this remind us never to give up on people. I have seen colleagues give up on clients simply because they stopped believing that recovery was possible. How about you? Have you given up on a friend or relative because they can't stop drinking or smoking or eating? To see someone through destructive, addictive behavior takes time—lots and lots of time. And it takes patience and love. If we give up, we're *all* lost. Healing can begin only when the person with the addiction summons the courage to stop their addictive behavior *and* we have the courage to see them through the recovery. If you know someone who needs help, try directing them to support meetings, therapists, or counselors who specialize in addictions. Perhaps you can first show them this movie as a wake-up call.

VOICE IN THE MIRROR

(Universal International, 1958), B & W, 102 minutes, PG-rated

HEALING THEMES:
Addiction to alcohol or drugs
Being in a relationship with someone who can't stop drinking
Giving up your addiction for a better way of life

Reaching out to those who need to heal from addiction
Coming out of denial
Making your life mean something

DIRECTOR: Harry Keller; SCREENPLAY: Larry Marcus; CAST: Richard Egan (Jim); Julie London (Ellen); Arthur O'Connell (William); Walter Matthau (Dr. Leon Karnes); Troy Donahue (Paul); Mae Clarke (Mrs. Robbins); Casey Adams (Max); Harry Bartill (Harry); Ann Doran (Mrs. Devlin)

SYNOPSIS: A young artist can't keep away from the bottle; he spends his money getting drunk and most of his time staying that way. He is confronted by his wife, who won't tolerate his drinking any longer. He's struck with an idea: What if he just starts talking about his drinking problem with other men and women who can't stop drinking? After some false starts, he and his wife eventually realize the dream of sobriety.

CINEMATHERAPY: *Voice in the Mirror* is a miraculous find. One night I was tossing and turning; I just couldn't get to sleep. At about two in the morning, I decided to watch TV. I couldn't believe it. Here was this movie, made in 1958, whose overarching themes were based on the principles of Alcoholics Anonymous. It had it all: the drunk who can't stay sober; the codependent wife who can't see her role in his alcoholism; denial, lies, and anger. And that's just in the first twenty minutes. Listen to Jim work on the people around him so he can get his alcohol. Watch as he puts his family last so he can have his booze. Notice the way he is attracted to those who have the same addiction. Of course, *he's* not addicted—no, not him. The other people are the ones with the problem. Heck, he just likes having a drink now and then. Do you know someone like our artist friend? Do the lies and stories he tells sound familiar? Maybe he reminds you of yourself. And what about his wife? Why in the world does she stay around? Maybe deep down inside she believes she deserves all the chaos. Did you feel their hope when they started reaching out to other people with the same problem? Can you see that helping someone else is really helping yourself? Recovery is a long journey. Whether you are the dependent—the alcoholic, drug addict, gambler, or food addict—or the codependent, you can experience the healing that comes from self-recovery. Like *My Name Is Bill W.*, *Voice in the Mirror* places these and other issues in the spotlight. Try attending Alcoholics Anonymous, Al-Anon, Adult Children of Alcoholics, or any number of recovery groups in your area. And when the time is right, you too will be able to hear the voice in the mirror and experience the miracle of wellness that comes with recovery. Maybe the time is now.

VOICES WITHIN:
THE LIVES OF TRUDDI CHASE

(ABC-TV, 1990), Color, 200 minutes, not rated

HEALING THEMES:
Trying to find the pieces of yourself
Understanding ourselves better
Going on when you feel you're falling apart
Learning something about multiple-personality disorder
Seeing yourself and making changes for the better

DIRECTOR: Lamont Johnson; TELEPLAY: E. Jack Neuman; CAST: Shelley Long (Truddi); Tom Conti (Dr. Stanley Phillips); John Rubinstein (Norman); Frank Converse (Peter); Jamie Rose (Truddi's Mother); Alan Fudge (Albert); Christine Healy (Sharon)

SYNOPSIS: Truddi has an awful secret: Her childhood was filled with abuse. As an adult, she can't seem to feel good about herself. In fact, she has other personalities that take over when times get too difficult. Truddi embarks on a journey of self-discovery in an attempt to live a normal life.

CINEMATHERAPY: The last thing I want to do is make light of Truddi's illness. Dissociative identity disorder, also known as multiple-personality disorder, is a serious psychological condition that requires long-term treatment. But the truth is, this condition is very rare. So why do I want you to see this movie? Each of us has different pieces to our personality and character that make us whole and help us decide who we are in the world. And that's how people see us. But we each see the same person from different points of view at different moments in time. Can you recall a friend saying something like "I met Frank's wife yesterday. She has such a great sense of humor. She has a wonderful personality"? Now you're thinking, "Did they meet the same person I know, the angry, spiteful woman who doesn't have a kind word to say about anyone?" The point is, our personalities change throughout the day. Some of our personality traits we like, and others we wish would go away and never return. Try watching *Voices Within: The Lives of Truddi Chase* from a different angle. Watch the way Truddi changes from one person to another, then focus on the personality of that person. What do you see in her personalities that reminds you of yourself? Do you like what you see? Keep in mind that she's not in control of her personality changes. Do you feel you're in charge of your personality, your moods? Do you know what you're doing but can't stop at that moment? Maybe you have problems with drugs or alcohol, which alters your personality. Do you know anyone who goes through personality changes because of substance abuse or a self-abusive activity like gambling or overindulgence in sex? This film offers a chance to experience healing by going at it from a different direction. And that's what it takes sometimes to come out of denial. Gather friends together and watch this picture. Get honest with one another. This one's going to be a real challenge.

WAITING TO EXHALE

(Twentieth, 1995) Color, 124 minutes, R-rated

HEALING THEMES:

Looking for a once-in-a-lifetime relationship
Having an affair
Sex for sex's sake
Turning to your friends for support
Knowing when to say it's over
Keeping secrets

DIRECTOR: Forest Whitaker; SCREENPLAY: Terry McMillan, Ronald Bass; CAST: Whitney Houston (Savannah); Angela Bassett (Bernadine); Loretta Devine (Gloria); Lela Rochon (Robin); Gregory Hines (Marvin); Wesley Snipes (James); Dennis Haysbert (Kenneth); Mykelti Willamson (Troy); Michael Beach (John Sr.); Wendell Pierce (Michael); Donald Adeosun Faison (Tarik); Giancarlo Esposito (David)

SYNOPSIS: Four Scottsdale, Arizona, women—Savannah, Bernadine, Robin, and Gloria—work at finding meaningful relationships with men. Each of them continues to get involved in empty relationships that are rich with problems, leaving them angry and unsatisfied with their lives. However, one thing is a constant for the quartet: No matter what, they have one another.

CINEMATHERAPY: As long as I can remember, I've wanted to exhale, not just for an evening or a weekend or a month, but all the time. I wanted a relationship in which I could be comfortable. I wanted to be with someone who would love me unconditionally. However, with each relationship came another disappointment. They didn't give me what I needed, let alone what I wanted. Sound familiar? Are you still waiting to exhale so you can be at peace with yourself? Are you becoming discouraged with relationships and life in general? What's the big secret, you ask? I'll tell you: The solution is very simple, but the act of following through with the solution is the most difficult thing I have ever achieved. You see, I realized that I was using people, relationships, sex, money, power, and so on, to feel better about myself so I could exhale. I was "using" people and things to center myself. If I was okay with my relationship, job, family, physical appearance, et cetera, I could, of course, finally exhale. But eventually, after years of self-induced pain and emotional failure, I learned that first and foremost I had to be okay with myself. I had to heal my own being before I could find a soul mate who worked as hard as I did to make me whole.

I don't mind saying that I am breathing much more easily now that I have reached that point in my life. No one can make me any better, or worse, than I am. I've learned to take responsibility for my life choices. I used to blame all my decisions on whatever relationship I was in at the time. "She made me do it," I would moan. Nonsense! *I* made me do it. It was my choice, my fault, and I own the responsibility for every inappropriate life decision I've ever made. Here's an idea: Now that *Waiting to Exhale* has been out for a few years, give it another look—or a look for the first time—and take a critical inventory of your life choices. Make a decision to become the best you can be before you choose to have someone else in your life. When you do, you will find yourself breathing, exhaling in peace. Now, that's healing.

THE WAR AT HOME
(Touchstone, 1997), color, 123 minutes, R-rated

HEALING THEME:
Nightmares
Problems at home
Parents who can't reach their children
Being unable to communicate with your family
Post-traumatic stress disorder
Running away from your problems

DIRECTOR: Emilio Estevez; SCREENPLAY: Emilio Estevez; CAST: Kathy Bates (Maurine); Emilio Estevez (Jeremy); Martin Sheen (Bob); Kimberly Williams (Karen); Corin Nemec (Donald); Ann Hearn (Professor Tracey); Carla Gugino (Melissa)

SYNOPSIS: A young man, Jeremy, returns home to his family after fighting in the jungles as a soldier in the Vietnam War. Jeremy's family expects him to be the same person he was before he left. In spite of his efforts, he cannot recapture the peaceful life he once led. In the end, he comes to realize that he must find himself before he returns home.

CINEMATHERAPY: In my opinion, post-traumatic stress disorder may be the most misunderstood emotional ailment in our society. It seems that few people truly understand the impact this psychological disorder can have on our lives. Why? Because in most cases it appears as if the person who is acting out is doing so intentionally—that they can control their actions but choose not to. This story gives us clear images of what Jeremy endured, so it is easy for us to understand why he is behaving the way he is. However, in the absence of such images, we are left bewildered as we try to cope with someone's actions. How does this relate to you and cinematherapy? If you are having problems understanding your spouse's behavior, or the behavior of your child, friend, or neighbor, *The War at Home* may give you helpful insight. Are your offspring becoming hard to handle? Maybe they are living in a war at school, frightened of a group of kids who may attack at any moment of any day. Is a member of your household having difficulty getting along with people? Possibly they are fighting a war in their mind, living with memories from their distant past that haunt them to this day. Do you live next to someone who seems to be paranoid, wants to fight over everything? Could it be they come from an environment that was like a war zone? In our society, some children are living in war zones: gangs, hostile families, city streets filled with traps that keep the child forever on edge. As these youngsters move into adulthood, they take these unwanted, uncontrollable memories with them. In the process, some lose control of themselves as they fight their childhood wars over and over again. Remember when you crossed the street to avoid an oncoming group of kids? Now try to imagine what it is like living that way every minute of each day. If you're having problems with anger and rage, get help. If you know people who cannot control themselves, reach out and give them the support they may have never had.

THE WEDDING GIFT

(BBC-TV, 1993), color, 87 minutes, PG-13-rated

HEALING THEMES:
Coping when someone you love is ill
Not knowing what's wrong with you
Learning to live with a debilitating illness
Believing you won't get better
Making sure your significant other will be okay without you
Considering suicide

DIRECTOR: Richard Loncraine; TELEPLAY: Jack Rosenthal; CAST: Julie Walters (Diana); Jim Broadbent (Derick); Thora Hird (Derick's mother); Sian Thomas (Aileen); Andrew Lancel (Nick); Anastasia Mulroney (Sally)

SYNOPSIS: Diana is a woman with a serious illness. Her doctors and nurses have little hope that she will recover. Derick, her husband, loves and takes care of her. Diana decides it's time that Derick got on with his life. She makes sure he has another woman in his life before she dies.

CINEMATHERAPY: When I was young, I could not relate to people who had an illness. I was impatient and had no time for those kinds of problems. Things have changed since then. I have someone in my life who means the world to me. I can't imagine being without her. At the same time, I could not tolerate living in pieces. *The Wedding Gift* is a beautiful story that examines all of these issues. Be honest: Could you handle your partner's becoming seriously ill? What would you do if they had a serious accident and required that you attend to them as if they were a baby? Would you want that done for you? I admired their relationship a great deal. This was a couple who was more than husband and wife—they were best of friends. What did you feel when you found out that Diana arranged for Derick to meet someone else? Could you do that for your significant other? Many people can't tolerate the idea of their mate being with someone else. Yet it's reality, isn't it? It's rare for both people to die at the same time. Someone has to be left behind. I find myself becoming afraid when I think about being without the person who makes up so much of my life. And what of Diana's choice to commit suicide? It's clear that she waited until she knew Derick had met someone he liked. Are you against what she did? She was tired of the pain and had given up all hope of getting better. She didn't want to be a burden to Derick any longer. What would you have done? In many ways, this is a love story. Try watching this as a couple. Feel free to express your emotions. Open up to each other's feelings. Diana couldn't heal herself, but you can experience the healing that comes from letting your partner into your life on a level that you've never before embraced.

WELCOME TO THE DOLL HOUSE
(Sony Classic, 1996), color, 87 minutes, R-rated

HEALING THEMES:
Living the life of the nerd
Wishing you were someone else
Feeling as if you're never part of the group
Being picked on
Learning about sex all the wrong ways

DIRECTOR: Todd Solondz; SCREENPLAY: Todd Solondz; CAST: Heather Matarazzo (Dawn); Brendan Sexton Jr. (Brandon); Daria Kalinina (Missy); Matthew Faber (Mark); Angela Pietropinto (Mrs. Wiener); Bill Beull (Mr. Wiener); Eric Mabius (Steve); Victoria Davis (Loleta); Christina Brucato (Cookie); Christina Vidal (Cynthia)

SYNOPSIS: The local junior high school has a few nerds, and Dawn is one of them. With a family that offers her no support, a brother who is just as much a nerd as she is, and a little sister who can do no wrong in the eyes of her parents, Dawn blunders her way from one day to the next.

CINEMATHERAPY: I would like to brag and say I was the hip, slick, and cool kid in school, but that would be a lie. If you want to know about my life, just turn Dawn into a boy and you've got it. Well, not exactly. At least Dawn could read, write, and spell. I had the distinction of being the dumbest kid in school. Just because Dawn is the focus of this movie does not mean you will be unable to relate. Maybe you were the person who picked on the nerds at school. Now that you're an adult, how do you feel about participating in that kind of behavior? Is there something you could tell your children about yourself that might help them to avoid doing what you did to others when you were young? Perhaps you were the tough kid, always pushing everyone around. What made you so mean? Why did you need to take your anger out on those who had nothing to do with the reason you were so upset? And what about Dawn's brother? I was so jealous of those kids whose siblings were popular. Why couldn't my sister be the prom queen or the valedictorian? Maybe I wouldn't have gotten in so many fights. I hope everyone watches this movie, young and old alike. Let yourself feel the pain from all the characters, not just that from Dawn's point of view. And when you're through, ask yourself a few questions: Why do we, as humans, need to torture one another? How is it that we are such hurtful, rather than loving, creatures? What role have you played in creating pain in the lives of others, rather than providing acceptance and support? How has your pain made its way into society? I know I promised you I wouldn't get on a soapbox, but allow me this one chance to state my case: Be kind, not mean to others. Help, rather than hurt. Be loving instead of hateful. If, after watching this picture, you can find any reason to treat Dawn, me, or others with such great disrespect and disregard, please write me and tell me the logic behind your behavior.

WHAT EVER HAPPENED TO BABY JANE?

(Warner Bros., 1962), B & W, 132 minutes

HEALING THEMES:
Learning to let go of the past
Persevering when anger and resentment rule your world
Responding to someone you know who is going over the edge
Living in the here and now
Dealing with your fear

DIRECTOR: Robert Aldrich; SCREENPLAY: Lukas Heller; CAST: Bette Davis (Jane); Joan Crawford (Blanche); Victor Buono (Edwin); Marjorie Bennett (Mrs. Della); Anna Lee (Mrs. Bates); Maidie Norman (Elvira); Dave Willock (Ray); Bert Freed (producer); Wesley Addey (director); Julie Allred (young Jane); Gina Gilleapie (young Blanche)

SYNOPSIS: Baby Jane was a childhood star. Blanche, Baby Jane's sister, became a successful screen actress and Jane became history. Much later, when Blanche is confined to a wheelchair, Jane begrudgingly takes care of her sister. Little by little, Jane plots to drive Blanche over the emotional edge. She almost accomplishes her mad goal.

CINEMATHERAPY: I'm walking down the street and I see someone who is dressed head to toe in a 1960s getup. You know the ones—they look as if they just came from a Dead concert and are on their way to a Rolling Stones revival meeting. And suddenly, *What Ever Happened to Baby Jane?* comes rushing back into my mind. Can you relate? Do you know anyone who is living in the past and refuses or is afraid to live in the present? Maybe they were a football hero in high school and they're still expecting people to get out of their way. Possibly they were the college president and can't let go of the power they once had. Or maybe they were physically very attractive and used to getting all the attention but have lost their looks over the years. What is it like to be around them? Are you that person? Are you having trouble letting go of the past and moving on with your life? Notice the way Baby Jane uses alcohol to get through her life. She drinks alcohol to numb her feelings. Who do you know who uses alcohol, food, drugs, violence, gambling, or shopping to numb themselves to life? How did the anger, sarcasm, and meanness make you feel? Listen to this telling line in the movie: "I want to live in a family where I'm not compared to anyone." Maybe that's what has pushed you to the edge, causing you to feel that you have to live up to a sister, brother, mother, or father. Growing up can be painful. We all have to accept the responsibilities that come with being mature. If we don't, we end up like Baby Jane, caught in the past and living for our memories. Learn to enjoy the rich colors, sounds, and smells of today. Embrace the moment and accept who you are in life. When that happens, you are living life on life's terms, one day at a time. *Note:* There are two versions of this movie. The remake was done in 1991. Give the 1962 version a try. There is something very haunting about seeing it in black and white.

WHERE THE DAY TAKES YOU
(New Line Cinema, 1992), color, 105 minutes, R-rated

HEALING THEMES:
Getting caught up in the drug life
Living with violence
Thinking of running away from home
Making it on the streets
Remembering difficult times in your life
Being taken advantage of

DIRECTOR: Marc Rocco; SCREENPLAY: Michael Hitchcock, Kurt Voss, Marc Rocco; CAST: Dermot Mulroney (King); Laura San Giacomo (interviewer); Robert Knepper (rock singer); Sean Astin (Greg); Balthazar Getty (Little J); Will Smith (Manny); James Le Ciros (Crasher); Ricki Lake (Brenda); Lara Flynn Boyle (Heather); Peter Dobson (Tommy); Nancy McKeon (Vikki); Kyle MacLachlan (Ted); Adam Baldwin (Officer Black); Rachel Ticotin (Officer Landers); Alyssa Milano (Kimmy); Leo Rossi (Mr. Burtis); Stephen Tobolowsky (Charles); Christian Slater (Rocky)

SYNOPSIS: King, Little J, Greg, Heather, and hundreds of other young people try to survive on the streets of Hollywood, California. They beg, borrow, and steal their way through long days and violent nights. When they try to escape the devastating street life, their chaos catches up with them and only Heather survives to live another day.

CINEMATHERAPY: I spent some time looking for a movie that truly reflected what living on the streets is all about. The one I chose is set in the backyards of the place where I spent a great deal of my own young adult life: Hollywood, California. Now, I doubt there are many runaways who will have a chance to watch this movie. However, I know there are more than a few parents who have lost children to the streets. And I imagine there are more than one of you who ran away, if only for a brief period of time, when you were the age of King, Little J, and the rest of the gang. "Living at home is never bad enough to run away. If that's the way they want to live, let them." "Why don't they just go back home and work it out? I'm sure if they talk to their families they can see their way through their problem." Those are nice thoughts that sound well and good, but if you've come from a home that is unsafe, where abuse, neglect, drugs, and poverty are the standard for the day, then living on the streets can seem pretty good. Can you relate to these kids? Were there times when you ran away as a defense against a difficult home life? Maybe you wanted excitement and felt that the streets had more to offer than home. Have you lost a child to the streets? Do you wish you could have understood what was driving them out of the house to such an unsafe environment? *Where the Day Takes You* gives us all a strong reality check. It takes us out of denial and forces us to look at what is happening to young people all over the world who are risking their lives on the streets. This is a wonderful movie to help you open up healing doors before it's too late. Sit down with your family and watch it. Spend time discussing what you saw, how it makes you feel, and what you need from one another to stop this from happening to you and your family. Now, that's taking action for your future. Every twenty-six minutes, a child runs away. Let's all try to slow that clock to a stop.

WHOSE LIFE IS IT, ANYWAY?

(MGM/UA, 1981), color, 118 minutes, R-rated

HEALING THEMES:

Having your world turned upside down
Becoming seriously hurt
Being forced to depend on other people
Choosing to take your own life
Responding when others try to make decisions for you

DIRECTOR: John Badham; SCREENPLAY: Brian Clark, Reginald Rose; CAST: Richard Dreyfuss (Ken Harrison); John Cassavetes (Dr. Michael Emerson); Christine Lahti (Dr. Clare Scott); Bob Balaban (Carter); Kenneth McMillan (Judge Wyler); Kaki Hunter (Mary Jo); Janet Eilber (Patti); Thomas Carter (John); George Wyner (Dr. Jacobs); Mew Stewart (Dr. Bair)

SYNOPSIS: A popular artist and sculptor wakes up in a hospital, paralyzed from the neck down. It doesn't take him long to understand that he will never be close to being the man he once was. In spite of efforts by hospital employees to stop him from taking his own life, his court petition allows him to die with the dignity he believes is his right.

CINEMATHERAPY: Like the subject of abortion, issues surrounding the right to die usually provoke a wide range of thoughts and feelings from people who believe we should, or should not, have the right to take our own life. More than any other movie I have seen, *Whose Life Is It, Anyway?* forces us to come out of our safe hiding places and look at this difficult question. I can remember as a child watching my grandmother die. It was horrible. I could not have been more than seven or eight. She had cancer and was in a great deal of pain. I was terrified of the idea that I would one day have to experience that kind of finale to my own life. I never shared my thoughts with my father, but I remember thinking, "If I were her, I would want to be put out of my misery. Who would want to live that way?" Now, I know those of you who feel strongly about intervening in God's life plan will find that thought abhorrent. And I certainly respect your feelings. But the big question still remains: Should each of us, as individuals, have the right to take our own life when and if we no longer wish to live? As you watch this film, you will not be able to ignore the question as it applies to yourself or to someone you love. Are you someone who wants total control of your life or death? Do you think it is a sin to take your own life? What would you have done if you were in Ken's condition? Possibly you know someone who has decided that they no longer want to live so they're taking their life slowly. Are they smoking, drinking, or taking drugs and dying a slow, emotionally and physically painful death? Make no mistake: There are a lot of ways to take your own life. Do you want the choice, or do you want someone to make the decision for you? *Note:* As of the writing of this book, only one state, Oregon, has a right-to-die law.

THE WOMEN'S ROOM

(ABC-TV, 1980), color, 150 minutes, not rated

HEALING THEMES:
Looking back at where you've come from
Being given more than you can deal with in life
Not feeling okay about sex
Thinking you're going over the edge
Becoming the person you never thought you could be

DIRECTOR: Glenn Jordan; **TELEPLAY:** Carol Sobieski; **CAST:** Lee Remick (Mira); Colleen Dewhurst (Val); Patty Duke Astin (Lily); Kathryn Harrold (Bliss); Tovah Feldshuh (Iso); Tyne Daly (Adele); Lisa Pelikan (Kyla); Heidi Vaughn (Samantha); Mare Winningham (Chris); Gregory Harrison (Ben); Ted Danson (Norm); Al Corley (Tad)

SYNOPSIS: Mira never thought that life would turn out the way it did—a marriage that ended in divorce, friends who are falling apart, and sons who seem to get along fine without her. She works to put her life back together, but it comes with a great deal of pain and struggle. When it's all over, Mira has a life—a place in this world—she can call her own.

CINEMATHERAPY: No matter if you are a woman or a man, you will grow from watching *The Women's Room.* For me, coming across this movie was a real gift. Here is a healing story that lets you pass through time. There is so much going on in this film that I strongly suggest you view it twice. The first time, just get the sense of the story. Watch the transitions in Mira's life and experience them with her. On the second viewing, work to get in touch with Mira, Lily, Adele, Ben, and the rest of the characters. Try to identify with one or more of them. Here are a few points to which you should pay close attention. Observe the way the subject of sex is handled by the female characters. Just listen to some of the phrases they use: "All a woman has is her reputation." A male character says, "Don't worry, at least I get pleasure." Why isn't it okay for women to enjoy sex the same way men do? Why shouldn't women be interested in having their sexual needs met? Each of the women in this picture speaks to this issue in one way or another. What are your feelings on the subject? Are you a woman who works at hiding her interest in sex because it's not the "ladylike thing to want"? Maybe you're a man who believes it's a woman's job to supply the sex, your job to supply the money. Did you notice how everyone had something to deal with? Smoking, drinking, having affairs, gambling, depression, suicide, money problems, and on and on goes the list. The character Mira reminds us that life is an incredible challenge. Part of that challenge is acknowledging that there are no guarantees in life, and that healing comes from accepting and taking charge of your life and who you are. Don't miss a minute of this one—Mira's relationship with her child, the loss of the life she once knew, returning to school, dealing with her age, and the ultimate emergence of her own identity. This is a terrific film to watch by yourself or with friends.

ZOOT SUIT

(Universal, 1981), color, 104 minutes, R-rated

HEALING THEMES:

Feeling you've been prejudiced against
Reacting when someone reaches out a helping hand
Trying to make your life better
Helping those who are in need
Seeing the different ways life can turn out
Trying to jump over life's stumbling blocks

DIRECTOR: Luis Valdez; SCREENPLAY: Luis Valdez; CAST: Edward James Olmos (El Pachuco); Daniel Valdez (Henry); Tyne Daly (Alice); Charles Aidman (George Sher); John Anderson (judge); Abel Franco (Emreque); Mike Gomez (Joey); Alma Rose Martinez (Lupe); Ed Peck (Lt. Edwards)

SYNOPSIS: It's the 1940s and war is all around us. Mexican-Americans are struggling to gain a place in the land of the free. The youth are finding their identity by becoming members of different groups—Vatos, Pachucos, and so on. Cruising and dancing are the entertainment of the day. Some wore the zoot suit to gain identity. In the barrios of Los Angeles, Henry, a leader of one of the gangs, is accused of committing murder along with three of his fellow Zoot Suiters. A trial ensues, and groups and organizations rally for fair adjudication, ultimately winning their battle.

CINEMATHERAPY: This is a unique movie. I saw *Zoot Suit* twice as a play before it was made into a movie. For the most part, the film is the play. Notice how the different cultures and generations battle one another to gain their own identity. No matter your age, you will be able to recall different battles, verbal or otherwise, that you might have gotten into when you tried to do it *your* way. That's part of growing up, being an adult, and experiencing yourself and your relationship to the world. Green hair, love beads, miniskirts, and nose rings are all different ways a person might choose to express himself. Some go to college and some don't want to have anything to do with school. We all make the statement; it's just that some make the statement more loudly than others. Take note of the prejudice in this movie. The Zoot Suiters were presumed guilty before they had a chance to make a case for themselves. One of the main reasons I wanted you to watch the film is its ending. The screenwriter makes a point of letting us know that life has no guarantees, that life can take many different turns. Maybe the message is not to fight life but rather to go with life. And isn't that the message we all need to hear about healing? "Let go." "Let it be." "One day at a time." Take note how alcohol, marijuana, and violence go hand in hand. Give this film a try. At the very least, you'll be entertained.

PART
THREE

USEFUL
RESOURCES

HEALING MOVIES PRESCRIPTION LIST

Therapist: _____   Date: _____

Client (s): _____

I would like you to watch the following movie (s) by: _____

_____ *Always* (1989)	_____ *Breaking Away*
_____ *American Graffiti*	_____ *Brian's Song*
_____ *American Heart*	_____ *The Bridges of Madison*
_____ *And the Band Played On*	*County*
_____ *And Then There Was One*	_____ *The Butcher's Wife*
_____ *Angel Baby* (1995)	_____ *Bye Bye, Love*
_____ *Angel Heart*	_____ *Can't Buy Me Love*
_____ *Animal Farm* (1955)	_____ *Casablanca*
_____ *The Apprenticeship of*	_____ *Cat's Eye*
Duddy Kravitz	_____ *The Celluloid Closet*
_____ *As Good As It Gets*	_____ *Chasing Amy*
_____ *Avalon*	_____ *Child of Rage*
_____ *Awakenings*	_____ *Choices of the Heart: The*
_____ *The Bad Seed* (1956)	*Margaret Sanger Story*
_____ *The Basketball Diaries*	_____ *Citizen Kane*
_____ *Bastard Out of Carolina*	_____ *Citizen Ruth*
_____ *Beautiful Girls*	_____ *City Slickers*
_____ *Bed of Roses*	_____ *A Clockwork Orange*
_____ *Before Women had Wings*	_____ *The Cocaine Fiends*
_____ *Bell, Book, and Candle*	_____ *Come Back, Little Sheba*
_____ *The Bell Jar*	_____ *Corrina, Corrina*
_____ *The Best Years of Our Lives*	_____ *Courage*
_____ *Bob & Carol & Ted & Alice*	_____ *Crazy From the Heart*
_____ *The Boston Strangler*	_____ *Curse of the Starving Class*
_____ *The Boy Who Could Fly*	_____ *Dancing in the Dark* (1995)
_____ *The Boys Next Door* (1996)	_____ *The Devil and Daniel*
_____ *Boys on the Side*	*Webster*
_____ *Breakfast at Tiffany's*	_____ *Disclosure*

_____ *Divided Memories*
_____ *Dolores Claiborne*
_____ *Doing Time on Maple Drive*
_____ *Don Juan DeMarco*
_____ *Dream Lover*
_____ *Drunks*
_____ *An Early Frost*
_____ *East of Eden* (1955)
_____ *Easy Rider*
_____ *Educating Rita*
_____ *84 Charing Cross Road*
_____ *The Elephant Man*
_____ *Elmer Gantry*
_____ *The End*
_____ *Equus*
_____ *E.T.: The Extra-Terrestrial*
_____ *The Fan* (1996)
_____ *Fatso*
_____ *Fever Pitch*
_____ *Fire in the Dark*
_____ *TheFirst Time* (1983)
_____ *Flowers in the Attic*
_____ *Fool for Love*
_____ *Forget Paris*
_____ *For Keeps*
_____ *The Fountainhead*
_____ *Fresh Horses*
_____ *Fried Green Tomatoes*
_____ *Georgia*
_____ *Girls Town* (1996)
_____ *The Good Wife*
_____ *The Goodbye Girl*
_____ *The Great Impostor*
_____ *Groundhog Day*
_____ *Gulliver's Travels* (1996)
_____ *The Hand that Rocks the Cradle*
_____ *The Heidi Chronicles*
_____ *Helter Skelter*
_____ *Home for the Holidays*
_____ *A Home of Our Own*

_____ *House of Cards* (1993)
_____ *How to Make an American Quilt*
_____ *The Hustler*
_____ *I Never Promised You a Rose Garden*
_____ *If These Walls Could Talk*
_____ *I'm Not Rappaport*
_____ *Imaginary Crimes*
_____ *In & Out*
_____ *Inherit the Wind* (1960)
_____ *Intimate Contact*
_____ *Inventing the Abbotts*
_____ *It's My Party*
_____ *Jack the Bear*
_____ *Jeffrey*
_____ *The Joker Is Wild*
_____ *Jonathan Livingston Seagull*
_____ *Keeping Secrets*
_____ *Klute*
_____ *L.A. Story*
_____ *The Lady Gambles*
_____ *Leaving Las Vegas*
_____ *The Lemon Sisters*
_____ *Lenny*
_____ *Like Mom, Like Me*
_____ *Little Darlings*
_____ *Little Man Tate*
_____ *The Locket*
_____ *Lorenzo's Oil*
_____ *Losing Isaiah*
_____ *Love, Lies and Lullabies*
_____ *Love Story*
_____ *The Man Who Shot Liberty Valance*
_____ *Marvin's Room*
_____ *Mary Reilly*
_____ *Mary Shelley's Frankenstein*
_____ *Mask* (1985)
_____ *Miami Rhapsody*
_____ *Mildred Pierce*

_____ The Miracle of Kathy Miller
_____ Misery
_____ Mr. Mom
_____ Moonlight and Valentino
_____ Murphy's Romance
_____ My Brother's Keeper (1995)
_____ My Left Foot
_____ My Life
_____ My Name Is Kate
_____ Nell
_____ Nine Months
_____ Norma Rae
_____ Now and Then
_____ The Odd Couple
_____ On a Clear Day You Can
     See Forever
_____ Once Upon a Time
     in the West
_____ The Other Side
     of the Mountain
_____ Out on a Limb
_____ The Outsiders
_____ The Pied Piper of Hamelin
_____ Pump Up the Volume
_____ Ragtime
_____ Rape of Love
_____ Reefer Madness
_____ The Restless Years
_____ The Right to Remain Silent
_____ The Rose
_____ Rush
_____ Safe Passage
_____ The Search for Signs
     of Intelligent Life
     in the Universe
_____ Shattered Dreams
_____ She's Having a Baby
_____ Shine
_____ A Simple Twist of Fate
_____ Single Bars, Single Women

_____ Sling Blade
_____ The Snake Pit
_____ Soul Food
_____ Stand and Deliver
_____ A Star Is Born (1976)
_____ Stuart Saves His Family
_____ Sullivan's Travels
_____ The Summer My Father
     Grew Up
_____ Sweet Nothing
_____ Table for Five
_____ Tales of Ordinary Madness
_____ Talking With
_____ A Thousand Acres
_____ Three Men and a Baby
_____ To Gillian on Her
     37th Birthday
_____ Torch Song Trilogy
_____ Trading Mom
_____ Trainspotting
_____ A Tree Grows in Brooklyn
     (1945)
_____ Trees Lounge
_____ The Turning Point
_____ The Vanishing (1993)
_____ The Verdict (1982)
_____ Voice in the Mirror
_____ Voices Within: The Lives
     of Truddi Chase
_____ Waiting to Exhale
_____ The War at Home
_____ The Wedding Gift
_____ Welcome to the Doll House
_____ What Ever Happened to
     Baby Jane? (1962)
_____ Where the Day Takes You
_____ Whose Life Is it Anyway?
_____ The Women's Room
_____ Zoot Suit

HEALING MOVIES PRESCRIPTION PADS

Here are two healing movies perscription pads. I suggest you use them as follows: Make copies and create a pad of blank prescriptions. Next, fill out the prescription pads for your clients, giving them the name of the movie you want them to watch or attaching the master movie prescription list. Finally, give the prescription to your clients as an assignment in their treatment. I'm sure you will find this to be an effective way to help your clients on their healing journey.

License/Certificate # _____

HEALING MOVIES PRESCRIPTION

Date _____

Name _____

I would like you to watch the movies listed below
by your next appointment _____ :

1. _____

2. _____

3. _____

Prescribed by: _____

Here's a suggestion from me:

- -

HEALING MOVIES PRESCRIPTION

Date _____

Name _____

I would like you to watch the movies listed below:

1. _____

2. _____

3. _____

Prescribed by: _____

SUBJECT INDEX

This index will help you identify movies within this book that focus on particular issues you would like to explore. Take the time to look through the twenty-one categories before making your viewing selections.

ABANDONMENT

(Death; loss of relationships; lack of support from friends, family, employers, etc.; and parents who leave their children and other family members)

Always (1989)
And Then There Was One
Angel Heart
The Apprenticeship of Duddy Kravitz
As Good As It Gets
Awakenings
The Basketball Diaries
Bastard Out of Carolina
Bed of Roses
The Bell Jar
The Best Years of Our Lives
The Boy Who Could Fly
The Boys Next Door (1996)
Boys on the Side
Breakfast at Tiffany's
Bye Bye, Love
Can't Buy Me Love
Casablanca
Child of Rage
Choices of the Heart:
  The Margaret Sanger Story
Citizen Kane
Citizen Ruth
Come Back, Little Sheba
Corrina, Corrina
Crazy From the Heart
Curse of the Starving Class
Damaged
Dancing in the Dark (1995)
Divided Memories
Doing Time on Maple Drive
Don Juan DeMarco
East of Eden (1955)

The Elephant Man
E.T.: The Extra-Terrestrial
Fever Pitch
Fire in the Dark
The First Time (1983)
Flowers in the Attic
Fool For Love
For Keeps
Forget Paris
Fresh Horses
Fried Green Tomatoes
Georgia
Girls Town (1996)
God Bless the Child
The Good Wife
The Great Impostor
Gulliver's Travels (1996)
The Hand that Rocks the Cradle
Home for the Holidays
A Home of Our Own
How to Make an American Quilt
The Hustler
I Never Promised You a Rose Garden
Imaginary Crimes
Inherit the Wind (1960)
Jack the Bear
Keeping Secrets
Klute
The Lady Gambles
Leaving Las Vegas
Like Mom, Like Me
Little Man Tate
Lorenzo's Oil

Losing Isaiah
Love, Lies and Lullabies
Love Story
The Man Who Shot Liberty Valance
Marvin's Room
Mary Reilly
Mary Shelly's Frankenstein
Mask (1985)
Mildred Pierce
Murphy's Romance
My Name Is Kate
My Left Foot
My Life
Nell
Ragtime
Rape of Love
The Restless Years
The Right to Remain Silent
Safe Passage
*The Search for Signs of Intelligent
  Life in the Universe*
Shine
A Simple Twist of Fate
Sling Blade
The Snake Pit

Soul Food
Stand and Deliver
A Star Is Born (1976)
Stuart Saves His Family
The Summer My Father Grew Up
Sweet Nothing
Table for Five
Talking With
A Thousand Acres
Three Men and a Baby
To Gillian on Her 37th Birthday
Torch Song Trilogy
Trading Mom
A Tree Grows in Brooklyn (1945)
Valley of the Dolls
The Vanishing (1993)
Voice in the Mirror
Waiting to Exhale
The War at Home
The Wedding Gift
*What Ever Happened
  to Baby Jane?* (1962)
Where the Day Takes You
The Women's Room
Zoot Suit

ABUSE

(Physical, psychological, sexual, or emotional abuse)

Awakenings
The Bad Seed (1956)
The Basketball Diaries
Bastard Out of Carolina
The Boston Strangler
Boys on the Side
Cat's Eye
Child of Rage
A Clockwork Orange
The Cocaine Fiends
Curse of the Starving Class
Dancing in the Dark (1995)
Disclosure

Divided Memories
Dream Lover
East of Eden (1955)
Educating Rita
The Elephant Man
Equus
E.T.: The Extra-Terrestrial
The Fan (1996)
Fire in the Dark
Flowers in the Attic
Fool For Love
The Fountainhead
Fresh Horses

Fried Green Tomatoes
Girls Town (1996)
God Bless the Child
Gulliver's Travels (1996)
The Hand that Rocks the Cradle
Helter Skelter
Home for the Holidays
A Home of Our Own
How to Make an American Quilt
Hustler
I Never Promised You a Rose Garden
Imaginary Crimes
In & Out
Inventing the Abbotts
Jack the Bear
The Joker Is Wild
Keeping Secrets
Lenny
Love Story
The Man Who Shot Liberty Valance
Mary Reilly
Mary Shelly's Frankenstein
Mask (1985)
Mildred Pierce
Misery
My Left Foot
My Name Is Kate
Norma Rae
Once Upon a Time in the West
The Outsiders

Ragtime
Rape of Love
The Restless Years
The Right to Remain Silent
Safe Passage
The Search for Signs of Intelligent Life in the Universe
Shine
A Simple Twist of Fate
Sling Blade
The Snake Pit
Stand and Deliver
A Star Is Born (1976)
Stuart Saves His Family
Sullivan's Travels
Sweet Nothing
Tales of Ordinary Madness
Talking With
A Thousand Acres
Torch Song Trilogy
Trainspotting
The Vanishing (1993)
The Verdict (1982)
Voice in the Mirror
Welcome to the Doll House
What Ever Happened to Baby Jane? (1962)
Where the Day Takes You
The Women's Room
Zoot Suit

ADOPTION

(Giving a child up for adoption or adopting a child, including becoming a stepparent through marriage or communal living)

Bastard Out of Carolina
Breakfast at Tiffany's
Child of Rage
Citizen Ruth
Flowers in the Attic
How to Make an American Quilt
Jack the Bear

Losing Isaiah
A Simple Twist of Fate
The Summer My Father Grew Up
Talking With
Three Men and a Baby
Trading Mom
Where the Day Takes You

ALCOHOL
(Abuse of alcohol from the perspective of the user and those involved with the user)

The Basketball Diaries
Bastard Out of Carolina
The Best Years of Our Lives
Bob & Carol & Ted & Alice
Boys on the Side
Breakfast at Tiffany's
Can't Buy Me Love
Casablanca
Cat's Eye
A Clockwork Orange
The Cocaine Fiends
Come Back, Little Sheba
Curse of the Starving Class
Dancing in the Dark (1995)
Disclosure
Divided Memories
Drunks
Educating Rita
Fool For Love
Fresh Horses
Fried Green Tomatoes
Georgia
Gulliver's Travels (1996)
Helter Skelter
Home for the Holidays
The Hustler
Imaginary Crimes
Jack the Bear
The Joker Is Wild
Keeping Secrets
Klute
The Lady Gambles
Leaving Las Vegas
Lenny
Love, Lies and Lullabies
The Man Who Shot Liberty Valance

Mary Reilly
Mask (1985)
Mildred Pierce
Murphy's Romance
My Left Foot
My Name Is Kate
Once Upon a Time in the West
The Outsiders
Ragtime
The Right to Remain Silent
Rush
The Search for Signs of Intelligent
   Life in the Universe
A Simple Twist of Fate
Single Bars, Single Women
Sling Blade
Stand and Deliver
A Star Is Born (1976)
Stuart Saves His Family
Sullivan's Travels
Sweet Nothing
Table for Five
Tales of Ordinary Madness
Talking With
A Thousand Acres
Torch Song Trilogy
A Tree Grows in Brooklyn (1945)
Trees Lounge
The Verdict (1982)
Voice in the Mirror
The War at Home
What Ever Happened to
   Baby Jane? (1962)
Where the Day Takes You
The Women's Room
Zoot Suit

CODEPENDENCY

(Supporting a person or persons in their dysfunctional behavior or relying on another person to identify your feelings or needs)

The Apprenticeship of Duddy Kravitz
Avalon
The Bad Seed (1956)
Bastard Out of Carolina
The Best Years of Our Lives
Bob & Carol & Ted & Alice
The Boy Who Could Fly
Boys on the Side
Casablanca
Cat's Eye
Come Back, Little Sheba
Corrina, Corrina
Courage
Curse of the Starving Class
Dancing in the Dark (1995)
Divided Memories
Doing Time on Maple Drive
Don Juan DeMarco
Dream Lover
Drunks
East of Eden (1955)
84 Charing Cross Road
Fatso
Fever Pitch
Fire in the Dark
The First Time (1983)
Fool For Love
Fresh Horses
Fried Green Tomatoes
Georgia
Home for the Holidays
A Home of Our Own
The Hustler
I'm Not Rappaport
Imaginary Crimes
Inventing the Abbotts
Jeffrey
The Joker Is Wild
Keeping Secrets

Klute
L.A. Story
The Lady Gambles
Leaving Las Vegas
Lenny
Like Mom, Like Me
Little Man Tate
Love, Lies and Lullabies
The Man Who Shot Liberty Valance
Mary Reilly
Mary Shelley's Frankenstein
Mask (1985)
Miami Rhapsody
Mildred Pierce
The Miracle of Kathy Miller
Murphy's Romance
My Brother's Keeper (1995)
My Left Foot
My Name Is Kate
The Pied Piper of Hamelin
Ragtime
The Restless Years
The Right to Remain Silent
Rush
Safe Passage
The Search for Signs of Intelligent
*   Life in the Universe*
She's Having a Baby
Shine
A Simple Twist of Fate
Single Bars, Single Women
Stand and Deliver
A Star Is Born (1976)
Stuart Saves His Family
The Summer My Father Grew Up
Sweet Nothing
Table for Five
Tales of Ordinary Madness
Talking With

A Thousand Acres
Three Men and a Baby
To Gillian on Her 37th Birthday
Trading Mom
A Tree Grows in Brooklyn (1945)
The Vanishing (1993)
The Verdict (1982)
Voice in the Mirror

Waiting to Exhale
The Wedding Gift
*What Ever Happened to
  Baby Jane?* (1962)
Where the Day Takes You
The Women's Room
Zoot Suit

DEATH/DYING

(Dealing with the loss of another person or coping with your own impending death)

Always (1989)
And the Band Played On
And Then There Was One
Angel Heart
Avalon
Bastard Out of Carolina
Bed of Roses
The Boston Strangler
The Boy Who Could Fly
Boys on the Side
*Choices of the Heart: The Margaret
  Sanger Story*
Citizen Kane
Corrina, Corrina
Damaged
Divided Memories
An Early Frost
East of Eden (1955)
Easy Rider
The Elephant Man
Equus
Fried Green Tomatoes
Girls Town (1996)
The Hand that Rocks the Cradle
Helter Skelter
How to Make an American Quilt
The Hustler
Imaginary Crimes
Intimate Contact

Inventing the Abbotts
Jack the Bear
Jeffrey
Leaving Las Vegas
Lorenzo's Oil
Love Story
The Man Who Shot Liberty Valance
Marvin's Room
Mary Reilly
Mask (1985)
Mildred Pierce
The Miracle of Kathy Miller
Moonlight and Valentino
My Brother's Keeper (1995)
My Life
Nell
Once Upon a Time in the West
The Other Side of the Mountain
The Outsiders
Ragtime
The Right to Remain Silent
Rush
Safe Passage
A Simple Twist of Fate
Sling Blade
Soul Food
A Star Is Born (1976)
Stuart Saves His Family
Sweet Nothing

Talking With
A Thousand Acres
To Gillian on Her 37th Birthday
A Tree Grows in Brooklyn (1945)
The Vanishing (1993)

The Verdict (1982)
The War at Home
Where the Day Takes You
Whose Life Is it Anyway?
The Women's Room

DENIAL

(The inability to see a truth or reality of a situation when involved in a relationship, work environment, family member, and so on)

Always (1989)
And the Band Played On
And Then There Was One
Angel Baby (1995)
Angel Heart
The Apprenticeship of Duddy Kravitz
The Bad Seed (1956)
The Basketball Diaries
Bastard Out of Carolina
Beautiful Girls
The Bell Jar
The Best Years of Our Lives
Bob & Carol & Ted & Alice
Boys on the Side
Breakfast at Tiffany's
The Bridges of Madison County
Can't Buy Me Love
Casablanca
Cat's Eye
Child of Rage
Citizen Kane
Citizen Ruth
A Clockwork Orange
Come Back, Little Sheba
Corrina, Corrina
Courage
Crazy From the Heart
Curse of the Starving Class
Dancing in the Dark (1995)
Disclosure
Divided Memories
Doing Time on Maple Drive

Drunks
An Early Frost
East of Eden (1955)
Easy Rider
Educating Rita
84 Charing Cross Road
The End
Equus
The Fan (1996)
Fever Pitch
Fire in the Dark
Fool For Love
For Keeps
Fresh Horses
Fried Green Tomatoes
The Good Wife
The Great Impostor
Gulliver's Travels (1996)
The Hand that Rocks the Cradle
A Home of Our Own
Home for the Holidays
The Hustler
Imaginary Crimes
Jack the Bear
Keeping Secrets
L.A. Story
The Lady Gambles
Leaving Las Vegas
Lenny
Like Mom, Like Me
Little Man Tate
Love, Lies and Lullabies

Marvin's Room
Mary Reilly
Mary Shelly's Frankenstein
Mask (1985)
Miami Rhapsody
Mildred Pierce
The Miracle of Kathy Miller
Murphy's Romance
My Brother's Keeper (1995)
My Left Foot
My Life
My Name Is Kate
The Odd Couple
The Outsiders
Ragtime
The Restless Years
The Right to Remain Silent
The Rose
Rush
Safe Passage
The Search for Signs of Intelligent
   Life in the Universe

A Simple Twist of Fate
A Star Is Born (1976)
Stuart Saves His Family
Sullivan's Travels
The Summer My Father Grew Up
Sweet Nothing
Talking With
A Thousand Acres
Torch Song Trilogy
Trainspotting
A Tree Grows in Brooklyn (1945)
The Turning Point
Voice in the Mirror
Waiting to Exhale
The Wedding Gift
What Ever Happened to
   Baby Jane? (1962)
Where the Day Takes You
The Women's Room
Zoot Suit

DIVORCE

(Ending a relationship—marriage or other intimate involvement—on a permanent or temporary basis)

Bastard Out of Carolina
The Best Years of Our Lives
The Bridges of Madison County
The Butcher's Wife
Courage
Curse of the Starving Class
Dancing in the Dark (1995)
The Devil and Daniel Webster
Divided Memories
Divorce
East of Eden (1955)
84 Charing Cross Road
The Fan (1996)
Fool For Love
Forget Paris
Girls Town (1996)

Jack the Bear
Lenny
Like Mom, Like Me
Little Darlings
Miami Rhapsody
Mildred Pierce
Murphy's Romance
Nine Months
Safe Passage
The Search for Signs of Intelligent
   Life in the Universe
A Simple Twist of Fate
Sullivan's Travels
The Summer My Father Grew Up
Sweet Nothing
Table for Five

Talking With
Torch Song Trilogy
Waiting to Exhale

Where the Day Takes You
The Women's Room

DRUGS

(Substance abuse by individuals and groups, or involvement with those who abuse substances or engage in other types of addictive behavior)

Angel Baby (1995)
The Basketball Diaries
Bastard Out of Carolina
Bob & Carol & Ted & Alice
Boys on the Side
A Clockwork Orange
The Cocaine Fiends
Courage
Curse of the Starving Class
Dancing in the Dark (1995)
Divided Memories
Easy Rider
Fresh Horses
Georgia
Gulliver's Travels (1996)
Girls Town (1996)
Helter Skelter
Home for the Holidays
Keeping Secrets
Leaving Las Vegas
Lenny
Love, Lies and Lullabies
Mary Reilly

Mask (1985)
The Outsiders
Reefer Madness
The Right to Remain Silent
Rush
The Search for Signs of Intelligent Life in the Universe
A Simple Twist of Fate
Stand and Deliver
A Star Is Born (1976)
Stuart Saves His Family
Sweet Nothing
Talking With
A Thousand Acres
Torch Song Trilogy
Trainspotting
Trees Lounge
The War at Home
What Ever Happened to Baby Jane? (1962)
Where the Day Takes You
The Women's Room
Zoot Suit

FAMILY

(Issues involving family and family members)

And Then There Was One
The Apprenticeship of Duddy Kravitz
Avalon
The Basketball Diaries
Bastard Out of Carolina
Beautiful Girls
Bed of Roses

The Best Years of Our Lives
The Boy Who Could Fly
The Boys Next Door (1996)
Boys on the Side
Breaking Away
The Bridges of Madison County
The Butcher's Wife

FOOD

(Problems with eating, including bulimia, anorexia, and compulsive eating)

Fatso	*Stuart Saves His Family*
The Search for Signs of Intelligent	*Talking With*
Life in the Universe	*The Women's Room*

FRIENDS

(Problems with friends, whether intimate or casual)

Always (1989)	*Fresh Horses*
American Graffiti	*Fried Green Tomatoes*
And the Band Played On	*Girls Town* (1996)
And Then There Was One	*The Heidi Chronicles*
The Apprenticeship of Duddy Kravitz	*How to Make an American Quilt*
As Good As It Gets	*The Hustler*
The Basketball Diaries	*In & Out*
Beautiful Girls	*Inherit the Wind* (1960)
The Best Years of Our Lives	*Intimate Contact*
Bob & Carol & Ted & Alice	*It's My Party*
The Boy Who Could Fly	*Jeffrey*
The Boys Next Door (1996)	*The Joker is Wild*
Boys on the Side	*The Lemon Sisters*
Breakfast at Tiffany's	*Like Mom, Like Me*
Breaking Away	*Little Darlings*
Can't Buy Me Love	*Lorenzo's Oil*
Casablanca	*Love, Lies and Lullabies*
Chasing Amy	*The Man Who Shot Liberty Valance*
Citizen Kane	*Mary Shelley's Frankenstein*
A Clockwork Orange	*Mask* (1985)
Crazy from the Heart	*Miami Rhapsody*
The Devil and Daniel Webster	*Mildred Pierce*
Divided Memories	*The Miracle of Kathy Miller*
Drunks	*Moonlight and Valentino*
An Early Frost	*Murphy's Romance*
Easy Rider	*My Brother's Keeper* (1995)
84 Charing Cross Road	*My Left Foot*
The End	*My Name Is Kate*
Fatso	*Nell*
Fever Pitch	*Norma Rae*
Forget Paris	*Now and Then*
The Fountainhead	*The Odd Couple*

On a Clear Day You Can See Forever
The Other Side of the Mountain
Out on a Limb
The Outsiders
The Pied Piper of Hamelin
Ragtime
Rape of Love
Reefer Madness
The Restless Years
The Right to Remain Silent
The Rose
Rush
*The Search for Signs of Intelligent
  Life in the Universe*
She's Having a Baby
A Simple Twist of Fate
Single Bars, Single Women
Stand and Deliver

A Star Is Born (1976)
Stuart Saves His Family
Sullivan's Travels
Tales of Ordinary Madness
Talking With
Three Men and a Baby
Torch Song Trilogy
Trainspotting
The Turning Point
The Vanishing (1993)
The Verdict (1982)
Voice in the Mirror
Waiting to Exhale
The War at Home
The Wedding Gift
Where the Day Takes You
The Women's Room
Zoot Suit

GAMBLING

(Problems with gambling)

Fever Pitch
The Lady Gambles

MEN'S STORIES

(Issues and problems from a male perspective)

American Graffiti
As Good As It Gets
The Basketball Diaries
Beautiful Girls
Bed of Roses
The Best Years of Our Lives
Breaking Away
Bye Bye, Love
Can't Buy Me Love
Casablanca
City Slickers

Don Juan DeMarco
84 Charing Cross Road
Forget Paris
Groundhog Day
I'm Not Rappaport
Mr. Mom
Nine Months
The Odd Couple
The Right to Remain Silent
Three Men and a Baby
The War at Home

MENTAL/EMOTIONAL ILLNESS

(Coping with those who suffer from a mental or emotional illness)

Angel Baby (1995)
As Good As It Gets
Awakenings
The Bad Seed (1956)
The Baskeball Diaries
Bastard Out of Carolina
The Bell Jar
The Boston Strangler
The Boy Who Could Fly
The Boys Next Door (1996)
Citizen Ruth
The End
Equus
The Fan (1996)
Girls Town (1996)
The Good Wife
The Great Impostor
Gulliver's Travels (1996)
The Hand that Rocks the Cradle
Helter Skelter
House of Cards (1993)

I Never Promised You a Rose Garden
In & Out
Jack the Bear
The Locket
Losing Isaiah
The Man Who Shot Liberty Valance
Mary Reilly
Mildred Pierce
Misery
Rape of Love
The Search for Signs of Intelligent
    Life in the Universe
Shine
Sling Blade
The Snake Pit
A Thousand Acres
Trainspotting
The Vanishing (1993)
The War at Home
What Ever Happened to
    Baby Jane? (1962)

PHYSICAL ILLNESS

(Help for those with a physical illness or who may be attempting to cope with another's suffering)

The Best Years of Our Lives
Boys on the Side
The Elephant Man
It's My Party
Jeffrey
Lorenzo's Oil
Love Story

Mary Shelley's Frankenstein
Mask (1985)
The Miracle of Kathy Miller
My Left Foot
My Life
The Other Side of the Mountain
Whose Life Is It, Anyway?

RELATIONSHIPS

(Emotional, physical, or business relationship issues)

Always (1989)
American Graffiti

And the Band Played On
And Then There Was One

SEX/SEXUALITY

(Issues that involve sex, rape, molestation, sexual identity, and so on)

The Celluloid Closet
Chasing Amy
Child of Rage
A Clockwork Orange
Dancing in the Dark (1995)
Disclosure
Divided Memories
Doing Time on Maple Drive
84 Charing Cross Road
The First Time (1983)
Fool For Love
For Keeps
Fresh Horses
Fried Green Tomatoes
Girls Town (1996)
The Good Wife
In & Out
Jeffrey
Klute
L.A. Story

Lenny
Like Mom, Like Me
Little Darlings
Mask (1985)
Miami Rhapsody
Now and Then
Rape of Love
The Restless Years
The Search for Signs of Intelligent
   Life in the Universe
She's Having a Baby
Single Bars, Single Women
Soul Food
Talking With
A Thousand Acres
Torch Song Trilogy
The Wedding Gift
Welcome to the Doll House
Where the Day Takes You
The Women's Room

WOMEN'S STORIES

(Issues and problems from a female perspective)

Always (1989)
As Good As It Gets
Bed of Roses
Boys on the Side
Breakfast at Tiffany's
The Bridges of Madison County
Casablanca
Divided Memories
Don Juan DeMarco
84 Charing Cross Road
Forget Paris
Groundhog Day
The Heidi Chronicles
Home for the Holidays

How to Make an American Quilt
Leaving Las Vegas
The Lemon Sisters
Little Darlings
Mr. Mom
Norma Rae
The Right to Remain Silent
The Search for Signs of Intelligent
   Life in the Universe
Single Bars, Single Women
Talking With
A Thousand Acres
Waiting to Exhale
The Women's Room

OKAY FOR VIEWERS UNDER FIFTEEN

(Movies that parents can feel comfortable showing their children)

American Graffiti

Animal Farm (1955)

The Boy Who Could Fly

Breaking Away

Brian's Song

Can't Buy Me Love

City Slickers

Trading Mom

SPECIAL ISSUES

(A wide variety of special issues, such as AIDS, philosophy, homosexuality, and abortion)

And the Band Played On—AIDS

And Then There Was One—AIDS

Animal Farm—Philosophical

Bell, Book and Candle—Magical

Boys on the Side—AIDS

The Butcher's Wife—Magical

Cat's Eye—Smoking

The Celluloid Closet—Homosexuality

Choices of the Heart: The Margaret Sanger Story—Abortion

Chasing Amy—Homosexuality

Citizen Ruth—Abortion

Corrina, Corrina—Race relations

The Devil and Daniel Webster—Philosophical

Doing Time on Maple Drive—Homosexuality

Dream Lover—Dreams

An Early Frost—Homosexuality

Elmer Gantry—Religion

For Keeps—Abortion

The Fountainhead—Philosophical

Girls Town (1996)—Suicide

Groundhog Day—Philosophical

In & Out—Homosexuality

Inherit the Wind (1960)—Religion

Intimate Contact—AIDS

It's My Party—AIDS

Jeffrey—AIDS

Losing Isaiah—Race relations

On a Clear Day You Can See Forever—Magical

Once Upon a Time in the West—Revenge

Out on a Limb—Metaphysics

The Pied Piper of Hamelin—Philosophical

Ragtime—Race relations

The Right to Remain Silent—Philosophical

The Search for Signs of Intelligent Life in the Universe—Philosophical

A Simple Twist of Fate—Serendipity

Talking With—Philosophical

Torch Song Trilogy—Homosexuality

The War at Home—PTSD

Whose Life Is It, Anyway?—Right to die

Zoot Suit—Race relations

SUPPORT, RECOVERY, AND OUTREACH ORGANIZATIONS

In this book, I recommend you make contact and become involved with support, recovery, and outreach organizations to help you, your family, and friends in the healing process. Below is a partial list of some of those organizations. Most organizations offer their support at no charge. Please keep in mind that the names of self-help groups vary from city to city throughout the world. Check with your local directory service for the proper listings and phone numbers. Don't hesitate to call directory assistance and describe what you are looking for. Most city phone services have a master list to refer to in dealing with these sensitive, personal issues. And you can now locate many of the numbers on the Internet.

ANONYMOUS GROUPS

Al-Anon (Alonon)
Alateen Anonymous (AltA)
Alcoholics Anonymous (AA)
Artists Anonymous (ArtA)
Cocaine Anonymous (CA)
Debtors Anonymous (DA)
Families Anonymous (FA)

Gamblers Anonymous (GA)
Hookers Anonymous (HA)
Narcotics Anonymous (CA)
Overeaters Anonymous (OA)
Pills Anonymous (PA)
Sex Anonymous (SA)
Smokers Anonymous (SA)

SUPPORT GROUPS

Adult Children of Alcoholics
AIDS Support
Al-Anon
Alzheimer's
Anger Management
Attention Deficit Hyperactive
    Disorder

Cancer
Incest Survivors
MADD: Mothers Against Drunk
    Drivers
Parents with Autistic Children
Toughlove
Victims for Victims

FOR THOSE WHO ENJOY THE INTERNET

Although not everyone loves to use the Internet, those who do may find these Internet Web sites of some interest. To my knowledge, there are no Web sites that discuss healing and recovery movies. You may enjoy reading some of the reviews and thoughts of those who watch movies for their entertainment value. When you are done, how about starting a Web site of your own?

ALT.CULT-MOVIES—
  news:alt.cult-movies
ALT.MOVIES. INDEPENDENT
CINEMANIAC'S HOME PAGE—
  http://www.odyline.com/-cine
Internet MOVIE DATABASE—
  http://us.imdb.com/
REC.ARTS.MOVIES.ANNOUNCE
REC.ARTS.MOVIES.CURRENT-
  FILMS

REC.ARTS.MOVIES.MISC
REC.ARTS.MOVIES.PEOPLE
REC.ARTS.MOVIES.REVIEWS
REC.ARTS.MOVIES.TECH
REC.MUSIC.MOVIES
REEL—http://Reel.com/
T@P: FILMS—http://www.
  taponline.com/tap/entertainment/
  film

. . . AND JUST FOR FUN

99-LIVES—THE VIDEO
  MAGAZINE
ALL-MOVIE GUIDE
ANDREW HICKS: MOVIE
  CRITIC AT LARGE
BEATRICE'S WEEKEND
  MOVIE WATCH
BEST VIDEO
BLACK EYE ON FILM
BOXOFFICE MAGAZINE

CAROLINE'S MOVIE REVIEWS
CLICK 3X
COMING ATTRACTIONS BY
  CORONA
COMIS LANDSCAPES
DINNER AND MOVIE.COM
DR. DANIEL'S MOVIE
  EMERGENCY
MR. SHOWBIZ MOVIE GUIDE

SUGGESTION BOX

Please fill out the form below and mail it to:

THE MOVIE DOCTOR
700 Leicester
Suite 9
Henderson, NV 89015
1-702-565-6218

Date: _____

Name: _____ (Optional)

In what part of the country do you live? _____

How old are you? _____

Are you a practicing therapist? Yes _____ No _____

Do you find this type of therapy to be helpful? Yes _____ No _____

What is your opinion of this book?

_____

_____

_____

Some of the movies I would like to see you include in the next edition of your book:

1. _____
2. _____
3. _____
4. _____

A few notes to the Movie Doctor:

_____

_____

_____

_____

INDEX